Waiter to the Rich and Shameless

Confessions of a Five-Star Beverly Hills Server

Paul Hartford

First edition paperback: 2015

Hillhurst Literary (Publisher)
Los Angeles, California

ISBN-10: 0-69-254358-9
ISBN-13: 978-0-69-254358-0

WARNING AND DISCLAIMER

WARNING: This book is written in the voice of a real waiter, in the way that most servers speak; if this offends you maybe you should go read "Alice in Wonderland" instead.

DISCLAIMER: Cussing, wild sex, drugs and rock 'n alcohol can be hazardous to your health. Don't try to re-create what you read in some of the chapters of this book!

DEDICATION

This book is dedicated to all hospitality workers, whether you're serving the Rich and Shameless or the poor and blameless, and to all corporate grunts plugging away in a 9 to 5 world, dreaming about getting out but not yet having the courage to actually do it.

And to my wonderful wife who stood by my side and worked so hard with me on this book. You rock, Honey!

TABLE OF CONTENTS

PREFACE

The events in this story are all true and celebrities' names have not been altered. According to my lawyer I didn't need to do so.

However, I have camouflaged and/or combined the identities of my co-workers to protect the innocent and the guilty.

In addition, in order to protect me from lawsuits, my attorney insisted that I change the name of the establishment. You'd better be right, Esquire junior.

But even so, you'll probably figure it out since it wouldn't take the Riddler from *Batman* to decode this one.

PROLOGUE

It's amazing that we all come across bartenders, waiters or waitresses pretty regularly in our lives, yet most people know very little about them or their work. More often than not, we don't pay much attention to who they are or what they're thinking. Like Oz, they seem to go behind the curtain, do some magic, and soon reappear with our most desired items. We don't really care to know more, as long as we get the dining experience we are expecting and everything goes well.

This is especially true of the rich and shameless who, rightly or wrongly, tend to regard all other humans as some form of servant. And yet, these servers, as we are now called, are thinking, feeling humans who are not only as individual as our guests, but hold hidden powers of persuasion, of timing, of quality control, over one of their most intimate experiences – eating. We waiters, waitresses and bartenders are also pretty much all-seeing and all-hearing – additional under-the-radar powers that most kindly servers would never abuse. In fact, if we do our jobs right, our customers will never even realize that we hold so much power over them. Secret super-heroes, yes, that's us. Operating under cover amongst the glitterati and movers and shakers of the world, yes, that's me. Doesn't it make sense to get to know us a little better?

I've worked in countless restaurants and nightclubs throughout my life ever since I was a mere sixteen years of age. And because I chose to be a musician, waiting tables and bartending suited me quite well with quick money, plenty of time to write songs, and no need to take work home. I've even managed restaurants in Boston and Los Angeles and what a disappointing crap job that was. But I never imagined back then that I'd end up serving at the swankiest eatery of the rich and famous right in the heart of Beverly Hills, California. Well, that's probably because I always thought I'd be a rich and famous rock star myself and be waited on all my life.

Anyone who's waited tables knows that a typical day can include any or all of the following: catastrophically losing an omelette down someone's back or spilling hot coffee in their lap; dropping a tray of glassware; arguing with the chef or busboys; working like a dog for no tips and indignant looks. Or in a worst-case scenario, all of the above occurring at the same time as: *Hey! Where's my food?! We don't have all day, you know!* And another corpulent gourmand screaming, *Waiter! I asked for my check ten minutes ago!* While yet another voice across the room yells: *Excuse me! I said medium rare! This steak is cooked well done!*

Working in a restaurant is not for the faint of heart.

And when you become a server at the top of the Hollywood food chain, the ordeals described above might still occur, along with high-level challenges unique to that habitat. For example, how many people can say they have saved Russell Crowe from certain embarrassment in front of his friends? Who has to single-handedly ensure that Johnny Depp's kids aren't poisoned by their food allergies? Who quietly serves a famous designer a cup of vodka so he can soak his bleeding tongue which was bitten by the starlet he just tried to French kiss? And who overhears detailed descriptions of celebrities' appalling sexual practices? Pauli, that genteel waiter silently and attentively serving their food, that's who.

While perfecting my craft of serving in the country's most storied and visible Hollywood canteen, another, more personal story simmered in the background. I found myself experiencing severe crises of conscience and identity. I lost myself and almost didn't come back. At first I found myself seduced by my famous guests' glamour and self-indulgence, then I grew accustomed to it and even started to identify with it, and finally I grew appalled by it. At the same time, I also discovered that the Cricket Room is so mismanaged that waiters quit at a regular rate and those who stay experience nightmares and opt for therapy. And yet, the challenges I faced – and created – in the Cricket Room during that time strengthened me in ways I could not see until I literally found my voice.

Waiter to the Rich and Shameless is not just a peek into the secretive inner workings of a legendary five-star restaurant; it is not just a celebrity tell-all or a scathing corporate analysis. It is a top-tier waiter's personal coming-of-age story, an intimate look into the complicated challenges of serving in the country's most elite and Hollywood-centric dining establishment while fighting to maintain a sense of self and purpose.

Welcome inside the chaotic, rarely-seen world of a reluctant five-star Waiter to the Rich and Shameless. My name is Pauli, and I'll be serving you tonight…

CHAPTER 1
ALMOST FAMOUS

A new start was what I needed – a do-over. I was only twenty-nine but desperately in need of a full-on witness protection level makeover. The rock band I'd been playing with for four years was breaking up, not due to lack of talent, but because our lives were all going in different directions. It was the fifth band in ten years to slip through my fingers. I had the gift, I had the look and I had the burning desire to make it in the music world. But it wasn't coming together. How many years does it take before you can say you really tried? I was getting sick of asking myself that question.

The new me began with my hair. Out of all the possible things I could change about myself, that seemed the easiest. The inside stuff is a helluva lot harder.

Long, curly handfuls hit the floor, the bleeding remnants of a dead, or at least dying, dream: rock 'n roll superstar. The barber tasked with changing my appearance from ragged rocker to upscale waiter must have seen what he thought was a tear roll down my scruffy cheek, but that's not possible. Rock 'n roll superstars, even dying ones, don't cry, dammit.

"You okay, mang?" he asked in his heavy Spanish accent, addressing me as "dju."

"Yeah, I'm fine. I think a hair got in my eye. Change like this is just hard though, you know?"

"Si, I know," he said, the clippers buzzing against my pale neck. "I come here when I was thirteen and it was muy difficult. But it was worth it. Now I am happy. You will see. Clean cut more better for work, no?"

Now I felt like a shithead. I was worrying about a haircut and this man had faced real challenges, like probably crossing a desert with nothing but a backpack and a dream. I hoped he was right and this shedding of long, sun-bleached hair was going to be more than symbolic. Shit. Dreams die hard, but now I needed a new one. I considered my employment options outside of music, and found there was really only one: the restaurant business, where I'd often found work during the in-between times that music couldn't pay the bills. This time, I wanted to work somewhere special. I had set my sights on a few of the classic spots around town, like maybe the legendary Cricket Room. It was Hollywood's premier hot spot, and had been for decades, frequented by big spenders from all over the world. I had to look the part, which is what brought me to Julio's Style Shop on Flower Street in downtown Los Angeles. He's good, works cheap, and I knew I wouldn't run into anyone I knew from the music world there.

I had to make it worth doing, losing my hair, changing my whole identity. It was only hair, I had told myself, but it had been a big part of the way I'd thought of myself for years. It was the image I presented to the world and it was symbolic of my complete dedication to my music career. I had worked hard to build a following, and those fans that had collected my posters, music videos, or seen my stage performances might not identify with me anymore. By giving up on a music career, was I letting them down? Did I really want to throw this all away, visible only in a scrapbook or in a photo on a Facebook page? I couldn't help but comfort myself by singing The Who's "Cut My Hair" over and over in my mind:

Why should I care
If I have to cut my hair?
...I have to work myself to death just to fit in.
...It's all a game,
'Cos inside I'm just the same...

Although my hair was just a symbol, it was the outward representation of everything I had been aiming for most of my life. And yet I didn't feel I had built much of anything at all. The numbers just weren't there. Lightning had not struck. Yeah, I had made some significant inroads in the music world, but I was no Steven Tyler even if I was better looking. He had that "it" thing going on and it had finally dawned on me that maybe I didn't. Time to switch lanes.

As Julio went about his buzzing, whisking, and powdering, I thought about the convoluted path that had brought me to this epic fork in the road. I wasn't sure which of the diverging paths to take. I couldn't yet see the one that would eventually lead me to the Cricket Room, but I knew I had to leave the path I had been following. By cutting my hair, I was making a commitment to follow a new dream.

I should probably introduce myself. My name is Paul but everyone calls me Pauli. Last name Hartford. My Sicilian family settled in Chicago where my parents met. Later they moved to Los Angeles for the California dream, making me a first generation Angelino. Then, for some goddamn reason, we moved to Scandinavia when I was about five. We stayed there even after my dad abandoned us during his mid-life crisis and went back to the States. Scandinavia's cold, and they eat a lot of fish and weird shit there, not to mention all their peculiar rituals and holiday traditions, which never resonated with me as a kid. Against all odds, my single mom managed to make a good life for me and my siblings. I'm third of four kids so that birth order puts me squarely at risk for ever becoming mature enough to succeed. I got the rebelliousness and charm of a middle child and the fun-loving, attention seeking self-centeredness of the baby in the family. Recipe for disaster.

Growing up in Denmark, I was exposed to European musical influences from the German operatic punk band Nina Hagen to the inescapable ABBA whom I never really liked. I grew up admiring bands and artists like The Police, Talking Heads, Lou Reed, Blondie, The Ramones, Aerosmith, The Cars, and David Bowie. But living in Scandinavia as not only an American, but one without a dad, I always felt like an outsider. Music became my refuge and best friend early in my life. In my teens, I took drum lessons and started teaching myself to sing and play guitar. I even got my first recording contract in Stockholm when I was seventeen. Who could give a crap if kids at school treated me like an outcast, when I had the world of music to retreat into where I got praise and attention. Musicians are all praise junkies and I was no exception.

One fine day as we were in the studio with our music producer putting the final touches on our first single, my brother Jimmy, who was the lead singer and will be known as Judas from now on, informed us that he was quitting the band to dedicate his life to Scientology. I could almost hear a needle being dragged across a vinyl record as I imagined our contract disappearing as if it had been written in invisible ink. Nothing could change his so-called mind; he was hooked. Game over.

When I turned twenty-two, I moved to Boston to be near my estranged father. I continued to work hard to develop my musical talents: I took singing lessons and began composing songs on my beat-up guitar.

Eventually my brother was delivered from the Scientology cult thanks to a de-programmer my father hired. A freed Judas begged to come join me in Boston. I was already working with three different

Berklee College of Music student producers who specialized in audio engineering. In return for letting them sharpen their skills on my original songs, I was getting free demos out of it. While Judas had been sidelined by his quasi-religious crisis and getting "clear" or whatever the fuck Scientologists do, I had continued to sharpen my musical style and abilities. By the time we got back on track, I had become the lead singer, with Judas singing only a few songs from our repertoire. By default, he was forced to work on his guitar playing skills just to keep up. He had lost a little bit of the spotlight and was secretly harboring resentment about the shadow he was standing in. Apparently, Scientology had not prepared him to play second fiddle.

We grew our hair long, as Bon Jovi was just becoming wildly popular, but our sound was more British, like the groups Gene Loves Jezebel or Tears for Fears. After an airing of a homemade demo on the #1 radio station in Boston, KISS 108, we were invited to an annual station party, where I managed to get our demo to one of the owners of a new up and coming label out of Florida.

When Miami-based Pantera Productions offered us an eighteen-month recording contract we immediately left Boston and a foot of snow to move to sunny Miami Beach, where we started yet another new band. This time, though, the producer wasn't getting us any deals and Judas and I couldn't seem to get along. It's not un-common for bandmates to get testy during long periods of inactivity, but our stress level kept building like a gathering storm with nasty black clouds on the horizon. Personal differences came between us that had little to do with the music, or lack thereof, and the band dissolved after just a year.

I had been pursued earlier back in Boston by a rich Asian investor who was dying to break into the music business. I managed to get hold of him where he was now living, in Los Angeles. He was thrilled to get re-connected and sent me a decent contract, including a year's living expenses and a paid ticket to Los Angeles. I took it. Anything to get away from the bad vibes in Miami.

There I was in my twenties, moving to the music and entertainment capital of the world with the promise of rock 'n roll glory waiting for me. It was the height of the glitz era of rock 'n roll – the Sunset Strip was loaded with longhaired freaks all dressed up like Mötley Crüe and Poison. It's funny, we all looked like girls back then (it was tempting when someone told me to go fuck myself), but the truth is we were young men daring to look like girls for the fuck-you of rebellion. I have to admit that I even found myself checking out some hot chicks now and then that turned out to be guys. Ouch! That can dent your self-esteem quickly, not to mention making you rethink your sexuality. Fortunately, in LA nobody gives shit like that a second thought.

The venues along the Strip are packed with the histories of every great rock band that ever existed – most of them started in LA or came here to make it. The Doors met here, the Eagles, Frank Zappa, Guns 'n Roses, Jane's Addiction, Metallica, Rage Against the Machine, Quiet Riot, Ratt, Van Halen, Red Hot Chili Peppers, The Byrds, Concrete Blonde, The Beach Boys – they all got their start in Los Angeles. LA is to rock what Nashville is to country music. I was stoked – ready to try it all again, as if for the first time, although in reality this was the third time I had been signed since my teens. Maybe the third time would be the charm.

This time around, I was working with a music producer who signed me to a recording contract with a wealthy production company which was funded by a major Asian label. I settled into sunny LA quickly – it was kinda like Miami with the warm weather and lots of Spanish, but yet a totally different, exciting vibe.

We began recording my songs with a group of talented professional musicians handpicked by my producer. We used some of the best recording facilities in the country, laying some basic tracks in a studio called One on One, which was known for producing the legendary drum sound on Mötley Crüe's *Dr. Feelgood* album. In true heavy metal fashion, the studio had a pool table and the Playboy channel playing on monitors 24/7. Metallica had just recently completed its album there so we used a lot of the same techniques that producer Bob Rock had originated. The sound we got was powerful. My confidence was soaring as the rock guitars roared, drums pounded, and my raspy voice reached for the rafters. The music came alive, and my voice had never sounded better.

After One on One, we moved to Fidelity in Studio City which was owned by Artie Ripp whose claim to fame was his discovery of, and partnership with, Billy Joel in the very early years. We spent about a month finishing up all the vocal, guitar and keyboard overdubs and then started playing live at all the celebrated clubs along the Sunset Strip. We called ourselves Jonathan Pauli. We were quite popular, especially at a hot Hollywood joint called The China Club. The stage and sound there were the best in town, and every Monday there were all-star jams with members of Kiss, the Doobie Brothers, and artists like Rick James, John Entwistle, Slash, Teena Marie, Michael Bolton, and Joe Walsh. We got a very favorable write-up in one of the biggest local rock magazines and we started to believe we were badass. My dream of being a rock 'n roll superstar was finally going to come true.

But my manager at the time was an idiot, a real clown who thought all you had to do was buy tons of cocaine and the record execs would come running. But just like in a shitty "B" movie, he got so addicted to the coke himself that he always looked sick and weird; powerful and important record executives stayed as far away from him (and therefore us) as they could. Instead, a herd of losers and drug addicts started hanging around the band – people who couldn't do a thing for us and made us look sleazy. I was stuck with him because he had paid for all the recordings. He basically owned my ass and at times I felt like he was my music pimp.

Astonishingly, we finally made a highly polished music video that we shot California-style, using a beautiful sun-drenched beach and starring my girlfriend at the time. She was the hottest girl I had ever seen and was a former Playboy model – the perfect LA music video diva. And there I was lip-synching in my mesh tank top, brown jeans, long girly hair (now lying like a dead rat in a pile at my feet) flying in the wind, primitive necklace, and a little facial hair, looking like Fabio. The video actually turned out great and just as we were getting meetings at record labels to showcase the music, the Nirvana wave hit. That was less than a year after we had finished mixing the album. Overnight my music was out of style and "Grunge" was the buzzword on every record executive's mind. Even the execs began wearing plaid flannel shirts to work. My timing sucked, like someone running to catch a bus that's just pulling out of the station.

It was a cruel joke. AOR (album-oriented rock) was dead, and it was goodbye Pauli, hello to angry depressed white rockers. How the hell was I supposed to fit into this? My deal with the production company was up, no more money. What could I do? So I took a job as a waiter. Wet dream over, hello dry white wine.

My first job in LA was at the El Torito Grill in Beverly Hills, an upscale version of the regular El Torito where they served designer margaritas and had a traditional Comal grill to make fresh tortillas for every table. I just slicked my rock 'n roll hair back into a ponytail and put my music persona on the shelf while I was working. I kept playing my music and performing all over the Hollywood area as often as I could, all the while working as a waiter at various restaurants and bartending gigs to pay the bills. The dream was like Freddie Kruger and wouldn't die, but it was bleeding and on life support.

After several years of feeling like my music career was stuck in idle, I decided to take a break from the music biz altogether, which was gut-wrenching. I had put so much hard work into it, and all of my love, passion, and hope, but had still come up almost empty-handed. It was hard to take. I asked myself, "How the fuck did I get here?" as the Talking Heads once said. "Is this the end of the road?" I finally felt that it wasn't worth it anymore, and decided I needed to make a big change.

As I sat down in Julio's chair, I knew I had to create a physical and symbolic break with my past and start anew. As each twelve-inch lock of my rock 'n roll hair fell to the floor, I thought of yet another song I had recorded that no one would ever hear. I had no idea what I would do with my life if I weren't pursuing that dream, but a new one was beginning to form.

Julio finally snapped me from my reverie by removing the cloth he had covered me with, shaking the rest of my former mane onto the floor, and spinning me to face the mirror. I was stunned! Who is this guy? I would have to get to know him again. I smiled and he smiled back.

"Dju like?" Julio asked, his eyes narrowed with concern.

"Yes, I like it a lot," I answered. And I meant it. This felt great. Not just lighter physically, but unlike Samson who had become weak when Delilah cut his long, flowing hair, I actually looked and felt younger, stronger than I had in years – as if a heavy load had literally been lifted from my shoulders. This guy staring at me in the mirror could do anything. He was someone to reckon with.

We shook hands and the new me gave Julio a huge tip, one I couldn't afford, but it felt right. I'd do without something else.

I took one last glance in the mirror, winked at the new guy, and headed out into the heat of the day.

CHAPTER 2
MODERN TIMES

My video vixen girlfriend and I broke up. You're shocked, I know. You thought it was gonna last like all those other LA rocker-model romances. Sorry to disappoint. Who knows, maybe she liked me better as a rock star, since she traded me in for a real one: Matt Sorum, the drummer for Guns 'n Roses and The Cult. By then I didn't care much what she did – she had revealed herself as a typical Hollywood bimbo and I was no longer interested in her scene. The old rocker me would have become moody and brooding, maybe written a song about getting dumped. The new me handled it well; fuck her, loser.

The new me also had to find a job, and I wanted to aim high. The legendary Cricket Room had always been just a distantly intriguing enigma to me. I didn't know anyone who frequented the place or anyone who worked there, but somehow I had always felt some sort of vague attraction to it. I had driven past its iconic façade on the way to Malibu Beach quite often, but it wasn't until I needed a better job that I actually considered applying for work there.

At the time I was working part-time in downtown LA as a nightclub bartender. The money was good there but year after year the clientele was the same every night or might as well have been, like interchangeable parts. They were as boring as beer guzzlers at the neighborhood bowling alley and I found that I had very little in common with them. I was feeling restless. It was time to move on. The new clean-cut me hoped and prayed that this would be the answer. I figured if this was to be my chosen profession, I'd better make it count and aim for the top.

It always seemed that the Cricket Room's trademark stucco walls held back a tidal wave of secrets and old Hollywood glamour. The more I thought about it, the more it drew me into its web. Hey, I looked the part now, not like some out of work rock musician looking to fill time between gigs. Maybe they'd hire me.

One day, just on a leap of faith, I decided to get dressed up, walk in, and apply for a job. It was noon on a random Wednesday and

Sunset Boulevard was chaotic. The street was filled with automobile bling-obsessed drivers showing off in their "Fuck you, no wait, fuck me!" sports cars and pseudo-macho Range Rovers that would never see anything so dirty as a range. But even with all the assholes buzzing by me like locusts in a swarm, I was able to appreciate the lush tree-lined streets of Beverly Hills on the beautiful drive to the Cricket Room. I could tune out the "now" and imagine how things had been in Hollywood's true glamour days, when boozy blondes were to be hidden, not displayed on talk shows, and leading men could really act.

Unlike the people you meet in Beverly Hills who look better from a distance, the property was more impressive close up. Designed in a Mediterranean Revival style with immaculate verdant gardens, I felt I had arrived at the end of the rainbow. They even had a designated parking lot large enough to accommodate all the Cricket Room employees. This is unheard of in LA with land costing by the inch instead of per acre. It was also the right day – they were accepting applications.

I walked through the foyer and into the grand dining room across the plush carpet with a design theme so large it stretched across the entire floor to make its point. An instant vibe of money and success emanated from the walls even though the restaurant was empty. The smell of riches was palpable. The wood was oiled, the marble was polished, and the wait staff looked like an elite regiment. Yeah, this was what I wanted to be a part of. This was special.

You see, people think of waiters to the rich and famous as powerless, people who can't do anything else, and the job as subservient and demeaning. In fact, the opposite is true. Even back in the old days, it's always been the "servants" who ran the show. For instance, in the new series *Downton Abbey* it's the butler, Carson, who commands everything going on in the castle. His employers even come to him for advice. When you can control someone's entire evening or special event, that's power. When you know their secrets and their habits, and they know nothing about you, that's power.

As I entered the HR office, after being directed there by a liveried doorman wearing white gloves, I came face to face with a friendly woman whose name turned out to be Aggie. Aggie smiled her best Human Resources smile and asked me for which position I was applying.

"Bartender," I said, and then I introduced myself and noticed her soft, curly blonde locks and a defining mole near her mouth. She had nice blue eyes and a calm air about her, reminding me of Marilyn Monroe, or maybe her much younger cousin. She presented me with a hefty stack of paperwork and I wondered if she were working here while pursuing an acting career.

"Fill these out please," she said.

With a playful, sarcastic grin I asked, "This isn't a government job, is it?"

She laughed and said that I should let her know when I was done so she could look it over. I was used to the old rock 'n roll way of hiring in which a recommendation and a cocaine connection pretty much sealed the deal. This place was a completely different story. In addition to running a credit report on me, they wanted my Social Security number, all of my work history, my contacts, references, banking information, a criminal background check and my DMV history. It was a more elaborate routine than I had been subjected to for any other restaurant job I had ever applied for. More like what one would expect from a large corporation rather than a glitzy show biz meeting place.

Aggie informed me after I had turned in my application that there would also be a mandatory drug test. "Are you okay with that?" Her smile had disappeared as though she were reflecting on the others who had fled the building when told of a drug test.

"Of course, sure, no problem," I replied confidently, my mind racing. *Fuck.*

I had an instant flashback to doing coke after work the night before at the bar downtown. Shit! *Well, nice try buddy*, I thought as I said goodbye to Aggie and her sweet smile. I remember her saying, "We'll be doing callbacks, so expect to hear from us soon." *Yeah, sure.*

"Okay, it was a pleasure meeting you, Aggie, thank you." There was nothing but smiles from everyone as I left the coolness of the building and was slapped in the face with the LA heat. The air was so thick you could practically eat it with a spoon.

Once I reached my car, I looked back at the beautiful property I was leaving behind. I closed the car door and started yelling, "Shit! Shit! Shit! What the fuck was I thinking? What kind of place is this? A fucking drug test for a bartender? Who the fuck would my employer be, the fucking Vatican? Of course, I've got drugs in my body! I'm a goddamn LA bartender! They should have a sign outside their goddamn office announcing that mandatory drug testing would be required. This was fucking entrapment! I'm gonna sue your asses!"

My rant over, I took a deep breath and got out of my car. I opened the trunk to grab an emergency cigarette. Hell, I don't even smoke any more, but when I get all steamed up like this, I have to. I let the nicotine rush to my brain, momentarily numbing my nerves and soothing my mind. The passion surprised me; I hadn't expected to care so much but suddenly I did. I wanted this job but I was probably fucked before I even got a shot.

As my anger dissolved, I gazed down at the paper Aggie had given me when I was leaving the HR office. There was an address and a name of the clinic where I had to go before they closed. I still had a few hours, though. Maybe if I ran up and down the Santa Monica stairs on Adelaide Drive for three hours, perhaps then I could sweat it all out. Or, what if I drank a couple gallons of that drug detox tea? Maybe that would accelerate the process. I said a silent goodbye to the place and drove straight over to the clinic on San Vicente Boulevard past the Beverly Center. Once again I could see that bus pulling out of the station, leaving my sorry ass behind.

With my head hung low and kicking at the sidewalk, I walked slowly along San Vicente until I reached the clinic. *I can't believe it. Why didn't I know this? I'm so naïve; this is Beverly Hills – of course they're gonna drug test me.* When I finally walked into the clinic, I showed them the paperwork that Aggie had given me and they photocopied my driver's license. I thought, *Oh great! Are they gonna share this with the fucking DMV?* I must have said it aloud because the girl said, "No, we keep it confidential. We'll just inform the HR department that you passed or failed and that's all, no details."

"Well that's a relief," I replied, surprised that she'd heard me. After the test, I drove home to Valley Village where I roomed with two other guys. We had rented a house with a pool and the garage had been converted into a big music studio. I plopped myself down on the couch and watched a stupid reality TV show marathon for the rest of the night, hoping to forget that I'd screwed up a great chance to change my life for the better.

Finally, bored shitless, I went to the computer, found a blog titled *Diary of a Waiter* and clicked on it:

> *The moment you are seated, in a carefully choreographed ballet wherein I play the lead, we will meet. You will not know the rest of the team assigned to your dining pleasure and comfort, but their roles are also very important. But I'm the one who will pretend not to notice your tears when your dinner date is late, the*

one who figures out what you mean when your requests are vague to the point of incoherence, and I'm the one you will reward for my kindness and patience with a huge tip. At least that's the way it's supposed to work.

You might not think so, at least at first, but waiting tables can be very exciting. It is a game of chance — you are at the mercy of whatever dumbass (or genius) is doing the seating. You never know who is going to land butt first in a chair or booth at your station. It's like Russian roulette, but without the bullets. At least you hope so. You are the pawn and the opposing pieces are shadows. You can lose (no tip) or win big, and the only control you have is your skill. You may be serving the dishes, but ultimately you must take whatever the shadow, now before you in full color, dishes out to you.

I have waited on homeless people with coupons, wannabe starlets with expired credit cards, and celebrities who are so wealthy they have to try extra hard just to spend all their money. It becomes a game to them.

In Hollywood, having a fat wallet trumps shirt, shoes, and civilized behavior for service.

After reading that, I wanted the job in Beverly Hills even more. If my life got any sadder, I'd have to switch from rock to country songs. The good old boys do a much better job of wailing the hell out of a guitar and singing about dogs, pickup trucks, and women with big boobs and small hearts.

Three days later, I got a message from Aggie saying that they wanted me to come in for a second round of interviews. I must've listened to that message twenty times to make sure it was my name she was saying and that I understood her right. When I called them back I was told to show up on a Wednesday again for an interview with the Maître d' and manager of the Cricket Room. Holy crap!

Have I mentioned how famous the Cricket Room is? It's meet-cute central for all of Hollywood's A-list players. It's been featured in books and movies for decades and is known around the world. Their logo is even featured on a famous designer's clothing. Fuck me, and they're calling me back? Me?

Maybe the nurse with the white coat had dropped my piss test in the toilet or shattered the vial on the cold marble floor. I'm not sure what kind of divine intervention was in place but it was definitely happening, because they would never have called me back for a second interview if the test had been done properly. I was one-hundred percent sure of that.

Well as it happened, the interview went very well. The guy I met with had a very strong Spanish accent and didn't ask me too many questions; I think he was just sizing me up. He kept staring deep into my eyes over his thick black-rimmed glasses like he was trying to do some Hollywood version of a Vulcan mind meld.

On my way out, I was immediately scheduled for a third and final interview, again on a Wednesday. This time I would be interviewed by the Director of Food and Beverage. What was it with all these interviews? I thought that they must have had my title mixed up with someone else's and that I'd wind up with a position in upper management. Who interviews a fucking bartender three times? The Cricket Room, that's who.

The following week when I met the Director, he was a bit stern, very formal in his demeanor, but we got along pretty well and I established that I was in fact only applying for the bartending job, not GM. Apparently, there was never any doubt in his mind, but I just couldn't figure out why they had to summon the Spanish Inquisition just to hire a bartender. I guess in Beverly Hills they do shit differently, at least on the outside.

Two days later I was called in to meet the real GM, which was just a formality, and thank God, because I was hung over. He did ask me more questions as if they weren't sure about hiring me yet, so I played his game. He was a strange-looking man, stiff as hell, in an expensive suit and tie. He reminded me of a mannequin with dyed brown hair and '70s-style tinted reading glasses like Saul wore in *Ocean's Eleven*. I pretended I was the Clooney character and tried for sophisticated nonchalance.

Once he was done making me nervous, which was clearly his power trip shtick, he shook my hand and said, "Congratulations, we're excited to have you join the team."

I smiled and breathed a sigh of relief, which probably smelled like a vodka martini. That's what George and I drink.

He pointed to Aggie and said, "That young lady will get you all set up with your uniform, medical and dental insurance, as well as an optional 401K plan."

I thanked him and told him that I was excited, too. Actually, I was. This was a big damn deal. George Clooney can go fuck himself. I got this.

Aggie explained the benefits program to me and said, "I was rooting for you, Paul."

"Thanks, Aggie. You are all so nice here, and you're obviously not on drugs. I don't know how you do it," I said jokingly.

"Prescription meds," she said and we both had a good laugh. I was still smiling when I got out to my car. Coincidentally, I was parked in the very same spot as on my first visit when I was saying goodbye, only now I was saying hello. Maybe I was catching that elusive bus after all.

There was only room for one daytime bartender and I had beat out twenty or more other applicants who didn't quite fit the bill. I wondered if one of those unlucky bastards had gotten my urine test results. I did remember seeing two of the other applicants there at the clinic. *C'est la vie,* as Chuck Berry used to say. I had struggled enough lately and this new job at the Cricket Room could just be my salvation. Somehow the prospect of working at this legendary, five-star oasis for A-listers kept my mind off almost everything else and made it easier to leave my rock 'n roll past behind. If it all worked out, maybe I'd start a blog and compete with the other dude I'd been reading. He sounded like a douche anyway.

The angels were smiling down upon me and I felt that if I listened hard enough, I could make out the fanfare of their triumphant horns announcing my victory. This was no longer the funeral march that I'd imagined being played as I'd walked toward the clinic for my drug test. It was more like Caesar's victory march. *Veni, Vedi, Vinci!*

A comprehensive training period began. I was issued a classic Cricket Room uniform, which reminded me of a butler's or ship steward's outfit. I looked very fancy with my hair cut short and no facial hair, which was not allowed. Fortunately, I had listened to some inner angel that had kept me from getting that neck tattoo I'd once considered. Suddenly, I felt all grown up – it was the first time that I'd ever had employment benefits. Medical, dental, and financial. I had never heard of a restaurant that provided benefits. They also gave me a fifty-page Employee Handbook – I had two days to read it and return the signed pages; it was ridiculous but mandatory, so I signed it without reading most of it. A change took place in me almost immediately. I felt safe, protected, dignified, and respected. A first. As a rock musician I got a lot of attention, but it was fleeting and insubstantial. This was *tangible* evidence that I was *worth* something. Management cared enough about me to insure my health and future financial stability.

It was cool during my training to learn that the Cricket Room bar uses the old-fashioned, classic "Club Service." If you ordered a rum and Coke, for instance, you would get rum on the rocks and the bartender would open a small bottle of Coke, pour the Coke from the bottle over your rum, and then you would keep what's left in the bottle of Coke next to your drink. No soda guns at all. The drinks always arrived on an elegant paper coaster emblazoned with the Cricket Room logo (an elegant green Cricket League shield). Patrons are also offered a trio of complimentary first class bar snacks, which are accompanied by a small linen napkin neatly folded in quarters. The whole presentation of even the simplest drink was one of elegance, class, and sophistication.

The night bartender, Don, had been there for years. He was the grandfatherly patron of the Cricket Room and looked the part. There was also a swing shift bartender named Mary who covered our days off. She was a fat, aging version of Pat Benatar from the wild frizzy hair and lots of makeup era. Mary worked two night and two day shifts and still had full benefits. She liked it that way because if she didn't she would have changed it. Mary was forceful, strong-minded and pushy as hell but we got along well because I did everything just the way she taught me. Otherwise, I'm sure there would have been a problem. I also treated her respectfully and never flirted with her - you'd be surprised how many guys would, just because they thought she would help them. This was a dream job and I sure as hell didn't want to fuck it up by being a smartass.

Mary was instrumental in helping me pass my ninety-day review. If she hadn't wanted me to pass, it wouldn't have happened. She was that trusted. She gave me detailed instructions on how to maintain the bar, polish the brass, dust the bottles, stock the glasses, wipe down shelves, and accomplish many more required tasks with near military precision. Every morning there was an hour of new side-work to be done and I paid close attention. It seemed that the night crew didn't do any of this. They probably figured they were the "A" Team and us day peons could do the grunt work. That was okay with me, at least for a while, but I had ambitions to move up, even as a probationary employee. I was inside those magical walls now and I wanted to take full advantage.

The ninety-day review marked the end of my trial period, and it entailed a strict grading of my grooming, product knowledge, punctuality, and attitude. If I hadn't done well, I would've been let go. I'd never heard of this kind of thing at any of my previous employers' establishments. I was taken aback at how "by the book" the place was run. But by then, I was rocking and rolling and my review was pretty much just a formality. There I was, finally on my own, and I could call myself the bartender of the Cricket Room. That was a status not many achieved and I was damn proud of myself.

During those ninety days, I had already gotten to know most of the local Beverly Hills regulars. My shift ran from eleven in the morning to seven at night, so I didn't see much of the legendary late-night craziness. But there were plenty of early birds who liked to drink their lunch from a martini glass, treating the olive as a salad.

One of Michael Jackson's many doctors enjoyed expensive chardonnay by the glassful. A local tycoon who bought and sold bankrupt businesses always carried at least five grand in hundred dollar bills rolled up in a rubber band. He liked black cherry vodka with a squeeze of lime and a bottle of club soda on the side. A female Beverly Hills court clerk poured out her sorrows into her Ketel One martinis. She drank them dirty so her tears wouldn't ruin the taste. Frequent customers included a couple of middle-aged trust fund slackers who claimed they had tour-managed for the Rolling Stones, which I later found out was a crock. Then there was the famous lawyer who would never look me in the eye. Mr. Rubin had lost all his money in a big legal scandal but he still had enough left to eat and drink well at the Cricket Room. Another interesting repeat customer was the congenial owner of a private jet company. Marcus drank about four martinis in an hour's time and got aggressive enough to start arguments with random women every time he visited. I think he was mad at his mother. Of course, there were always one or two looky-loos, tourists or writers from out of town who were too stupid to recognize the celebrities sitting right next to them. If it wasn't one of the Jonas brothers or Justin Bieber, they didn't give a shit.

On the surface, it was the most civilized job I'd ever had, but I wasn't fooled by the assortment of white-collar drunks lined up in front of me. A vice is a vice, a drunk is a drunk, no matter what the booze costs. You can be a useless piece of shit drinking high-end Scotch whiskey just as easily as you can drinking swill at a neighborhood dive. You just feel better about yourself.

After the ninety days were up, I really enjoyed being the captain of my bar with no one looking over my shoulder. I was inspired by the one-on-one contact with guests from around the world and the fact that I didn't have to rely on anyone else – cooks, bar-backs, etc. – in order to do a great job. I was totally self-sufficient behind the bar. It began to feel as if the Cricket Room bar was my own living room. I was in complete control. My days were filled with talk about international issues, politics, and show biz, the main occupation of this industry town and shaking up fresh-raspberry lemon drop martinis, key lime martinis with graham cracker rims, mojitos and glasses of fine Champagne for the ladies. The men drank an occasional mint julep, vodka martini, or Macallan 18 at twenty-five bucks a pop as if they were just bottled water. I even started reading more newspapers and trade magazines so I could converse intelligently.

One evening as I was cleaning up, getting ready to go off duty for the day, I looked around the room. The mirrored wall behind me was lined with sparkling, softly backlit glass shelves boasting thousand-dollar bottles of cognac and all the finest liquors of the world. As I stood behind my intimate, solid oak bar outfitted with brass rail trim, it was a good feeling. It dawned on me all over again that the Cricket Room was truly a unique place. And not just as a bar frequented by Hollywood's elite, but because there was no other place quite like it in the world. It had history and tradition. This was a rarified atmosphere that deserved to be treated with damn near reverence.

It also demanded a high level of commitment and integrity, two qualities that were necessary while pursuing my music career. So it wasn't too much of a stretch – I felt up for the challenge. The rocker slouch was gone, replaced by squared shoulders and prideful chin. I had slid into a long line of tradition and I felt like I belonged.

I took my position as a dignified bartender to heart. I cleaned up my language, started paying more attention to the details of service, and brushed up on my etiquette. Thanks to the international clientele, I also got in touch with my European roots more than ever before. Living in Western Europe where respect for history, art, and good taste are all ingrained in society, it has a deep, almost unconscious effect on you. Their culture of service is more refined and developed than ours in the US. Over there, schools for service personnel are considered gateways to an honorable profession. I came to believe that the Cricket Room had been founded on these principles.

As time went on, I started to relax enough to get to know some of the staff. Our hostess, Ariella, was the real-life embodiment of Jessica Rabbit. She wore her skirt short, her heels high, and her blouse bursting with feminine exuberance. She was something else. With her thickly but expertly made up eyes and face, she impressed every man and woman who walked in the door. Her demeanor was professional in the dining room but behind the curtains, she could hang with the guys and handle the raunchiest of conversations. Though the company openly discouraged dating colleagues, I'd had my eyes glued to her from the first day.

Then there was Lola, the always blasé sous chef whom I had to deal with when my guests ordered anything solid to accompany their liquid lunch or early dinner. Lola was a tall blonde with no particular body features that worked in her favor. Her hair was short, her eyes sky blue and droopy, and she only moved fast if she was mad. Then she'd rush around the kitchen with short quick steps, dropping the F-bomb every other word. Lola was a classic example of a burnout and her attitude was one of indifference to nearly everything. It was always a battle to get perfect food from her to serve my guests, but I was protective of them and fought her every time she slapped some shit on a plate that looked nothing like it was supposed to. Fuck her, my customers were more important than her apathy and I let her know it. Needless to say, she was not fond of me.

During my first six months at the Cricket Room, I became friends with one of the most original and talented waiters anyone could ever hope to work with. His name was Jens, pronounced with a soft J as Yens. Jens was about thirty-five years old, blonde, slim as a twelve-year-old boy, and Danish. He spoke French, German and English as well as Danish, and he had had a thorough culinary education. He'd attended schools in Russia, Tokyo and in Denmark to study the culinary arts and he knew all there was to know about fine food, fine wine, and the art of five-star food service.

Jens stopped at the bar one day right before the lunch rush and struck up a conversation with me. It turned out that we had traveled to many of the same countries and in light of my having grown up in Denmark, we instantly hit it off.

Nowhere in Los Angeles was there another waiter who could match all of his attributes. I used to watch him through the glass that separated the bar dining area from the main dining room, animatedly describing our signature dishes, or selling great California cabernets, white burgundies or exquisite champagne to delighted patrons. He always bowed and smiled as he poured. He had a built-in desire to serve and gave those he served attention far beyond their expectations. He was quick-witted and charming and there was nothing you could throw at him that would stick. The consummate professional, he was skilled at making people feel comfortable. No matter who they were, he could relate to them and find something to say that was appropriate. There were never any complaints from the guests as far as his service went, but his fellow wait-staff complained a lot. They all grew jealous of his popularity and the many guests who began asking specifically for him to serve them.

The gay boys who worked the day shift thought they controlled the dining room, but soon found out that they were being upstaged by Jens, and were in fact losing some of their regulars to him. Customers could tell instantly that he was sincere, really cared about them, and that the others were just performing for tips. It was entertaining to watch the dance play out in silence, through the glass, like an old silent movie. I'm sure many of those early movie stars drank and dined here. Maybe their ghosts even haunted the grounds and were at least partially responsible for luring me behind the walls.

The managers all liked Jens because he would come in a bit early and set up the entire garden area with perfectly-pressed linens and make sure every table had full salt and pepper shakers and polished stemware for water. He had tremendous energy and passion for the business. The kind you don't find very often these days. Jens's extensive knowledge and dedication to the culinary and service arts became an inspiration to me and I found myself constantly learning lessons about food and table service from him.

He made a strange request one morning: he asked me for a Bloody Mary made with Akvavit to cure his hangover from the previous night. From that day on, every morning I had a Danish Mary waiting for him in a white Styrofoam cup. You could say it was my tuition for the grand education he was giving me.

Behind the bar, everything was under control on my watch. My guests were introducing me to check totals I had only dreamed of, as they would order Beluga caviar and drink Dom Perignon by the glass. The hockey great Wayne Gretsky ordered both but added a shot of Stoli vodka that he knew I kept in the freezer. Gretzky was a no-nonsense guy, not exactly loosey-goosey, just straightforward and tended not to chit chat. This was just before the U.S. Fish and Wildlife Service listed the Beluga sturgeon as a threatened species. Nowadays the guests have to settle for Ossetra caviar from Iran. There's a lot of stuff to know in the food and beverage service business, at least at this level.

With Gretzky at the bar, I spied Warren Beatty seated in a booth with his hand in the air, furiously trying to flag down a server to wait on him. Instinct told me to approach him immediately. I quickly looked around for our Maître d' but he was nowhere to be found. Even though I hadn't been trained to serve the tables, watching and listening to Jens had given me a false sense of confidence and I boldly approached Mr. Beatty. He was pretty angry.

"What the hell is going on here today? Can you get my guest something to drink? What do you want, Sam, an iced tea?" Sam nodded. "Yeah, get us two iced teas and don't put that orange in it just a bunch of lemons on the side, okay?"

I nod as I'm writing furiously in my captain's pad.

"What do you want, the fish, Sam? Yeah, waiter, we'll both have the sea bass, broiled not grilled, no butter just a little olive oil, no salt and some steamed broccoli and sautéed spinach, but sauté the spinach with garlic, would you? And no salt on anything, right, Sam?" Whoever the fuck Sam was, he nodded again. "And bring us some of that flat bread, the 'lavask?' You know, the hard cracker bread?"

"Yes, sir, would you like some mineral water?" I asked when I finally got a chance to say something.

"No, we'll have some green tea after lunch with some blueberries and blackberries for dessert, and don't put any sugar on them – just *au naturel*, okay? All right, thank you."

"Thank you, Mr. Beatty."

I repeated his order back to him just to make sure I'd gotten it right.

"Yeah, yeah, and hurry up with the bread and iced tea, please."

"Yes, sir."

All of a sudden, I'm a waiter and my guests at the bar are left without a host. How does it happen in a place like this that a superstar like Warren Beatty with Hollywood glamour practically tattooed on his forehead can be sitting unnoticed, reduced to waving his hand in the air? It wasn't long before I realized that there's a different movie playing behind this particular silver screen, one not so obvious to anyone at first glance.

CHAPTER 3
COCKTAIL

Bartending is a very special, unique line of work. It's much more than serving drinks – it's a calling. Bartenders serve many functions: we are often sounding boards, philosophers, psychologists, marriage counselors, dating coaches, emotional stand-ins, devil's advocates or even confidantes. Sometimes we can even be teachers: students lined up facing us on barstools, eyes fixed, relaxed and engaged, paying complete attention to the story being told or wisdom being imparted. What you never discuss, unless you're the Evel Knievel of bartending, is politics and religion. You can lose tips, teeth, or your job by taking the wrong side or insulting someone's beliefs.

Holding court in a temple of history, tradition and elegance like the Cricket Room was the Holy Grail of bartending. There was no other place like it and I constantly worried whether it could survive in today's culture where cheap, fast, and crude were valued above class, dignity, and quality. So far so good; we were raking in the dough. The level of celebrities, however, couldn't hold a burned-at-both-ends candle to the elegance of Cary Grant, Doris Day, Marlene Dietrich, and the other stars of Hollywood's heyday who were frequent guests here.

Sometimes in quiet moments, I stood behind my bar soaking in the atmosphere, feeling like king shit, and thought about why I was there, in that special place. For a bartender, this was hallowed ground. Hearing Cricket Room celebrity stories from the past, often told by guests, other employees, and even management, made me jealous, but not of the people who witnessed them. I just wanted something similar to happen to me. I wanted to see movie and reality show stars have impulsive arguments, emotional meltdowns, and passionate hookups. I also wanted to help them blow ridiculous bundles of cash at my bar. So far, my only real celebrity encounter had been with Warren Beatty, and aside from being impatient, he'd behaved perfectly. Why couldn't he have stood up in the booth, started throwing dishes, and ripping off his clothes? Now that would have been something. I wanted chaos and mayhem, dammit. Bring on the crazy. Somebody come in and let your freak flag fly high and proud. I was anxious for a chance to prove that I had the training and maturity to handle it. I was prepared for anything short of murder.

For the first six months though, working the bar had been uneventful. No guest ever stumped me with some fucked up made-up drink request, and even if they had I would have just made something up and served it. People who pull that crap on bartenders never know the difference if you serve it with confidence. It's all in the attitude.

The drinks ordered were all old school. By the glass: French Champagne like Veuve Clicquot and the occasional Dom at a mere $100 a glass; high-end wines from our rotating list of fourteen wineries from around the world; vodka martinis (mostly Ketel One, Grey Goose or our most expensive at the time, Ultimat, in its signature cobalt bottle); gin martinis (Bombay Sapphire and Tanqueray); lots of Old-Fashioneds and Manhattans (mainly mixed with Maker's Mark Bourbon); aged Scotch whiskey (primarily Macallan 18 and 25 and an occasional Balvenie or Lagavulin for those who wanted to grow hair on their backs); and basic mixed drinks. Negroni, a bitter concoction of gin, Campari and vermouth, was ordered mainly by Italian and French guests. Singapore Sling was Hunter Thompson's favorite when he had been a famously frequent guest, especially during the '60s and '70s. Every year, Hunter Thompson fans would actually come in on his birthday to drink Singapore Slings in his honor. I could easily picture the iconic writer sitting at the bar, wearing his trademark tinted glasses, smoking a cigarette, discussing world events or politics. Ahhhh, the bad old days.

One day I was furtively checking out some skinny, goofy-looking guy at table number one who wore large cartoonish glasses and sported a hairdo that looked as if he'd gone to clown school, then seen a ghost and been electrocuted at the same time. It took me a minute until I realized that I was looking at Phil Spector, who was famous for his music and in later years for his murder trial. Many of the songs you know were either written or produced by this little twerp. He was sitting with a blonde girl who looked a hell of a lot like Lana Clarkson, the woman he later murdered. But according to court testimony, it couldn't have been her because he claimed to have met her for the first time at the House of Blues on the night she was killed. Sorry, I don't believe that. I know what I saw. This was months before Ms. Clark-son's murder, and I doubt Mr. Spector would mistake the Cricket Room for The House of Blues since he was our regular guest. The wigged-out Spector is now serving prison time, no doubt singing soprano to his girlfriend, Inmate #70238956, a/k/a Butch.

It was lunchtime and two old regulars who had been coming to the Cricket Room for at least twenty years were sitting at the bar. Mr. Peterson said he preferred the lounge's bar atmosphere to our formal dining room. By now, the stool's imprint is permanently worn into his butt, not that I've looked mind you. Mr. Peterson of the Peterson publishing empire and his wife always came to my bar to have lunch, but Mr. Peterson would complain about how terrible the food was. He loved to tell me stories about the good ol' days, and how they all used to dine like kings at his old restaurant, Scandia, on Sunset Boulevard. He'd bought the restaurant in the 1970's from the original proprietors, Ken and Ted Hansen, who had made it into a number one celebrity dining spot that had competed with the Cricket Room of the time.

The waiters had worn red jackets, the captains differentiated in black jackets, and the service was reputed to have been beyond impeccable. One guest recalled that if you dropped your napkin, a swarm of staff would descend upon you to replace it and lay it in your lap. The food, as he described it, was Scandinavian-inspired luxury continental cuisine. Having lived there, I'm highly skeptical of the cuisine, but I always let him talk (read: brag) uninterrupted. Scandia's sumptuous interior was elegantly designed with exotic paneled woods that today's tree huggers would despise, copper and brass fixtures, bright red chairs, royal blue and white china, and crystal vases. The kitchen had received many awards for its gourmet cuisine from the '50s through the '70s. Mr. Peterson even admitted to me that he had no idea how to run a restaurant and finally in 1989, after losing money for ten years, he had to close his beloved old-school eatery. Now he came to my bar to relive the old days, which sounded quite similar to the Cricket Room's heyday. Today, if Frank Sinatra suddenly arose from the dead, the Cricket Room would be the only place in the LA area where he'd feel comfortable. We might even let him smoke.

Right next to Spector and his blonde mystery date was Warren Beatty at his usual table, number two. This time he was getting good service. Somebody probably still has teeth marks on their ass from the chewing out they got for his last visit, even though I had saved the day by jumping in to help. Someone of Beatty's stature should not have to even ask for service, let alone wave his hand like an idiot flagging a taxi.

Next to Beatty on table three was Steven Tyler, a rock and roll peacock in his flashy outfit. Without the crap all tied into his hair, his ten pounds of jewelry, and his over the top outfits, he would look more like somebody's skinny grandfather than a rock legend. But legend he is; I'm a huge fan and would have loved nothing more than to act like a fan and run up to him for an autograph. That, of course, was not done at the Cricket Room and would have gotten me fired immediately.

Suddenly I felt as if I had truly arrived, and this was the Cricket Room I had been hoping for. "Fuck yeah, this is more like it."

As I was gazing at these iconic figures from behind the bar, a memory flashed back to me from my waiter-ing days in Boston. I was working at a trendy spot on Boylston Street when Tyler walked up to me and asked: "Hey! What kinda beers you all gots?" As if he were rapping out the lyrics for "Walk This Way." He was just about to order an Anchor Steam when his wife Cyrinda intervened. They later went to a table where Joe Perry, Tom Hamilton, and their ladies joined them. Mid-dinner, Steven went to the bathroom and did not come out, even with the band and Cyrinda pounding on the door. Finally, the restaurant staff had to unscrew the hinges. And there they found Tyler, passed out cold. They quickly paid their bill and dragged Tyler's limp body out with Perry and Hamilton holding him up. He certainly looked a lot more alive and healthy this time. It would have been cool if he'd remembered me, but he probably didn't remember that night at all, let alone me.

During my early days at the Cricket Room, it seemed to me as if I was being auditioned by many of the old regulars. Just a feeling I had – that they needed to make sure I could pass muster and maintain their standards. They would subtly test me in conversation to see if I could politely keep up my end of the discussion. Could I remember their names? The details of their usual drink orders? The strength, the two cherries in the old fashioned, the blue cheese stuffed olives, the two drops of vermouth in their Plymouth martini, the brand of bourbon in their Manhattan rocks? It became evident that I was passing their tests because more and more locals began showing up and the bar was becoming busier by the day. I liked to think some of that booming business was due to my bartending skills and charm, but it may have been coincidental. Celebrities like to say they "cherish their anonymity" and love to "fly under the radar" but that's bullshit. They crave attention and adulation; it's why they're in the business. So they love coming to a bar that's known for celebrity clientele. It makes them feel special, and it's my job to encourage that delusion.

I served Sheryl Crow and Lance Armstrong after they had

attended a fundraiser for the Democratic National Party. Crow looked very plain-Jane in person and Armstrong looked like a thousand other thin, fit guys you'd see anywhere. I didn't even know who Crow was until she handed me her credit card. The same went for Claire Danes. Girl-next-door types you might see at any bar or Denny's in America. For a while, Selma Blair was hanging out a lot and bringing her then-buddy Matthew Perry. They were always funny and entertaining, never rude or arrogant, but too antsy to sit still for too long so I never really got to know them. When certain actors become known for a signature role, like Perry is with his role on *Friends*, people often expect them to be the character instead of themselves, whether it's being funny or a superhero. In person, they more often than not just want to act like normal people out for a drink or a meal. They may have chosen the Cricket Room because it's special, has great food and service, and not like others in their business who come for the snob appeal.

They have normal-people problems too: Taryn Manning's credit card was declined and we ended up picking up her check. She was quite embarrassed and said she'd come back to pay but she never did. And this was after her big breakthrough in *Hustle & Flow*. *Yo, it's tough out there for a pimp!* Maybe she forgot, or simply was too embarrassed to return and pay her debt, but I lost a lot of respect for her.

Not one but two James Bonds came in: Roger Moore and Pierce Brosnan came in two days apart. Moore had a cranberry juice, no ice. I wanted to ask him, "Shaken, not stirred?" but I refrained since he might not be drinking for a reason. He's probably heard it a million times anyway. He was looking a bit bloated and old, actually. Brosnan had a couple of Ketel One Martinis "shaken!" with olives. He was cool and approachable but his phone kept ringing so we really didn't talk much. He's so good looking (and taller than I expected at six two) that women's heads turned and he got a lot of attention.

Ozzy Osbourne, who had a house account, approached me at the bar. He sort of did his little wobble-float walk and then stopped, facing me, and said: "Gimmieashodabsoluvoka."

I picked up the Absolut bottle and raised my eyebrows. "This, sir?"

"Yeajusgimmieashod quick," he said, so I filled my aluminum shaker with ice and prepared to chill him a nice shot of vodka.

"NohIdonwaninieyes."

"No ice?" I repeated. He shook his head. I was about to pour it straight out of the bottle into a shot glass when he stopped me with,

"Makeyadubel."

"A double," I repeated. He nodded his head, and continued nodding approvingly as I poured two shots into an old-fashioned rocks glass. He almost grabbed it before I stopped pouring, gulped it down in two slurps and then wobble-floated away. Nothing like a double shot of warm Absolut. He left an herby-scented trail of patchouli hippy perfume in his wake and a question mark on my face. I felt as if someone should jump in and present me with a certificate for interpreting a foreign language on the fly. But no matter how bad Ozzy had fucked himself up, he was still the coolest dude on the planet. I think he could have had a pile of shit on his head and people would have thought it was cool.

There were two young guys at the bar who had just gotten two of their scripts signed with National Lampoon Films and were celebrating. This kind of celebrity encounter was just what they'd come in hoping for.

"Wow, dude, that was fucking surreal!" they said regarding Ozzy, and then they asked how much per shot for the Louis XIII, a top shelf cognac by Remy.

"A hundred and fifty," I said.

"Give us one each."

And before I could lift the damn bottle, Ozzy was back. "Gimmia nu-uh dubulshod."

So we did it again, only this time I knew the drill, he gulped it down and as he was leaving I asked, "Put these on your house account then, sir?"

"Yepuputweypercentip."

"Thank you, Mr. Osbourne." He waved his hand and just wobble-floated on out again. Everyone in the bar was too mesmerized to speak or even attempt to approach him. He had that effect. It was like seeing God. You didn't run up and ask God for an autograph. Well, Ozzy either.

I served the two scriptwriters their once-in-a-lifetime glass of Louis XIII, which they had no idea how to drink but would brag about it to their grandkids one day. One of them shot it and the other one tried to sip it but really didn't like it at all so he shot his too. They high-fived each other and giggled – a funny sight. Coupla lucky newbies with big dreams and more money than brains.

I went back to thinking about Ozzy: *Isn't Ozzy supposed to be clean and sober?* According to the press at the time, he was on the wagon. No wonder he was in such a hurry. Sneaking shots behind Sharon's back, eh?

As time went by, I had my share of attention from women who frequented the bar. I'm not a bad looking guy, but singers and bartenders have one thing in common: women think they're hot. One of my fans was nicknamed The Stalker by Ariella. She told me an elaborate story about how she was the ex-girlfriend of the actor Ed O'Neill and also had dated Andrea Bocelli. The Stalker would come in around noon and sit there for four hours telling me her life stories and all about her men and her "spiritual" relationships. Most of her stories included some actor or rich businessman with whom she had connected on the Internet and had managed, with her good looks, to lure into a rendezvous. The constant name-dropping was just a bit too much at times but I had to listen with a smile. Her ego translated my smiles into interest in her. I would serve her the same thing every time: chopped salad, no bacon or cheese, side of ranch dressing and a diet Coke with lots of ice and a lemon wedge. For someone so supposedly "spiritual," she ate like a typical faux-Zen Angelino obsessed with her weight and appearance.

She was very pretty; tall with dark brown hair, a great body probably from Yoga, but a small chest. She never wore makeup, and she didn't need it. It didn't take a genius to determine that she was a time bomb so I kept things very professional and never called her outside of work, even though she left me her number on several occasions. There was a direct phone line to the bar and she somehow got the number and always called to make sure I was working before she'd come in. I heard that she never showed up when I wasn't working. She was truly exhausting, always asking me what I thought about her relationships, etc. Who did she think I was, Dr. Phil? If I had been, I would have advised her to stop sitting in a bar for four hours a day and trying to seduce a bartender who didn't give a flying crap about her, but I'm not and I didn't. My job is to listen, not opine.

This went on for a whole year and I'd be lying if I said that the thought of going over to her apartment in Hollywood and having hot sex with her hadn't entered my mind. But I knew that with this one, it would be a big mistake. I actually eventually grew so incredibly tired of her stories that I could feel my mind go into hibernation within a few minutes of her arrival. She was the intense kind of woman who I could see boiling somebody's pet rabbit or hiding a huge chef's knife under the bed. No thanks. There were too many easier ways to get laid without risking body parts or pets.

During that same time period there was a divorcee from Mulholland Estates in Bel Air who began showing up. She would come to my bar and pour her heart out about how lonely she was. She tried to lure me in by describing how quiet it was up there in her big house all alone and how she wanted to cook for me and serve me a candlelit dinner. She dropped me her number but I kept stalling, mainly because she had that fake plastic surgery face and the boob implants so common in Hollywood. She was a nice enough woman, but to top it all off she was actually kind of heavy and I couldn't get past her plastic-looking *Planet of the Apes* face. To me, almost everyone who has had that amount of plastic surgery ends up looking strange, like a certain new breed of people that live mostly in LA. Do they all go to the same doctor? I just couldn't see being with her. What would Mom say? Probably something like, "She looks like there might be big clips in the back of her head holding it all together." Sex on demand or not, she was just too creepy and I was scared to see her naked.

Just as I had wished, every day started surprising me with something out of the ordinary. The tourists and regulars kept coming, but Paul McCartney came in one evening with his then-wife Heather and ordered a couple of margaritas with salt and lime squeezed into them. I was truly honored to have the world's best songwriter of our time at my bar. He looked great and his wife wasn't bad to look at either. I shook his hand and told him that I was a huge fan and that it was my greatest pleasure ever to have him at my bar. He was very humble and thanked me in his trademark Scouse accent, but was much more interested in regular everyday chitchat with his wife than chatting with me. They weren't able to sit too long before other people noticed them so they had to be moved to a private table. I was sad to see him leave but psyched that I had had the brief opportunity to meet him. I never charged for the drinks – are you kidding me? (Mr. P signed off on it.) It's a Beatle for God's sake! How many people can say they served a drink to a Beatle and his wife?

I served the Donald, his ex, Ivana, and their daughter, Ivanka Trump, but all at separate times. Ivanka is absolutely a real quality woman. She's beautiful and very classy; she's a real pearl in the classical sense. Ivana used to come in with her Italian tennis-playing boy-toy Rossano who was at least twenty years her junior. She was always sweet and very courteous. She always ordered a Goose Martini and Rossano would have an espresso. I've got to admit I could see what the guy saw in her – she definitely had something special in addition to the obvious, even with the huge age difference. Maybe she was his homeroom teacher and he was her teacher's pet? I almost asked if he had a note from his mother, but of course didn't.

Months later, Trump himself came in with his then-fiancée Melania. Diet Coke for him and a Goose Cosmo for her. She was definitely impressive-looking. Trump left without paying, meaning no tip for me, so I had to transfer the check to his table. What a jerk, but that's already written all over his face anyway – you don't need me to tell you that. When he enters a room he has that demeanor of parting the seas. "I'm here now. Everyone can breathe." It's amazing what a gorgeous woman like Melania is willing to overlook for a measly few billion.

Broadway Joe Namath showed up one day and had three Grey Goose Martinis, shaken, with olives. He sat at the bar and told me that he was building a house around the Brentwood Park area to be closer to his daughter. Thank God he didn't talk about football because that's one thing I don't know shit about, having grown up in Europe and all. Joe had a great vibe about him and it wasn't long before he was swarmed by rich locals at the bar calling out his name, "Hey, Joe, remember me?" Or "Hey, Joe, we met at blah blah blah," one after the other. He paid for his three drinks and got out of there quick. I shook his hand, he left me a Grant, and I've got to say, that guy never stopped smiling from the time he came in until the time he left. Never saw him again, though. But I heard he came back several times after that from Don, who served him.

Paul Magers, an award-winning news anchor from the Twin Cities, signed a deal with CBS News Los Angeles and bought a house up the street from the restaurant. He would come in to unwind after work and talk about how it felt to return to LA after being in the frozen north for years. He liked his Chalon chardonnay and house-smoked Balik salmon. Nice guy, good tipper, even if he was wearing TV makeup. I always enjoyed serving him.

Stan Lee (comic book writer, editor, publisher, media producer, television host, actor) would sit at one of the tables very close to the bar and insist that I come out from behind the bar to serve him. He was going through a real revival of interest his work, and his comic book creations were famous again, especially *Spiderman*. This was right after the first movie starring Toby Maguire. Lee had also created the *Fantastic Four*, the *Hulk*, *Iron Man*, *Thor* and the *X-Men*. So when

Hollywood started making big-budget movies featuring Stan Lee's characters, we started seeing more of him. Even though he was getting on in age, nothing dampened his smile. One time I introduced a regular customer of mine by the name of Mr. Hart to Mr. Lee. They talked for a long while and Stan ended up signing some stuff for him. Mr. Hart was so thrilled that he tipped me seven-hundred bucks, the biggest tip I ever received as a bartender.

During my period as a bartender, I also waited on numerous rock stars, which always touched a nerve for me:

Bon Jovi: Boring, doesn't drink alcohol. Just kind of walks around for everyone to notice him and then gets bored and leaves. He's as boring as his singing suggests, even though he had been my "hair" inspiration. To his credit, he's been married to his wife for twenty-four years and has always kept a good image. Gay?

Richie Sambora (Bon Jovi bandmate): Likes to drink decent wine, is happy-go-lucky, and doesn't mind talking to strangers. He picked up the tab for himself and his guest, keyboardist David Bryan (who looks like he's been living large). Sambora excitedly expressed his appreciation for Steely Dan whom he had recently seen perform live. Nice guy, though he's got the reputation of a player with the ladies. Rock on, dude. Rock on.

Mick Jagger: A wiry fucker and still just drinks iced tea. Was joined by a female publicist and another businesswoman. He let them drink their wine and once their guard was down he laid out his points and got them to agree, and before they knew it, he was gone. Handled like the true businessman that he is. I love his hair and his rubber face.

Johnny Rzeznik (Goo Goo Dolls musician and vocalist): A shy, quiet, romantic, who drinks light but prefers a dark candlelit table to court his young girlfriends. It's fun to watch him mesmerize them by taking them to the most exclusive dinner spot in Los Angeles and gazing deeply into their eyes from behind his long bangs.

Billy Corgan (Smashing Pumpkins): The same as Johnny only a lot taller and his girls are at least fifteen years his junior; he seems like one hell of a serious, scowling bald man. He drinks inexpensive Napa Cabernet by the glassful like a conventional suburban housewife on a tight budget. What kind of rocker is that? Seriously, buy a good bottle, impress me, snarl-face! By the way, when you sing you sound like an angry baby! Maybe somebody smashed his pumpkins.

Neil Diamond: No introduction needed. Fan or not, everybody knows this crooner. Red wine drinker. This guy's a freak. He likes 'em younger, baby, yeah! No smiles; has a very serious attitude. He married his manager who has the convenient last name of McNeil and is *thirty years* his junior. Just seeing Mr. Diamond reminds me of the story about him coming offstage at The Last Waltz, saying, "Top that!" to Bob Dylan who was standing in the wings. Dylan famously said, "What do I have to do, fall asleep?" My sentiments exactly.

Simon Le Bon: Rented our private dining room to try on stage outfits for his new tour with Duran Duran, is British, tall and good looking in a pretty-boy kinda way. Le Bon sat at the bar for a while and I served him a glass of Moët Champagne. He seemed very sophisticated for a rock-star, a pretty mellow old fellow, I'd have to say. He didn't embarrass himself.

Harry Belafonte: An old school musical genius. Drank Myers Rum on the rocks with a lime squeeze. He still has the fire in his eyes.

Diana Ross: Champagne and smiles. When she walks in the room, the piano player always plays "Mahogany" and she shouts in excitement, "They're playing my song!" She's been coming regularly for years, gracefully prancing through the restaurant like the diva she is.

50 cent: Is far from the hood he portrays in his music and never wears a bandana or tank top to the Cricket Room. He developed a vitamin water product with Glacéau called Formula 50 and assumed a stake in the company. Coca-Cola eventually purchased Glacéau for $4.1 billion, and *Forbes* estimated that 50 Cent walked away with $100 million after taxes. He likes sweet fruity drinks and yo, he ain't no thug.

Puff Daddy, Diddy, P. Diddy, Sean "Puffy" Combs: He's changed his name more often than an identity thief. Nobody likes him in the whole Cricket Room, no one, not even the regular guests. He's impolite and disrespectful, definitely has a chip. One night on his way out, he asked the hostess for a toothpick. Ariella very politely held the container so he could pick one out. Diddy picked through the selection and discarded the ones he didn't want on to the floor by her feet, kept one for himself, and left. We couldn't figure out what was wrong with the ones he discarded since they were all wrapped in plastic. Maybe this was during his "I'm a rebel" phase. Or it was his time of the month.

Ludacris: Loved the guy. He's full of funny comments and surprisingly insightful conversation. Alizé and pineapple. Line 'em up! Another rapper who is no thug and is completely different in person than on stage. Shorter than Puffy but no chip there. He knows who he is; nothing' funny about that in spite of the ironic name.

Nelly: A clean-cut rapper and entrepreneur with a soft voice who would come in to romance some young girl while his huge bodyguard looked on. His signature facial Band-aid was removed. He was too quiet, I couldn't hear a damn word he said.

Jay-Z: That's one tall mother at over six feet. Beyonce knew what she was getting in on with that guy. A smiley happy dude who seemed good-natured to me.

The funny thing is, all the rappers ordered stupid ass drinks. It stood out to me because they all have tough-guy images and you expect more coolness. Maybe it's because they all pretty much came from nothing and never had a chance to develop a taste for classic cocktails – like they learned the names of drinks from TV shows or lousy "B" movies – and here they are at the elite Cricket Room but really don't know how to drink. I always found myself making them Pina Coladas, Mai Tais, Malibu and pineapple juice, Alizé or Hpnotiq with pineapple juice, banana Daiquiris, strawberry Coladas. Those sweet froufrou drinks are disgusting! There's only one sweet drink that qualifies in my book: the classic Mojito made from scratch with raw sugar or sugarcane juice, although it's a pain in the ass to assemble. But if you're gonna drink that other shit it has to at least be by the pool or in the Florida Keys and it should be a Rum Runner topped with 151: Bacardi light, Captain Morgan, Malibu, spill some grenadine, cranberry, orange and pineapple juice, blend it smooth with ice, top it with a sugared lime wheel and a 1/2 oz. shot of 151 lit on fire. Hollaaaa! And eat some fried cheese sticks or jalapeño poppers while you're at it. Come on, guys, man the fuck up.

Despite this illustrious parade of celebs at my bar, I noticed that most stars usually don't want to sit at the bar because sooner or later they will be approached by some idiot asking them stupid questions that they just don't feel like answering. So most of the celebrities end up at dinner tables where their privacy is more easily guarded.

During my time as bartender at the Cricket Room, I was never bothered by any managers or anyone interfering with my job. Once in a while my boss would bring some new agreement for me to read and sign but it was usually pertaining to the wait staff and since I also served some food at the bar I would have to look it over and sign it too.

Being a bartender in this place was an absolute dream. With only seven chairs and some standing room, I got to know guests on a personal level, and they knew me by name. It wasn't even the Cricket Room anymore, it was Pauli's Bar and we were all in love with our own little world. It was far away from the eyes of Big Brother. Since there were around fifty-five dining tables, the establishment kept all of their focus on the diners, as we know from experience that diners are way more prone to complain and bar patrons are easier to keep happy – you just have to manage their blood alcohol level and make sure they don't get too happy. At the Cricket Room bar I carefully managed my patrons' drug of choice and made sure we always had interesting topics to talk about. Even my European patrons were becoming regulars.

After my third year behind the bar, the management decided I was also going to handle table service at the few tables that were in the front of the bar, mainly during the early hours of lunch when I wasn't too busy. I didn't realize it then but they were grooming me to become a waiter. They were instructing me on how to perform five-star food service at the bar as well as educating me on all the ingredients in each dish. I also learned a bit about how the kitchen works and details about the food and wine pairings. Since I was a bartender and not a waiter, the kitchen staff was always nice to me. We had a good deal going. Their friendly demeanor had much to do with the alcoholic drinks I secretly obtained for them, and my friendly demeanor had to do with the top-notch food they would provide to me in return. There was a constant food-for-drink tradeoff, usually bartered through the food runners so it looked legit, as if they were bringing it for me to serve to a guest. Instead, I would be the one furtively enjoying lobster, Kobe burgers and steak tartar that I had hidden in my supply cabinet in the employee hallway.

It's odd that in the combined twelve years I spent as bartender at the club downtown and at the Cricket Room, I had now managed to forget all about my bad experiences as a waiter. I lost track of the vast differences between the two jobs and the ways in which guests and even the kitchen staff relate to you. I should have kept all that in mind, but I was seduced by the glorious atmosphere of the Cricket Room and intrigued by the confidence our Maître d' was placing in me to handle the art of food service their way. I should have stayed behind my polished mahogany bar, been the cool guy mixing exotic drinks for the 1% of society, and continued to turn down more ass than most guys get in a lifetime.

CHAPTER 4
THE PARTY

I was surprised at how well I had fit right into the scene at the Cricket Room. I wasn't a celebrity fucker but I did enjoy rubbing shoulders (and only shoulders) with people who had become A-Listers. It also helped that I enjoyed characters, including my colleagues, who had roles of their own to play and played them well. There was always a lot of pride evident in the staff; everyone knew they were privileged to work there.

Who knows why I was so fascinated by jocks, jerks, and jump-your-bones bimbos that populate Hollywood today. Maybe it was the contrast between their trashy behavior and what I perceived to be the class acts of previous stars and starlets. Memory and history do have a way of whitewashing the truth. Ever heard some dork tell you how great high school was? And you just know he lived with a permanent wedgie and carried breath freshener and acne cream in his hand-me-down-jacket pocket.

Or maybe it was my own dream of rock stardom that just wouldn't go away; it was always a mosquito buzzing in my head. Could I gain some sudden inspiration or learn some magical method for rocketing to fame and fortune? Maybe. And in the meantime it couldn't hurt to work amidst the Hollywood glitterati in the most famous bar/restaurant on planet Earth.

One of my new friends – a consummate performer in his own right – was my Danish colleague Jens. Our common Scandinavian background made our soon to be prodigal bond even tighter. We were both making enough money to begin to party somewhat in the manner of the degenerate show biz types we served at "The Room." Don't get me wrong – we didn't need any inspiration on that front. If a full-time waiter or bartender in a popular, busy establishment tells you he doesn't party like a rock star every chance he gets, he's lying. The work is so unrelentingly stressful – physically and mentally – and so damn exhausting, we have to let it all out every now and then. And lest ye be taken aback by the debauchery I plan to relate in these pages, let it be known that I am no angel, and yet no different from any serious server

I've ever had the pleasure of working – and partying – with.

As for Jens and me, it also helped that we shared the exact same work schedule. One perfect So-Cal spring day Jens invited me over to his girlfriend's condo in Sherman Oaks. The complex had two swimming pools with hot tubs attached; her unit was just a two-minute walk from one of the pools. It was a very lush and quiet complex with most of the tenants at work since our days off were during the workweek.

Jens gave me a tour of the unit; it was a two-bedroom, two–and-a-half bathroom townhome with Brazilian dark-wood floors and elegant furniture, a balcony facing the pool and another in the back. The fridge was stocked with food and there was ample wine and booze to be had as well. Jens instantly offered me a Margarita. Why would I say no? Even if it only was one o'clock in the afternoon on a Wednesday, anytime was party time for Jens – if he wasn't working.

A couple of dips in the pool and a few margaritas later, Jens started to share stories about his past. His gift for storytelling was one of the reasons he was a waiter who people remembered. As we were paging through loose photos from his life in Ibiza which he kept in a shoebox stashed under the bed in the guest bedroom, he became even more excited and energetic. Every guy has that secret stash of pictures that he hides like buried treasure and digs up every so often to count the gold and polish the jewelry. Valuables he can't share with his wife or girlfriend because she wouldn't understand, or simply wouldn't want to. The big drama comes when they're discovered and long, stuttering explanations ensue. But I digress...

He had pictures of himself bartending in some kind of club with a dance floor covered with soap bubbles and semi-nude girls everywhere. There were pictures of Jens partying on a yacht; pictures with hot, horny girls on both arms, one with a leg twisted around his and the other with her tongue in his ear. The more pictures I saw, the more I realized that this guy was a true party animal. In every picture he was either shirtless or wore his shirt wide open to the navel. He looked like the new Scandinavian version of Hugh Hefner holding court in his own debauched Playboy pen. I can't stress enough how in these party pics he looked nothing like the stiff, starched, formal service-oriented waiter to the stars whom I had come to admire.

He wore ropes upon ropes of sterling silver jewelry like a rocker or rap icon. There were Maltese crosses on his belt buckle; long, heavy chains around his neck; super cool sterling skull rings on his fingers. He even had a heavy sterling silver ring made with his actual family crest on it. He wore the latest in Italian casual fashion, back when Diesel was becoming all the rage. As it turned out, his taste in clothing was a few years ahead of its time. Just a year later everybody was wearing $300 jeans and distressed designer clothes that looked worn but cost a fortune. Jens had been doing it for years. The guy had style.

Although in the eyes of some, the squares, he looked like a fag, I thought he was the coolest guy I knew. Now I admired him even more.

Jens's favorite music was not really what I considered music. It was club music. Like House and Trance, most of it was instrumental. I assumed he had developed his musical taste while living in Ibiza and Marbella and hanging out in discos. He had also had a fair amount of experience DJ-ing at clubs and parties. As we dug through his shoebox full of photos of half-naked girls in beds surrounded by empty liquor bottles, he reached deep into his closet and returned with his "other" shoebox. It was chock full of dollar bills, twenties, fifties, hundreds.

"Pauli," he said, "this is the money I keep hidden from Christie. It's my emergency fund, you know? I've been putting three hundred a week in here and now I'm itching to start spending it." He lifted it all out, and there had to be close to twenty grand. This was the real buried treasure.

"You ever try opening up an account in an actual bank?" I asked sarcastically. "Don't you think this is dangerous?"

"Yeah, uh, come on, of course, Pauli, I have an account; this is just the stuff I keep for *me*."

Once he took all the money out, there were a few baggies of pills and coke and drug paraphernalia left at the bottom. He tried to play it off as if he were surprised. "Wow, I didn't even know this shit was here! We should do some!"

He finished the thought by cutting up lines of coke on the glass table and snorting up the biggest one. "Oh shit, this stuff is clean!" he said while he handed me the glass snuffer tube, which was a fancy version of the cut off clear plastic drinking straw that most people use. This thing had a rounded end that fit in your nostril more comfortably and the other end was just slightly flared. *Oh, shit*, I thought to myself, *I thought this part of my life was over.* Apparently not. I reached for the glass straw and snorted a line. It's not often you get free coke.

Immediately, the white light shot through my brain like a blast from a Star Wars laser gun. My senses were blasted into a higher realm and all light, color and sound became exceptionally vivid. I could feel the drug flood into my bloodstream and give me a sense of relaxed alertness mixed with an air of confidence and extreme focus, as if each moment were its own beautiful photograph frozen in time and then surpassed by the next. I was high! A fleeting thought passed through my now electrified brain: random drug testing. I laughed at the irony, buoyed by my almighty, drug-induced confidence. *That'll never happen to me!*

Jens laughed too – I'm not sure why – but he instantly became very excited, convinced that he had found a new partner in crime. "We should get the hell out of Sherman Oaks and go to the Viceroy Hotel on Santa Monica Beach," he said, bouncing all over the place in a state of complete delight. When Jens gets crazy about hanging out with somebody, he starts making big plans. "You don't have to go to work 'til Friday, right?" I nodded. "That's awesome, Pauli, neither do I! Let's go!"

Next thing I knew we were in Jens' green Jetta screeching and lurching towards the beach. We headed straight for the Viceroy and grabbed a cabana by their tiny little pool. By the time I had gone to the bathroom, done my business and washed up, there were two bottles of 1995 Piper Heidsieck chilling by the cabana and Jens was sprawled out like he owned the place. We were like characters in a movie, maybe *Get Shorty*, completely convinced we were all-knowing, all-seeing hunks who owned the world. We were the pearls in an oyster known as LA.

Just twenty minutes later three people I had never met before showed up. One guy's name was Andrei – he was a tall, dark-haired man with a heavy Russian accent, and he'd brought two girls with him. One girl's name was Victoria – she was cute, in her late thirties, and thin but curvy with long dark hair twisted up in braids. The other was a blonde named Susan, who was a bit younger. Susan was bubbly, genuinely attractive and had a fine, full hourglass figure that made her look like a movie star from the 1940s. Of course, the first thing going through my mind was that we now had two girls and three guys. Then I remembered that Jens already had a live-in girlfriend. But the question remained, which one of them was with Andrei?

We occupied that cabana for the rest of the day and part of the evening. We were all drunk and Susan and I continued to hang out and have a good time while Jens yakked it up with Victoria. Andrei was always on the phone and kept disappearing. The bill at the cabana came to five hundred bucks, so I gave Jens two hundred cash thinking that Andrei would be putting in a couple of hundred too but he never did. I suspected he was a dealer and something of an amateur pimp, not really a friend of Jens.

Jens had booked a room on the penthouse floor for the night, The Monarch suite. This guy was like a professional partier. Once we got up there, things *really* got crazy. The two-room suite was awesome. There was a balcony off the living room overlooking the sea. The sun had set but you could see the moonlight reflecting off the waves below. I had never partied at quite this level with any other waiters I'd worked with. With record execs, it was normal enough but not with run-of-the-mill restaurant employees. They were usually too broke to spend money on coke, champagne and hotel suites. A big night out after work generally consisted of lots of cheap alcohol and weed, loud music, brash women, and maybe a game of pool, not a swim in one.

Andrei emptied out a quarter of an ounce of cocaine on the glass coffee table in the living room. There was a knock at the door and in walked another sexy blonde girl in a red Scotch tartan miniskirt, knee socks, pigtails, and a tight white shirt tied above her belly-button.

"Hi, I'm Victoria." She shook my hand, and I turned to Jens who had a really crazy look on his face, probably from doing too much coke. He had a sleazy porn face going now and I barely recognized him. I briefly wondered if he'd made some money on the side by playing bit parts in pornos.

Victoria seemed to be a popular name for sexy party girls for some reason. This one was probably another actress wannabe that populated LA like fireflies on a summer night. She most likely told herself she was studying for a future role – Heidi does Hollywood.

"Yep, that's right, Pauli, another Victoria," he said. And as she sat down beside him, he put his arms around them and said, "I'm going to give it to both of them," looking at them with his crazy porn eyes. By that time I was getting extremely high, as we all kept drinking Piper Heidsieck. I literally began feeling ecstatic and having an out of body experience. It was wonderful, weird, fascinating, and frightening all at the same time.

Andrei was long gone, probably off to deliver coke or broads somewhere else. I noticed that Jens was playing a game on the blonde Victoria in which he pretended to ignore her; he didn't invite her to snort a line of coke when he did, which as anyone knows is common druggie courtesy. Doing coke in the company of others and not sharing is just rude. Even degenerates have some rules they live by. Jens was breaking one of the most important ones.

She was left perplexed, staring at the luminous white lines as they twinkled and teased her for a full thirty minutes before she finally got the nerve to ask him for a hit. *Bingo!* That's what he wanted apparently – for her to beg.

He played dumb. "Oh, you want some of this? Sure, help yourself," he said highhandedly. "As you can see, we have got enough to last us for a couple of days," he added as he let out a stale gargled laugh. Who was this guy? Certainly the elegant waiter I knew from the Cricket Room had disappeared in a champagne-bubble-coke-powder haze.

When she bent over to snort her line, Jens grimaced and said, "It's okay, Miss Hoover, slow the fuck down, it'll be here all night!" Blonde Victoria casually ignored his comment, pinched her nose, took a deep breath like a pro, and then bent over to kiss Jens. Her ass was facing me and Susan so we had a front row seat to the real Victoria. Her skirt rose nearly to her waist as she bent and we saw that she wasn't wearing panties. This was almost too much for me to take. *La Dolce Vita* with no missing scenes. Holy hard on, Bat Man. Even with the booze and drugs, Little Pauli was suddenly as awake as a heat-seeking missile.

Susan giggled as if this were an everyday occurrence in her world. She pulled me closer, slid her hand in my waistband, and asked if I wanted to go into the bedroom. Does a horny bear fuck in the woods? Of course I did! But should I? I still wasn't sure if these were friends, hookers, or what they were. Hot was as far as I'd gotten. And really, at that point I didn't give a shit about their pedigree or life beyond the hotel room we were in.

Jens catches on; apparently he still has a few brain cells firing. "It's fine, Pauli, go ahead!" Right before I close the door, I hear him yell, "Don't get the sheets dirty!"

Susan went into the bathroom and I heard the sound of running water. I turned on the television and started watching a rerun of *Sex in the City*. Samantha was in her frilly lingerie, seducing some young guy. I remembered a stupid joke about a Chinese restaurant featuring "Cream of Sum Yung Gai" and laughed. Simultaneously, I had an attack of performance anxiety and wondered if I would be able to perform well in bed with all the coke in my system. Was I about to embarrass myself?

I started thinking of the excuses I might use as Susan slowly exited the bathroom wrapped in a white terrycloth hotel bathrobe. Her blonde hair was wet and slicked back, but her makeup was still intact, and boy, did she have hips. Once she let that robe glide off her body and I saw her voluptuous naked body, I didn't need excuses. We had amazing steamy sex and the buzz I had going actually enhanced the event to a level of intensity I hadn't experienced for quite some time. There were fireworks exploding all around the room. Or were they just in my head?

When we finally came out of the bedroom, I wasn't prepared for the full-on porno scene that greeted us. Both Victorias were spread out naked on the floor, one was doing the other and the other was doing Jens. My first reaction, of course, was, *Awesome!* Then I immediately became uncomfortable. This was a bit much even for a former European and rocker. Whoa.

"Oh, I'm sorry," I said, apologizing for barging in on their perverted debauchery that was also extremely hot.

Blonde Victoria, who was on her back with Jens' junk in her face and the other woman giving her a complete gynecological exam, opened her eyes as fast as her thick black eye makeup allowed. "Oh, that's all right, why don't you two come over here... oooh, that feels great, honey... and join us. We'd all love to see what you two feel like!" Her eyes slammed shut, she moaned loudly, and went back to pleasuring Jens who was pleasuring no one but himself.

What the fuck! This was my big chance to make every man's fantasy come true but I just wasn't comfortable enough with these people to do it. Having sex with a stranger was one thing, but a massive orgy was another. What if Jens started talking about it at work, what would people say? I pulled a Woody Allen and sort of choked, "Eh, that's okay, you guys are doing, uh, so well without us, we'll just go downstairs for a drink and be back in a while."

Susan didn't flinch – she must've been used to this stuff and I wondered again if she was a professional, or just a friend of Jens' who likes fucking strangers. I excused myself as I climbed over brunette Victoria, and almost changed my mind about leaving as she brought blonde Victoria to ecstasy. I grabbed the glass straw to hit the coke again. I said I was uncomfortable, not reformed. Walking away from crazy sex was one thing; walking away from free coke was just stupid.

Susan and I made it down to the lobby bar right in time for last call. When we got back up to the suite it was two in the morning, just an hour since we had left. Jens had moved his sex party into the bedroom and I swear to you, this is no joke: I was shocked to see Jens in the master bathroom spraying blonde Victoria with a golden shower as she sat in the bathtub. The whole thing should have been shot in a San Fernando porn studio for raunchy late-night reality TV. She looked like she was getting off on it. Jens turned around and laughed that evil laugh of his and the other Victoria slammed the bedroom door shut in our faces. That was the last image that I had in my head for the rest of the night. They didn't sleep. They had plenty of coke in their bodies to fuel their obscene orgiastic extravaganza. To sleep would have wasted valuable coke and porn time.

Susan and I talked about everything and nothing, and then she fell asleep on the couch as I slept on and off in the chair with my feet on the coffee table. I noted that Jens had since moved the coke elsewhere. The next morning around ten, I woke up and peeked at Susan who was still asleep. I sat there for a while playing through Hustler-type flashbacks in my head. It felt totally surreal; I hadn't understood what Jens was capable of. This was my first time socializing with him outside of work. That must have been what it was like when first meeting Mr. Hyde after only knowing Dr. Jekyll. Like meeting a completely different person.

I grabbed a bottle of water and drank it down quickly. I had that terrible day after cocaine feeling, kind of like a vampire at a sunny pool party. My brain was burning; I felt dirty all over and knew the best remedy would be a Bloody Mary. I grabbed the ingredients out of the minibar and mixed a nice one, spicy with lots of hot sauce. There had even been a lime and a lemon on the fridge, but no celery. How thoughtful of them. I imagined that they'd be charging Jens $35 for this drink and the bottle of water. The way I felt, it would have been worth it at twice that price.

Susan awoke as I took my first few sips. She looked pretty, bathed in the morning sunlight as it bounced off her jade green eyes. It was like seeing her for the first time, sober. I walked out onto the balcony and asked her to join me when she was ready. It was a perfectly clear morning, mid-70s already. It was an "I Love LA" kind of morning. As soon as the drink got to me, I started feeling better.

"Susan? Would you like me to make you a Bloody Mary?" She was already drinking from a bottle of Fiji water. She paused then said, "That would be terrific."

Hmmm, "terrific?" I haven't heard that word in a long time.

Then it dawned on me that in spite of our having been *very* intimate and that we now knew each other's bodies very well, we actually knew nothing about each other. Knowing someone's got a birthmark on the inside of their thigh, or that they are very ticklish in certain areas, does not make a relationship. Were we even having a relationship? Did I want one with her? The thought crossed my mind but then quickly drowned in my beckoning Bloody Mary.

I smiled but said nothing and mixed her a drink with the same passion I had mixed my own, adding a squeeze of lemon and lime. We decided to go downstairs and have breakfast and some very necessary cappuccinos. While I was downstairs, I got a text from Jens asking where the hell I was. When we got back upstairs, Jens and his two brides were enjoying a huge room service breakfast. It looked like they had ordered everything on the menu except that Chinese dish I mentioned earlier. They were probably out of that one by now.

We all spent the rest of the day hanging out on Venice Beach, drinking at the Waterfront Café. The girls were prepared and had brought beachwear with them. I bought a pair of cheap sandals and cut my pants off about three inches below the knee. I went to the bathroom with Jens and he tried to give me some Ecstasy and some coke but I declined and said, "I'm already having such a great time, why risk it, right?"

We both laughed. "Listen, Pauli, my girlfriend Christie…"

I interrupted him, "Yeah, I was wondering how you manage that, you do live with her right?"

"Yeah, I've got to call her. Listen, just say that you wanted to surprise me and that we went to San Diego to visit your family or something."

"I do have a cousin there, sure."

"Okay, I'm gonna call her now," he said, and when he did, he and Christie immediately started arguing. Apparently just the sound of his voice launched her into a tirade.

I grabbed the phone from him and tried to calm her down saying what he had instructed me to say. She was obviously upset and rather quiet while on the phone with me. Afterward, they argued about some chores he was supposed to have performed around the house. It culminated in a shouting match and he hollered a few choice obscenities in his guttural accent, ending with, "Fuck you, bitz!" And he hung up on her. I was startled by his quick changes, like flipping a switch. But then again, he'd gone from classy waiter to porn star so what was my problem with instant rage? Maybe I should have just enjoyed the show and stopped thinking so much. After all, I was impaired to put it mildly.

The rest of the night went off without a hitch and I didn't refuse Susan's invitation when she pulled me into the bathroom at the "Canal Club" in Venice that night. It was hot. And very quick. I was getting the hang of this porn king thing. A line of girls were waiting to get in when we finally emerged. The first one gave me a pissy look on my way out but I could have sworn a few others winked at me. I love this sleazy town. I wondered if Susan would mind if I made a U-turn but the thought bubble burst quickly.

I stuck to alcohol all night and Susan drove me home around two in the morning. Jens stayed at the Viceroy again with blonde Victoria, whom I found out later was an actual porn star.

When I saw him at work that Friday, around eleven, he looked like shit, though he was clean-shaven and his uniform and hair looked unbelievably sharp. The party from the night before had probably just ended. His voice was raspy and low from no sleep; there were bags under his eyes the size of silver dollars, and his skin was breaking out like a girl's on the first day of her period. It took a long time for the image of him with two women to fade. Anytime I needed a little "stimulation" all I had to do was call up that image and *boom*. Instant flag salute.

But Jens quickly proved that nothing could get in the way of his love of serving guests in the Cricket Room. He juggled several tables with ease, sold wine and champagne like a seasoned sommelier, and acted as though nothing was bothering him. It was as if it were just another day at the Beverly Hills Cricket Room.

Around one o'clock, I walked through the kitchen to get to the waiters' stocking area, and I caught a glimpse of Jens rounding the corner with a bottle of '92 Corton Charlemagne and two glasses carefully balanced on his silver tray. He walked casually over to the big 30-gallon trashcan on the way from the service bar and made a pit stop. I thought he was going to take a swig from the bottle, but instead as he was elegantly holding his tray away from his body, he bent over the can and puked twice. Then, still holding the tray perfectly, he walked over to his glass of iced tea, rinsed his mouth out, gargled a bit, and gingerly wiped his lips with a cloth napkin that lay folded on his wrist.

I watched him walk out onto the restaurant floor, carrying that perfectly balanced tray as if nothing had happened. He poured a taste of wine for the host at the table, then served the lady first, bowing politely while maintaining eye contact with the guest. He never missed a beat. That was the moment when he officially became my hero, albeit a hero who had gotten his balls polished by two professionals,

Later on, he came over to my bar. "Pauli, make me a Danish Mary before I crash and burn."

"You got it, buddy, I'll put it in a Styrofoam cup right there for you. Have you even been home yet?"

"Thanks, no," he said with a laugh. "And I'm not looking forward to it. She's pissed off beyond belief."

Thinking about the deep shit he was in with Christie, I snickered cautiously. Martin Scorsese, who was drinking at my bar, turned around to face Jens.

"Rough night?" he asked. Apparently one of the world's most famous directors could recognize a hangover when he saw one.

"Yeah, but worth every minute of it," said Jens.

Scorsese chuckled knowingly and saluted Jens with his glass. It was a one-scoundrel-to-another salute if ever I saw one. At that point, I didn't even know he was Scorsese but I kept thinking he would look like Scorsese if he had gray hair. The eyebrows were the same. Our conversation was light. We talked about nothing for almost an hour and there he was, drinking Coppola Claret, which in retrospect definitely seems like cannibalism.

I realized later that it was indeed Scorsese, damn it! Mr. P, our Maitre d', confirmed it. I decided I would not miss any more opportunities like that. I was disappointed in myself for not recognizing a man as famous as Scorsese and began to reluctantly spend a few minutes a day paging through People magazine, Variety, and other tabloids in order to stay current on celebrity 411. In retrospect, though, I think Scorsese enjoyed being spoken to as an average guy without having to defend or explain his work to someone he didn't know. It was a valuable lesson. Once it all clicked, I realized that I wanted to be more informed for my own sake but I also understood that the celebrity guests would appreciate a discreet, anonymous approach. No more fan boy shit for me. I hadn't been acting like a fan boy, but I needed to reign in my thoughts so I didn't feel like one either.

Bottom line on the party: It cost me a fortune in hard-earned savings but was worth every penny. Would I do it again? Probably

not, but it's a memory to get me through dry spells. I never saw Susan
again.

CHAPTER 5
THE WAY WE WERE

Whatever you know of greater Los Angeles and its districts like Hollywood, which is west of downtown, or neighboring cities like Beverly Hills which lies west of Hollywood, you probably don't know just how beautiful it all is. LA is hillier than most people imagine and because you have the interplay of ocean, valleys, and mountains, the weather can be as dramatic as anything filmed in the famous studios. We get raging fires, strong Santa Ana winds, fog, and days so beautiful they make you ache to be outside. Early mornings are magical; the pewter gray fog drapes itself over the hills, folding down into the shallow valleys, and giving the whole metroplex an other-worldly look. I've lived all over and there's no place like LA. Guess that's why I've stayed so long. And lest you think I'm just a sentimental pussy, let me assure you the availability of gorgeous women and the uninhibited party lifestyle don't hurt. You won't see Jens and me on a Chamber of Commerce poster, however. Just keeping it real. What Vegas is to gambling, LA is to beautiful and/or talented people.

And it's been that way since the early days of the movie industry, when The Cricket Room got its name. Way back in the 1930s, there were mostly rolling green fields in Beverly Hills and only a few buildings to mar the otherwise pristine landscape. Across the street from the pastel stucco Mediterranean-inspired edifice was a large park and a cricket pitch. Among the game's fans and players at the time were many A-list Hollywood actors as well as studio heads, who in those days were often lured from Hollywood to Beverly Hills for a day's getaway of fun and games. Afterwards, the players, coaches, and fans would gather at the restaurant to celebrate, and the place started to make a name for itself. The game of cricket was just intriguing enough, just unique enough, to appeal to the elite senses of the wealthy. They never passed up a chance to appear more "in the know" than their peers. Cricket was the perfect sport, a diversion worthy of nose-in-the-air snottiness, and yet fun. It smacked of European privilege, always a good thing for Hollywood types. They could dress up in their summer whites and be photographed sipping champagne from crystal flutes, having fun and kissing each other on the cheek like American royalty.

With this entrée, the Cricket Room began to charm Hollywood society thanks to its stunning architecture, cloistered, beautifully appointed dining room, and lush garden veranda dripping with bougainvillea. It had a fine menu, and the stringent door policy provided total privacy that attracted celebrities and tycoons from all over the world. The Cricket Room was an exclusive hideaway where old Hollywood could come to play after dark, undisturbed by prying eyes and uninhibited by provincial morality. They might as well have hung out a sign that said: No Riff Raff or Regular Folk Allowed.

There are famous pictures of Frank Sinatra, Dean Martin, Sammy Davis, Jr., Marilyn Monroe, Marlene Dietrich, and Humphrey Bogart all holding court at various tables. The comedian Jackie Gleason was a regular at the bar. It seems their ghosts still come by now and then for a laugh or two. Over the years, there have been many ghost stories and "sightings" from staff members. I myself have seen doors flung open with no one in sight on some of my closing shifts while covering for Don who was on vacation. It was mighty creepy especially since I was all alone and everyone else had gone home.

For most of the Cricket Room's history, you couldn't get past the Maître d' unless your face was your calling card or you were personally known to him. The Maître d' was notorious in those days for strategically, and sometimes brilliantly, connecting different people. If he liked you and felt you were worth the crapshoot he would introduce you to the most powerful players in Los Angeles. Many an acting, writing, or directing career got its start from the Maître d's introduction at the right time. I've had many people tell me about how they started their careers in the Cricket Room and they still come back to pay homage to this special place.

My immediate boss, Mr. P, was the subject of a bit of history himself. As the latest in a long line of legendary Maître d's, he has been working at the Cricket Room for almost thirty years. He started as a busboy straight out of a Mexican high school, and in those days he could barely speak English. He was always a very hard worker. His superiors took notice.

After several years as a busboy, he had gotten to know most of the guests by their first names. Young Mr. P became so good at his job that he started covering the waiters when they took a break. They liked it because he did all the work and they kept the tips, sharing with Mr. P only what suited them. He never complained and seemed happy only to be of service.

Once the waiters discovered that he had a talent for serving guests, they trained him in table service and allowed him to cover their duties so they wouldn't have to work as hard and could spend more time screwing off in the back room smoking, eating, or drinking and horsing around. There are two worlds in a restaurant, even one like the Cricket Room: what the guests see in the dining room, and what goes on in the back. No matter how famous the guests, the real drama usually happens in the back, where tempers flare, there are fights, food is thrown, drugs are used to fight fatigue, and love affairs spark and flame out like fireworks. A waiter may have just thrown up in a trashcan, popped a pill, kissed a girl, and punched a line cook, but when he steps foot into the dining room he is calm, collected, smiling and focused on service.

About eight years after Mr. P started as a busboy, one of the waiters, Ponce, indulged in a few too many drinks courtesy of his buddy the bartender. Ponce went on break and was unable to complete his shift. The Maître d', Nino, asked Mr. P to put on Ponce's jacket and take over his tables. The jacket stayed on for another ten years until he finally became Maître d' himself.

Like his predecessors, Mr. P knew all of the regulars by name; he knew where they worked, where they lived, what they ate, what they drank, who their families and friends were. He most likely knew uncouth details about their lives too, overheard but never repeated.

Each holiday season regular guests came by with wonderful gifts for him: gold watches, expensive shirts and silk ties, baskets of imported chocolates and best of all, cash. There were four regular guests who always gave to the whole staff and would come in with two to four grand in wads of cash and then Mr. P distributed the largesse among the floor staff and the kitchen workers, as he felt appropriate. You wanted to keep on his good side or your holiday tip could be fucked.

Though Mr. P was not technically a tipped employee, and earned a straight salary from the restaurant, he made a bundle seating guests who wanted certain tables and who didn't mind paying dearly for them. He accepted their donations gracefully but never expected them. He has always remained incredibly humble and grateful.

I will say this much for Mr. P: he's not greedy. He's always been fair with the guests and the staff and retained an aura of old-world class in the way he treated all comers. For someone with such a severe language barrier when he first came to work at the Cricket Room, he evolved far beyond most people's expectations and still runs the floor of the most important restaurant in all of Southern California.

The Cricket Room has always been the place to see and be seen, and in the old days, elegance and class prevailed. Every male guest was required to wear a dinner jacket at lunch and dinner upon penalty of expulsion, no matter who you were. Or, if you were important enough, the Maître d' would provide one for you. Even Johnny Carson was once asked to put on his tie. He described the event on *The Tonight Show*, joking that he wore the tie, but removed his shoes since they didn't have a shoe policy.

In those days, women were not allowed to enter unaccompanied or wearing slacks. Can you imagine? Supposedly, Marlene Dietrich was 86'd (restaurant jargon for refused or removed) for showing up one day in pants. Back then, they were concerned with quality as opposed to quantity, and they didn't hesitate to turn people away who didn't adhere to the rules.

It was then, as it struggles to remain today, strictly a classy old-school gathering place for Hollywood celebrities and moguls, the wealthy gentry, and all manner of business tycoons. The cricket pitch is long gone, given way to commerce as the price of land exploded, but the restaurant has not much changed. It remains as a monument to Hollywood's glamorous history and traditions. "I'm ready for my close up, Mr. DeMille," and other famous movie lines have become an ingrained part of American culture. "Say hello to my leetle friend." Two California governors came from "the biz" – Ronald Reagan and Arnold Schwarzenegger.

No paparazzi have ever been allowed inside the building or even permitted to wait outside in the parking lot. It's still the only public place in town where, once you're on the property, no one but the walls knows what happens inside. Oh, and the staff, like me, but for the most part we're forced into a vow of silence like members of the priesthood.

There's an enduring story about Frank Sinatra, who was always reputed to have mob ties. As the story goes, he was sitting at his usual table, number three, partying with his boys. He always traveled with a gang and was never seen alone. Now Frank wasn't a very soft-spoken guy and in those days before political correctness made people wary of them, Frank and his buddies used racial slurs when speaking to one another. That was just the way they spoke: *greaseball, WOP, guinea, kike, spook*. As the story goes, there was a Jewish guy at a nearby table who was quite prominent in the entertainment business. He started to smolder with anger as he listened to the steady stream of loud racial slurs the gang directed toward each other. Though the conversation was amongst only them it could easily be heard at nearby tables. Neither the wait staff nor the Maitre d' would dare step in and ask them to quiet down. No one wanted to wake up with a horse head in their bed.

The Jewish guy (who must have been a real dumbass) walked up to Frank's table and stared Sinatra in the eye. With a measured, deliberate tone, he asked Sinatra to keep it down. Sinatra didn't take kindly to the intrusion. He became enraged and started smacking the guy around, just going ballistic on him and yelling, "Why don't you mind your own business! Mind your own business, you fucking bastard, who the fuck do you think you are coming up to my table and interrupting our conversation!"

The guy didn't fight back, he was shocked, and he was ducking and trying to avoid the worst of it. Sinatra's boys had to tear Frank away from him because he was in one of his rages and he would have given him a thrashing. It was all over in less than a minute but it quieted the Cricket Room down for a while. The guy was bleeding out of his ear and the side of his face. The Maître d' came over with handkerchiefs and ice but the guy just sat there with his head in his hands.

When Sinatra's boys came over to see if they could patch things up, the gentleman said, "I don't want anything from you guys. I just want an apology from him, that's all." About a half hour later when Sinatra and his party were walking out, Sinatra took out a bundle of cash – three or four thousand in Benjamins – and threw it on the guy's table. "Here's your apology, and be careful whose conversations you interrupt in the future."

The guy never sued, and even if he had, no one in that room would have testified, not a single patron nor the staff. Sinatra knew that. He was the Chairman of the Board, the king of the entertainment world and no one was gonna dare cross him.

Of course, I had heard this and many other tales of the Cricket Room, all hidden behind those famous stucco walls, and they are definitely part of the lore that attracted me to the place. That, and its reputation for being the apex of the Hollywood food chain. And if I was going to work in this business, why not aim for the top.

There are also countless stories detailing what my colleagues experienced firsthand not long before I arrived. The high-drama legacy continues to the present day. For example, the convicted murderer and legendary music producer Phil Spector was often the subject at the time. Although there are many stories about him, two really stick out to me, in addition to the Lana Clarkson date I'm pretty sure I witnessed. Spector had been dining with some friends at table one and there had been a bit of table jumping as well, as there always is among the elite. This is common on tables one, two, and three as those are visible from the entrance, and certain old-school celebrities always like to sit there. It's like putting their brand on the place. "Hey, I'm here. Notice me!" Nowadays, the Johnny Depp and Brad Pitt types prefer a much more private table and the same goes for the big time directors and producers. Stars of old used to seek publicity, but now with 24/7 media, they're more likely to seek privacy. They like to be able to talk unmolested and we Cricket Room wait staff are trained to be nearly invisible.

But Mr. Spector always liked to sit at table one, so people would sit down with him and his friends and see who could tell the best stories. On this particular night, Spector was still seated in his booth at closing time and had drunk so much that his eyes were rolling around in their sockets. Finally, after everyone had left, he stood up with the help of the Maître d'. He was wet all over the front of his pants and the velvet booth was soaked underneath him. He had pissed himself. Classy, right? Don the bartender came around and helped the Maître d' walk Mr. Spector out to his Rolls Royce and waiting driver, and off they went to his little castle in Pasadena to take his wig off and put on his striped English jammies. Maybe an adult diaper too.

Another time Spector was leaving the restaurant with one of his girlfriends and just around the corner from the valet parking booth, our head valet, Devin, heard a girl yelp loudly. He rushed to check what was going on and saw Phil in his date's face screaming at her and shaking her violently. Devin boldly tapped on Mr. Spector's shoulder and asked, "Is everything all right here, Mr. Spector?"

As Spector turned to face Devin, he drew his gun from his shoulder holster and pointed it at Devin's stomach and said, "Mind your own business, kid." Devin threw his arms up in the air and backed away slowly. Devin would later have to testify in the Lana Clarkson murder case regarding Mr. Spector's habit of flaunting weapons. As Spector did at an infamous session for Leonard Cohen's *Death of a Ladies' Man* during which he'd stuck a gun in Cohen's neck and said, "Leonard, I love you."

Cohen answered, "I really hope you do, Phil." Guess he did 'cause he didn't kill him.

Of course, the judge knew Devin by name long before the trial; the judge was also a frequent guest at the Cricket Room and Devin had parked his car several times. Beverly Hills is a small town and it all seems to fit inside the Cricket Room on any given night. If you work there long enough you will see everyone who is anyone, and many who only think they are.

Regrettably, Anna Nicole Smith was thrown out of the Cricket Room back in the late 1990s for rude and obnoxious behavior. My friend Joey in security had to subdue her as she was screaming obscenities after having too many pills mixed with alcohol. As she proceeded being abusive and swinging at the security guards, Joey threw the cuffs on her and made her sit on the edge of the flower-bordered ramp in front of the restaurant by the u-shaped driveway. She was still screaming right up until the cops showed up. Once the cops arrived, she started crying and saying she was sorry. People think she was a shitty actress, but she could sure turn the tears on and off like a faucet.

Finally, after she had apologized to the security staff, they unlocked the handcuffs and it was agreed amongst all parties, including the Beverly Hills Police, that she was never allowed entry again. If she did show up, she would be arrested. It must have been one hell of a sight, the Beverly Hills Police pulling out of the driveway with big ol' Anna Nicole Smith in the back seat, with all of her expensive eyeliner and mascara running down her face like a river of black mud. Drugs really do change people, don't they? Hard to believe this story about one of my favorite blondes. It's sad the way her life ended. I wish I could have served her and gotten to know her. Something makes me think she was a nice person deep down and was just changed by the pills people keep pushing at her to control her. Such a waste of beauty and talent.

Speaking of waste, Bobby Brown and Whitney Houston used to frequent the establishment in the late 1990s too. They set up a house account and Bobby would come up to the bar and spend money like crazy. He didn't make that money, so why not? One time, after arguing with Whitney, he arrived in a fury and asked to buy an entire bottle of Louis XIII Cognac. Back then, it was a lot cheaper than today's prices – we charged only $3,000 for the full bottle. Made by Remy Martin, the Baccarat crystal bottle is 150 centiliters (a magnum) and bears a fleur de lis crystal stopper. If you've been to a nice bar, you've seen it. Brown asked to put it on their house account and then asked Don the bartender to pour it on the rocks with Dr. Pepper. Seriously. Dr. fucking Pepper. And top-shelf cognac.

The bartender could barely contain his laughter. Bobby Brown will own that one forever. He remained at the bar for about forty-five minutes, and then asked the Maître d' to bring the bottle to his driver who was waiting curbside. Bobby wandered aimlessly around the restaurant as if looking for someone to talk to for a while and then he left, looking lost and estranged. He was a douche but you couldn't help but feel a little sorry for him.

Gore Vidal came to my bar early in my tour of duty and spent hours with me telling me all about his long history with the Cricket Room. He described how his mother, the infamous alcoholic, Nina Gore, used to frequent the restaurant leaving him, at the early age of six, for hours to run around the lobby and play. He also disdainfully recalled how she had dismissed a chance to buy into the young establishment during a low period of diminished revenues the owners were experiencing at the time. "She declined, that stupid bitch," he said, much to my astonishment. He then said that I looked Italian and would fit right in on the Amalfi Coast where he had a huge house built into the mountainside. When I mentioned my dream of visiting Capri he expressed that he had enjoyed many a good time there with friends, sipping prosecco under an umbrella by the shore.

He then snarled and spat out: "You'd better wait until mid-September or you'll be run over by bloody tourists." Sometimes it was hard to follow him; he was brilliant and complicated, but always fascinating to listen to. Mr. Vidal would become a frequent guest of mine later on.

Over ten films have been made at the Cricket Room location including very famous scenes from Eddie Murphy's *Beverly Hills Cop* and Hunter Thompson's *Fear and Loathing in Las Vegas*. Countless movie and music deals have gone down at Cricket Room tables, dating back to the golden days of Tinseltown. Every single day, I'd see famous producers or directors meeting with talent (onscreen personalities), trying to woo them into working on their next project. Today's Cricket Room is no longer private and restricted like it once was, and just about anyone can get in. Prestige has been traded for profit and bottom-line numbers.

Yet even by current standards, it's still a totally unique culture – unlike any other in the world. Thanks to its strict, highly responsive security team, today's Cricket Room is still exclusive, buzzing with even more of Hollywood's brightest movie icons. Its patrons are closely protected from paparazzi and looky-loos hiding phone cameras in their shorts. When you're called to a meeting at the Cricket Room, you know you've really arrived.

The glow left by the Cricket Room's storied past helped get me through now and then. When reality TV stars are whining, their fake boobs bursting out of designer clothes they didn't buy, and crotchety tycoons with over-whitened teeth are hanging onto their youth, making fools of themselves with girls a third their age, I close my eyes and imagine the whiners and perverts of the good old days, and it warms my heart.

CHAPTER 6
TRAINING DAY

There are a thousand versions of the old joke, "Waiter, there's a fly in my soup!" Here's an old one I find hilarious, probably because at the Cricket Room, we'd *never* be allowed to respond to a guest in such a smartass manner:

5 February 1919, Ruthven (Iowa) *Free Press*, pg. 3, col. 1.

Lots of professional baseball players pride themselves on their gift of repartee, but out on the road even the smartest of them are beaten at that sort of game.

Ty Cobb, king of players in the business, smart as he is, was tripped up by an ordinary waiter.

In a small New York hotel one day Ty loudly called the attention of a waiter to a fly in his soup.

"Very true, my dear Mr. Cobb," said the waiter, "but why should you worry when there is not a chance in the world of your catching it?"

More than four years had passed and I was still the daytime bartender in the Cricket Room. The glow of glory days gone by was still there. The stars still came and went with regularity. Ghosts still roamed the premises, reluctant to leave their famous "haunt." But I was feeling kind of stagnant. I realize that might sound ungrateful; I had really wanted this and now that I had it I was grumbling. But the rock 'n roll animal in me was growling, getting restless. Bottling up all that stage energy was getting vexing, even with all the partying.

The pay was more than decent - fifteen bucks an hour plus tips and great benefits, unheard of for a bar salary anywhere else. Tips from the big spenders could be huge; big enough to really make a difference in my lifestyle. I had bought myself a beautiful BMW that turned heads even in Hollywood. I took two long vacations to Europe with my family, feeling more wealthy and successful than many of my friends. I also visited New York City several times just for the change of scenery and to enjoy the raucous nightlife you can only find there. The choice of things to do and ways to spend money was massive, especially compared to the torpor of LA with its lazy, slow beach vibe.

This is what I had imagined rock 'n roll success would have given me if I had gotten my big break. Well, not quite, but compared to where I was four years ago, this was the big time.

Let's just say that staff at the Cricket Room was well compensated for our discretion. There are things I will tell you here, but there are an equal number of secrets I won't spill because a bartender is the next best thing to a priest for confessing sins. I take that seriously. Not much short of a subpoena will drag shit out of me about my guests. And Mr. P? Imagine all the secrets he's got bottled up in that head of his!

I was debt-free, enjoying life, accumulating a sizeable bank account, and partying with Jens on a regular basis. Yet in my gut I felt something essential was missing. I hadn't written a single note of music in almost five years. I realized I wasn't quite ready to give up that dream of being a recognized songwriter and performer. Though I might have successfully turned off the creative spigot, I couldn't hold back the flow forever. The artist inside of me was yearning to dust off my microphone and howl again.

I loved my job but grew to hate my schedule because the day shift was so tiring. No real time to do anything before work and by the time I finished and got home it was eight o'clock and I'd be too drained and uninspired to write any music. As a musician, I had found I could be most productive by working at night and using my days to compose my music. I liked that schedule; it had always worked for me. I felt I needed to make a change and tried to figure out a way to work at night again. Unfortunately, it didn't seem that Don, the crotchety old night bartender, would be leaving anytime soon. He really didn't make that much more than I did, maybe about two-fifty a week, but it was his schedule I was after. I didn't see much hope, but then one day, like my arriving on the perfect day to apply for the job, things fell into place.

One otherwise normal week, three night-shift waiters all dropped out within a ten-day period. One waitress, Ann, took a job working as a stewardess for a private charter jet company. Another younger guy, David, went to work for a financial investment company downtown. ("Yes, sir, I'm qualified to manage your billion-dollar portfolio. I'm a waiter. I know all about responsibly managing vast sums of money.")

And then there was poor Álvaro, a hardworking immigrant from Spain, who had a heart attack in the middle of a busy night shift. Oh boy, did that ever cause a scene! He fell to his knees in the center of the dining room, loudly yelling out in pain. The tray he was carrying crashed to the floor, baptizing several horrified guests with wine, pasta, and our then-famous blue cheese bread. His dramatic collapse seemed more like an actor in a bad movie than a heart attack victim.

Two other waiters picked him up and took him downstairs to the changing room. He sat on the sofa for a while looking quite pale but refused to be taken to the hospital. Once he seemed to stabilize, they left him alone to rest and went back to work. When Mr. P wouldn't allow Álvaro to resume working, fearing liability, he tried to go home and collapsed again on his way to his car. Luckily, William in the security booth saw him on one of the surveillance monitors and called an ambulance.

Álvaro ended up recovering fully after a peripheral arterial bypass but he was out of commission for almost eight months. He was our most senior waiter, in his early sixties back then, and I know for a fact that he still works there. He's a small man with glasses, built like a skeleton, and sporting suspiciously strangely colored hair. It's a shade of burnt orange not seen in nature. He used to wait tables in his high-heeled Euro boots mostly because he was so short. At least with the boots he could almost reach five-six. I guess he had a complex regarding his height because even though the heels hurt him he wouldn't stop wearing them, not until after the vascular leg surgery, when the doctor explained that he not only needed orthotics but he also needed to wear special shoes from then on. With regular shoes, he was nearly face to face with guests seated at tables. It was comical but customers loved him. Every night he worked was like an episode of *Little People*, showing him overcoming his height, age, and medical challenges. Little fucker worked hard, I'll give him that.

So there it was before me: a clear opportunity, my big chance to not only go on a night shift schedule but also to begin working as a waiter in Los Angeles' most infamous restaurant. Switching from bartending to waiting tables may not seem like a promotion, but it was, and the main reason is that tips are much larger when you wait tables. The checks are larger, thus the tips increase. It's also much harder work. And you put up with more crap because while you're responsible as a bartender for mixing the drinks, when waiting tables you're serving what others have prepared. You are dependent on kitchen staff, bussers, and runners to help get the job done.

I put to work all the experience I'd gotten from my previous server jobs and all the knowledge I had absorbed from watching Jens. He was a master of his vocation; he turned serving A-listers into sheer poetry. He knew when and how to party, and when to serious the hell up and get the job done. He was a class act and I only hoped I could be halfway as good as him. I just wanted a chance to try.

Here's a little story about Jens: one evening I watched in awe as Jens served a table of four (we call it a 4-top) seated on the lush patio. He had taken one young woman's order and said, "Excellent choices," then turned to the other woman in the party (it's always ladies first). He took her order, said thank you, and turned to take one of the gentlemen's orders.

The woman interrupted and said, "Hey, excuse me, is my choice not excellent? You said her choice was excellent."

Instead of becoming irritated as a normal waiter might, Jens said with a smile, "Madam, if we might change your loin chop to medium instead of well done, and add shaved pecorino and some fresh Alba truffle to your risotto, your selections would also be 'excellent.'" She looked a bit startled and unsure about her meat being cooked medium, but she agreed.

"Excellent choice, madam," Jens replied, and continued taking the orders.

Not only had he turned an awkward confrontation into a win (and she would no doubt love her juicy chop and fragrant risotto), he had boosted his check total by about fifty bucks. Not just suave demeanor and grace under pressure, but brilliantly disguised upselling. Did I mention he's my hero? My porn star, drug using, classy waiter hero? What a dichotomy; how does he pull it all off?

When I asked to be transferred from daytime bartender to PM-shift waiter, Mr. P asked me, "Is dis really what jew want?" in his thick accent. I said that I had been waiting for a night shift spot to open up behind the bar and we both agreed that that wouldn't happen anytime soon. Once the Spanish Inquisition (meaning questioning by the other department heads) had decided that this would work well for the restaurant, there was just some simple paperwork to make the transfer happen.

I was downgraded to a lower hourly wage of around eight bucks, but the tips were to be triple what I was getting behind the bar because the checks and the number of guests we served were much larger. Best of all, it was paid out in cash by the restaurant at the end of each night. This could fuel my craving for a taste of the Hollywood night scene for a long time. If Jens needed another sinner in his world of debauchery, I could finally pay the tab. Being a player, babe-banging, chick magnet was expensive, especially in LA with all the gorgeous girls around. It was an infinite sea of sin.

I immediately found myself working with a much bigger team of employees. Behind the bar, it had been "My World," run according to my rules. Like Frank's anthem, it was my way. And I ran it tight, like a German train schedule, consistently providing my guests the fine experience they deserved and the graceful, personable service they expected. People come to a bar to either relax or have a good time, so tending bar becomes a balancing act between being efficient, savvy, and competent, and making it look easy. You can't look stressed or tense; who wants to leave a bar more uptight than when they came in?

The bar isn't the main attraction at the Cricket Room, so none of the managers really gave a shit as long as there weren't any guest complaints. I basically had carte blanche to run it the way I saw fit. Sweet. In the restaurant, however, the waiters, the sommelier and kitchen staff are the heart of the money machine, and the machine was pressed to the limit every day and night. Upselling was mandatory, turning tables without rushing guests was too, and the bigger the checks the more a waiter was valued. No one gave a crap if your mother just died or your dog got run over. You were expected to per-form on cue and smile doing it.

Mr. P was our hard-working leader and he ran the floor the best way he could, considering he was required to function as both manager and Maître d'. Speaking in his thoroughly mangled Spanglish, he was very straight and direct with his instructions. My training as a waiter, I was told, would take two weeks and I would first do the busboy job, then food runners' job, and then finally shadow a waiter for a week. I thought that sounded great because I would not only get to see what everyone did, I would also learn how to do their jobs in case we were short handed one night. I prided myself on being a team player, especially if the team consisted of two Victorias and a Susan.

I'd also get to see what all the food looked like coming out of the kitchen and become familiar with every item on the plate. This was especially important because of the high profit margin we turned on each of these very expensive items. They had to be world-class in quality and presentation. Many guests have been in again and again, so they know what to expect: a high level of excellence and consistency. I was also excited to get a feel for how the kitchen worked and at what speed certain dishes could be delivered. This is essential since it would be my job to time the firing of each dish. Like the blogging waiter I mentioned earlier, I also had to know the different cuts of meat; wine pairings (even though there's always a sommelier, you better know your shit if a guests asks); the difference between Japanese Wagyu beef and USDA prime cut steak (one steer has his own masseuse and gets sloshed drinking beer, the other is corn-fed in his prison cell, and Wagyu is three times as expensive); and the types of seafood that are on the menu or offered as specials. I was up for it. At this price level, people love to show off to their companions and often ask whether fish is out of the Atlantic or Pacific Ocean, wild or farmed. Seriously, who gives a flying crap? But they will ask and I better damn well know and sound convincingly arrogant while doing it.

My first day started with getting to know the staff, which I had interacted with rarely as a bartender. In the kitchen, we had the head sous-chef, Lola, whom I already knew a bit. She looked perpetually tired and unhappy to be there. She had never liked waiters, but then what sous-chef does? (A sous-chef, by the way, is an assistant chef.) Lola functioned as expediter at the line during service, yelling at cooks and compiling the waiter's orders as they come in.

At the grill, we had Miguel and Johnny. They were both experienced grill masters while still only in their thirties. These poor little bastards' arms were covered in burn scars that made them look more like war veterans than culinary aces. And they were constantly berated all night long by Lola. It was their job at the grill station to cook the majority of the menu items themselves: the meats and poultry, burgers and vegetables, fries, and potatoes. If you've never been in a commercial kitchen, you'd be shocked at how stupid loud it is, and how hot. With open-flame char and flat grills cranked up, stove burners all going full blast, heat lamps to keep the food warm, the only refuge is the walk-in cooler. Sometimes there was a traffic jam in there of people just trying to cool off. Or hook up, but that's another story.

Philipina and Harvey at the cold station prepared salads, shucked oysters, assembled cheese plates and the like. Those two were a frickin' joke. I learned they had been at the CR for ten years and were still working for the same salary. I've never met two people more burnt out or less ambitious in my life. They were on a treadmill and seemed not to care. Philipina does everything extra slowly and Harvey will never, ever make eye contact with a waiter. They move as if they're auditioning for roles in a zombie film. Once I figured out their burnt-out M.O., I realized that I must never make a mistake with the cold items because it would take way too long before I got my replacement dish. I cannot explain how they kept their jobs for so long; maybe management types felt sorry for them. They were not going anywhere, though, so I had to learn to work around them.

Moving on, we had Martino the pastry chef whose apparent mental disabilities would later earn him the name "Patzo the Clown" ("pazzo" means "crazy" in Italian) for always forgetting to put the 20-minute soufflé in the oven and for disappearing from his post without letting Lola know he would be absent for a while. He should have had a role in *La Strada* or *I am Sam* for that matter.

He wasn't actually a bad guy though – he always gave us sweets and desserts whenever we wanted them. We often crowded around him like kids on the playground. I really liked him. I think I had a soufflé every night during my first year of being a waiter there thanks to Patzo, our constant benefactor. Are they fattening? Yes, and it's the kind of fat that takes an extra long time to shed too, I can confess to that. Maybe I shouldn't have considered Patzo a saint; I should have shouted, "Get thee behind me, Satan!" each time I saw him. His temptations were unhealthier for me than Jens' ever were. The easy accessibility of food and drink has led to the demise of many a waiter and bartender. A restaurant is like a crack house for sugar addicts.

Finally, on the sauté side as we called it, we had Nico, my Italian homey. He handled the pasta dishes and many of the pan-roasted and sautéed fish and seafood dishes. Nico was a thin, tall, good-looking guy in his thirties. All the chicks thought he was awesome until he smiled. His teeth were brown and crooked, but as long as he kept his mouth shut he'd be getting girls left and right. He was always good to me even before I started as a waiter. Nico would cook me anything I wanted, at any time. He was a happy guy with a great attitude, and we had an unspoken "paesan" bond.

Now let's meet the busboys, shall we? That's a job title the PC police have been after for a long time but can't seem to change, but whatever you call them, they're incredibly important. Most waiters come up from busboy jobs. If conductors keep the trains running on time, it's the busboy equivalents who keep the restaurant running. Career-wise they're on the first rung of the ladder with everybody above shitting down on them.

Juan, a Mexican (you're shocked, right?) father of two, had a healthy head of coarse black hair and a huge beer belly that hovered over his skinny legs like a dirigible over two sapling trees. His arms looked like lengths of rope. I guess the only thing that had grown on him since his teens was his belly. He was in his forties and had been working two full-time busboy jobs for ten years and showed no signs of wanting more responsibility. He owned a modest home in the San Fernando Valley, about thirty miles away, so his biggest gripe was always LA traffic. He was funny and loved to laugh, always with a joke about stupid LA drivers. When Juan was stressed or behind in his work, he'd appear cross-eyed and looked stupid even though he wasn't. I often found myself quietly chuckling at that. He also drank so much club soda I was sure that his pee must've been carbonated. He probably didn't pee, he spritzed. When I told Jens my theory, he said he might start drinking gallons of club soda just to see what kind of bubbly "showers" he could rain down on blonde Victoria.

José was a short, round, grey-haired man who was just over fifty. He had one work pace, medium-slow, as if he were a robot. Nothing short of a Taser was going to jolt him into moving faster. José disliked most waiters because they often requested that he do crazy things – things that were included in his job description. To him, insisting that he do his job – like clearing the dessert dishes – was unreasonable. When you asked him for something he would call you by the GM's last name as if saying, "Okay, Boss Man," but that was just José's way. José loved to goose people's butts – especially the gay waiters. I often caught them scolding him and he would reply, "Come on, puta, jew know jew like it."

All in all, José was an okay guy to talk to. He also liked to joke around and laugh. Much like Juan, he was not a serious guy. There were other busboys too but they came and went so frequently that I could hardly ever recall their names. They were like replaceable and forgettable extras in our little movie.

Our food runners were Paco and Marino. I always seemed to be working with Paco, which was cool because he always agreed with me. Of course, he did – I was the one tipping him. He got me, though, and he was always amused when I would lash out at people who kept screwing up. But what I really liked about Paco was that he would try hard to do his job well and I could respect that. Paco had a quiet demeanor and although he was of Mexican descent, he looked as Spanish as the actors who have played Zorro. I also suspect he'd had drug problems but had gotten himself sober. I can always tell a tweaker apart from the rest of the crowd and Paco was definitely a former user. Just call me the drug whisperer.

The next evening, Mr. P took me into the dining room to teach me the table numbers and how to set up a table properly. Each tabletop was to be set with an appetizer knife and fork as well as a dinner knife and fork, with the knives to the right of the plate, of course. The appetizer silverware was placed on the outside next to the dinner silverware. To the left of the appetizer fork was a plain, small bread plate with an old-fashioned butter knife balancing on the right upper and lower edges. A stemmed water glass would be placed directly above the dinner knife and a stemmed white wine glass placed slightly to the left above the water glass. Centered between the silverware there had to be a logo plate (sometimes called a charger) which is extra heavy, trimmed in gold, with the restaurant's green shield logo emblazoned in the center of the plate. On top of the logo plate was a specially-folded white linen napkin with the restaurant logo embroidered on it, facing the guest. The napkin would cover the logo on the plate but as soon as the host had seated a guest he (or she) would remove the napkin, open it up with a flourish, and lay it the guest's lap, leaving the logo on the plate exposed. The higher the prices on the menu, the more ritual comes with the meal. And the Cricket Room is expensive. You get plenty of pomp and circumstance to make you feel very special. It costs the restaurant nothing, but validates in the guest's mind that the special treatment is worth every dime. Suckers, yeah, but I guess if that's what it takes to make someone feel special, or generous at check time, who am I to argue?

Before the night shift could begin, waiters had to polish everything on their tables. This table detail included: polishing the sterling silver salt and pepper shakers, the logo plates, all the silverware, and all the stemware. We also were expected to check the tablecloths for holes, check under the table to make sure that nothing had been left behind during the lunch shift, brush off the seats, and light the sterling silver table top candle lamps. Salt and pepper shakers had to be completely full and the white porcelain sugar caddies had to contain five packets each of raw sugar, white sugar, and every brand of artificial sweetener known to man. All packet labels had to be facing in the same direction. Uniformity and attention to detail was mandatory or you would be called on it. This was the dining room's version of *mise en place*, a French phrase meaning "putting in place." The silver candle lamps were also polished once a week by the stewards (an expensive word for dishwashers).

Serving tables at the Cricket Room was to be performed in a specific manner and there were precise Rules of Service, as they were called, and those rules were not negotiable. Each waiter had to touch on over twenty points at each table during the course of dinner service and many points were to be carried out within specific time limits. But hitting every point within the specified time limits was nearly impossible. Only the best reached that level of service; Jens was one of the few who could do it and I wanted to achieve it as well.

After Mr. P had given me a printed "Rules of Service" list, he told me that I would have to memorize it, and within a few days I would have to serve a table of the executive party to see if I could pass the "Captain's Table" test. Keeping my job at that point would depend on hitting those twenty points on the nose. *Jeez*, I thought, *these people are anal as shit. It's only food service, right? Or would I be doing brain surgery for dessert? Maybe a little fucking rocket science?* But merely food service or not, it was important to them, and keeping my job was important to me. I also knew the clientele of the Cricket Room expected top-notch service. They might not know if their waiter missed one of the twenty touch points, but if a guest happened to be one of the monthly secret shoppers, the Maitre d' would certainly find out.

Then Mr. P described all the service imperatives that were <u>not</u> in the "Rules of Service" but were nevertheless expected. *Fuck, there's more?* At round and square tables that were free-standing, at which you were able to access both sides of the guest, Mr. P explained that he wanted plates of food to be served from the guest's left and empty plates removed from the right. Beverages should be served and removed from the guest's right. Napkins were to be removed from the guest's setting and placed in the guest's lap from the right, upon arrival, if not already done by the host or hostess. However, in the booths or on deuces (tables for two) that were up against a window or wall, Mr. P told me to follow his serving rules but only if possible. He stressed that I should always be aware of the guest's comfort and always use discretion, ultimately serving from the side that was least intrusive to the guest.

Mr. P went on to teach me the position numbers of all the tables. For example, as we faced a booth he said position number one would be furthest to the left and it would go up from there, moving clockwise. It definitely got trickier at the free-standing tables but it all made sense to me and I learned the drill quickly. The reason that waiters have to make note of position numbers on orders is so that the food runners can put down each plate in front of the appropriate guest without having to ask the guest or announce the dish. Mr. P explained that I must always be polite and remember to never, ever, argue with a guest. If I ever were to have a problem with someone, he told me to just come and get him. "Jew can never to take matters into jur own hands." *Great, so I'm responsible for everything but have no ability to take control.*

He continued to describe how I must behave, always excusing myself before setting anything down, or removing anything from the table. I was never to reach across a guest while serving, but if I were forced to, I must always pardon my reach. To me this whole approach seemed very old-school but then again this whole place seemed to be an anachronism right out of the 1930s. The world had evolved in over seventy years but not the essence of the Cricket Room. The winds of turmoil, change, and chaos might swirl all around the outside of the building, but inside it remained the calm, sophisticated, and sane oasis it had always been.

That was kind of cool, actually, and one of the reasons I was drawn to it. I fell in love with the place and this new challenge was very appealing to me. I couldn't wait to become a world-class waiter, maybe one in Jens' league.

At this point, you may be wondering why the hell I'm going into so much detail about how the Cricket Room operated. My purpose is to differentiate that very unique place from the jillions of other dining establishments and bars, and make clear just how special it is.

Every table in the Cricket Room was set with long, draped white linen over a long table skirt in a hue that accented the color scheme of the dining room. Hardly any of the tables were a uniform size, which added an interesting feel to the different sections of the restaurant. There was the front dining area, with which I was already familiar. This section had a bit more festive and less formal air because it was close to the bar and the live entertainment. Included in this section was a recessed area we grew to call The Cove, as it included one four-top and five super cozy deuces. The Cove was surrounded by garden view windows. This space saw many proposals for marriage made, make-up gifts exchanged, and no doubt some indecent proposals as well.

In the main dining room, the atmosphere was definitely much more formal. All the tables were grander and seated at least four, but some could fit up to twelve guests. You'd be correct to imagine these tables with a movie producer at the head, and his cast of stars seated around him like apostles.

All the tables had a nice floor-to-ceiling view out to the garden, and along the massive sliding glass windows were a line of five two-tops. The outdoor garden area was lush with flowers and plants as well as a large, beautifully lighted pepper tree. This area was especially popular at lunch or on warm nights, and offered quaint booths for four tucked away amid the surrounding greenery and flora.

The Cricket Room also had a secluded private room for small banquets or very private guests who made good use of it for a more intimate dining experience. This room was unknown to the general public. It was never offered; you had to be "in the know" to request it but still it stayed booked.

The atmosphere in the restaurant sparkled, with candlelight reflecting off the fine silverware and shimmering glassware. I'll never forget the first time I stood looking over the dining room after the table lamps had been lit, in those brief moments before the first guest is seated. It was magical.

The view into the garden was like something out a 1940s-era romantic movie with enchanting tiny lights accenting the entire patio. You could imagine Lauren Bacall dining there with Humphrey Bogart, him kissing her hand romantically, her large sultry eyes looking deeply into his. She was some dame.

The restaurant even sounded exclusive and civilized, with any ambient noise softened by the thick carpet, royally plush furniture, and long table coverings. The style and feel was as far away as you could get from "contemporary modern" and just as traditionally warm and regal as you'd want from a classic old-school, five-star eatery, without feeling like you were in your Grandma's mansion (if she had had one). It was classy, cozy, and very well-maintained to capture intimacy at its fullest.

During my first week, it became very clear to me that not much was expected from the busboys. Their job was to bring bread and butter to the tables, and to clear plates (sometimes). It was very hard to get them to remove stemware, dessert plates, and coffee cups, or to pour water. I noticed quite early on that the teamwork between the waiters and the busboys was not very good, and it was even worse between the waiters and kitchen. Only the food runners worked well with us. The main reason for this disconnect was, of course, jealousy over money. The waiters made a small fortune in tips while everyone else got to help them do it. The pressure on the waiter to perform was intense but the rewards were far beyond my expectations. Luckily, the company had a policy of promoting in-house, so at least employees knew that there was opportunity available if they could measure up.

I became very friendly with Ernesto, a Honduran waiter who had one of the jolliest laughs I'd ever heard. It started low and ended in a giggle. Ernesto loved to joke around but was also extremely helpful in teaching me much of what I had to learn very quickly. When we were busy Ernesto was very organized, his service was quick and efficient, and he had a good grasp of the English language. He had done well for himself working two jobs as a waiter – he owned a nice house in the suburb of Arcadia that he had done a lot of work on himself. He would often talk about his wife and kids and how he cherished his time off with them. Ernesto never worked on Saturday or Sunday. "I can't stand the crowds," he said, and even if he could make an extra fifty bucks, he would have had to work twice as hard because weekends were all about quantity not quality. Ernesto always had a little secret stash hidden deep within one of the cupboards in the back service area. He was good friends with the bartender – I think that was his little recipe for happiness.

Since I hadn't really worked the night shift before, most of the wait staff was new to me. There was Daniel our token queen with the fair skin, rosy cheeks, brown eyes, wavy dark brown hair, and a slim athletic body that was almost girlish. You could tell because he didn't fill out his uniform too well. Daniel was a very jovial chap and would often sing old songs from musicals like *My Fair Lady*, *Fiddler on the Roof*, and *Westside Story*. Even his speaking voice was very singsong; you get the picture. He fairly floated around the dining room, unwittingly amusing staff and guests alike.

Then there was Matt, the angry and tough gay man who appeared straight but had never been with a girl in his life. He said he knew at a very early age that he was gay and never denied it. Matt was smart and had many different interests. He confessed that since he'd been at the Cricket Room, he had studied film, finance, and law. He just couldn't seem to find the right avenue out of the restaurant business, yet getting out was all he wanted. I think that's what made him so angry. That and the fact that his father had abandoned him as a kid, which I could identify with. Although my dad's disappearance only lasted a couple of years it left a deep scar on the family forever.

Germaine, a quick and witty man in his forties with a full head of short strawberry blonde hair was a fat ass who filled out his uniform to the brim. He was the gayest straight man I had ever met; all he ever talked about was women, but with a slight effeminate cadence. "Pauli, go take a look on table three. She's so hot!" Germaine loved to talk to the guests; I would often pick up his slack and make a little extra cash because he was too busy engaging the guests in conversation.

There was only one female on the PM server team and that was Amy. She was skinny with no ass at all, bright blue eyes, and super short, dark hair. Amy was in her early forties and not bad looking at all. She had a good attitude and guests liked her a lot. Amy loved to talk and tell extraordinarily long stories. It was really painful because she had terrible breath, and the restaurant business is very fast-paced with no time for long stories, period. Her breath was beyond toxic; I've never known a live human being with worse breath, actually. I always avoided asking her questions because I didn't want to get trapped in one of her malodorous long stories. She was a sweet woman but we never actually talked very much.

Shakil was an oddity: a fair-skinned Indian man with a stereo-typical Indian "would-you-like-a-Slurpee" accent. He was in his late forties, of medium build, and had pitch-black hair. As a Muslim, he'd had to escape India as a young man when hostilities grew between his religious group and the Hindu majority. At first, he had lived in Scandinavia but discovered that was not his cup of glögg and chose a life in California's warmer climate. He married an Indian woman and they now have two kids in junior high school. I'm not sure how they managed but he owned a condo an hour away from Beverly Hills. He, like many other immigrants, was a very hard-working guy and this certainly showed when he was on the floor at the Cricket Room. Shakil had a tendency to be a bit too nervous and almost every night he screwed something up just from his nerves. Improving his English would have definitely helped him.

As I've said, Jens was the best waiter on the floor and I was excited to be working with him, though he only worked two night and three day shifts. Jens had been blocked from earning complete night shift status because he had tried to steal a fifty-dollar tip that a guest had very clearly designated for Mr. P on his credit card slip. Mr. P interviewed Jens before he went home that night and Jens made up some flimsy excuse and that was the end of Jens moving up any further. He really should have been a full-time PM waiter. Maybe it was my saving grace, because Jens and I together spelled trouble.

And finally, there was Ariella, our hostess with the mostess. Ariella wore her brown hair long, with bold frosted streaks; her eyes were blue as the sky and her skin fair as Cover Girl Ivory #105. Ariella was Barbarella – tall and seemed larger than life in high-heeled pumps. Austin Powers would have said, "Yeah, baby, yeah! Shagalicious!" Male guests almost fell over when they saw her and it wouldn't be long before they made a move on her. Little did they know... Well, more on her later. She and Matt (Angry Boy) were best friends who later became known as Will and Grace after the TV show of the same name.

That, with the exception of high-turnover positions, was the cast of characters in our little nightly charade. The guests pretended to be polite, we pretended to give a shit, and everyone went home happy.

CHAPTER 7
A STAR IS BORN

I t was my third day of waiter training. On my scooter on the way to work, I saw a three-car pile-up on one of those infamous five-way spaghetti intersections on Sunset Boulevard in Beverly Hills. A rich old man with a lead foot, who probably got confused, crashed his brand new Lexus LS into a black Range Rover. A Mexican gardener in an old light blue pick-up truck had to swerve out of the way and so crashed into a giant telephone pole. Scattered all over the street were broken bags of cement mix, rakes, a couple of lawnmowers, shattered pieces of light bezels, as well as most of the front end of the Lexus. There was even a canteen of gasoline leaking fluid into the street.

The hunchbacked old man was out of his car, along with several of the other drivers, pointing frantically to the traffic light, but we all knew what had really happened. It's a mind-bending intersection and if you don't steal your left turn you could sit there all evening during rush hour. The old man's car was totaled, and he was lucky to still be standing, while the Range Rover was barely dented and the driver never even bothered to come out of his car.

Although I couldn't see through his tinted windows, I assumed he was on the phone, probably with his attorney. The only person with an apparent injury was the poor Mexican guy, who was sitting on the curb with his head in one hand and rubbing his back with the other. He seemed to be hurt, but hopefully he was faking it – maybe he thought it could be the unfortunate opportunity of a lifetime. His truck was in sad shape, though maybe it had looked that way before the accident. No blood on anyone, thank God.

Crap! I'm running late. I crossed the grassy median to ride on the sidewalks the rest of the way. Illegal, I know, but who gives a crap. There weren't any cops on the scene yet but I could hear them coming.

I parked my scooter next to the railing near the employee entrance. As I entered the building, I rushed past the security gate, swiped my card, and entered my employee number as I waved hello to Joey inside the security booth. I picked up my company-provided uniform and rushed upstairs through the fire exit stairway. Entering the men's locker room, I passed a small gathering area where a few employees were sitting on comfortable couches. One of the dishwashers was hunched over and sleeping, with the TV blasting a soccer game in Spanish. I saluted the busboys, "Hey, Jose. Hey, Juan."

"What up, Puta, you late!" said Jose. I let his comment roll off my shoulders and hurried toward my locker. No time to tell him to go fuck himself and the donkey he rode in on.

I rolled the combination to the locker with one hand and with the other hand, I was already throwing off my clothes and putting on my clean, pressed uniform. My polished work shoes sat in the bottom of the locker waiting for me and my tie hung, pre-tied with a double Windsor knot, on the top hook. I glanced down at my TAG. Seven minutes to go. I put my work shoes on, threw on my dinner jacket, and grabbed a brand new captain's pad, as well as my corkscrew, table crumber, and sleek, thin, silver flashlight. I also filled my shirt pocket up with Big Brother logo-emblazoned pens. With a glob of hair gel in my hand I ran to the bathroom, dampened my hair in the faucet and hurriedly applied the gel and combed through. Now, I looked like a Goodfella gumbah, ready to serve the rich and famous.

With only two minutes to go, I rushed upstairs and through the kitchen, still buttoning my jacket. I greeted the sous chef, "Hi, Lola," sliding on the tile floor like Tom Cruise.

"Hi," she said with her usual blasé expression. "You're late."

Nothing anyone did was ever going to change her so why bother with repartee. "Not yet!" I said, gliding past her.

When I rounded the corner, I saw most of the dining room staff already standing at attention. I typed in my employee number again and threw my hand down on the electronic ID reader. It's three minutes past six. *Crap!* I turned around just as our very serious Maître d' entered from the dining room.

"Hey, Mr. P," I said as if nothing were wrong. In his strong accent, he told me, "Fix jor tie, Polli." Daniel, my rosy-cheeked, effeminate, show tune-singing, new-to-me colleague helped me straighten my tie. *Oops.*

Now we were all lined up in front of Mr. P under the stark supermarket-type lighting for our nightly pre-shift meeting at the kitchen food service counter, also known in kitchen lingo as the line. Vincent the sommelier, whom I call Vino (clever, huh?), and the whole staff, stood in a row like soldiers before battle, all of us in clean, pressed uniforms adorned with four gold buttons on our dinner jackets. Underneath the jacket was a plain silk black tie against a starched white shirt, black double pleated gabardine slacks and perfectly polished black shoes to boot; classic black and white ensemble. We were so military, if we'd had weapons we could have done some damage.

Mr. P inspected each one of us to see that our uniforms were acceptable. Though our look may be a bit old-school, we're definitely the best-uniformed wait team in the city. Notwithstanding the Hooters girls. Those uniforms rock.

Mr. P proceeded to read through the station assignments and gave the busboys their designated patrol areas. His accent's so thick that I turn to Matt with a questioning look on my face. Matt shrugged his shoulders with a clueless smile. I elbowed him in the ribs and he let out a gasp. Jose and Juan caught our horseplay and giggled. Mr. P glanced up over his glasses with an intense look, not the least amused, and we all straightened up as he read on. He's so serious he could have been General Patton laying out a battle plan. I was genuinely straining to understand him – was I supposed to kill the Germans, or the Japanese? And which tank was mine? What I could almost discern is, "Kate Hudson will be coming in tonight around eight-thirty, and she'll be on table 43. Warren Beatty is already here. Penelope Cruz will be coming in with some family members on table six at nine o'clock." Then he mentioned a whole bunch of other stuff that I quite frankly couldn't make out. I'm guessing that the bulk of it was the same bull crap as usual: *'Remember that we will be shopped any day now, so make sure to use all the 'Rules of Service.' You must mention the guest's name at every table, you have blah, blah seconds to greet your guests and blah, blah minutes to bring the drinks, and you must try to upsell at every table."* It goes on and on and at this point it's just the corporation speaking through Mr. P the way the evil spirits in *The Exorcist* speak though their victims. I just hoped I wouldn't make Mr. P's head spin around or cause projectile vomiting. Not a very high goal, I'll admit, but at that point in my training it was all about absorbing the rules and surviving every day by becoming a little smarter and more Cricket Room worthy.

Once he had made himself fully misunderstood, Lola, our illustrious and impassive sous-chef, stepped up to introduce the soup of the day as well as our dinner special. Mr. P walked back out to the dining room, assured his troops were prepared for battle. Er, I mean service.

"Hi, guys," she mumbled with no enthusiasm. "The soup of

the day is cream of wild mushroom, consisting of porcini, shiitake and black morel fungi garnished with roasted truffled pine nuts. Prepared from a vegetable base."

"Does it have cream in it?" asked Paco.

Jens couldn't resist. "No, dumbass, it's consommé. She just wanted to throw you off by calling it 'cream of.' Of fucking course it has frickin' cream in it!"

Everyone snickered. "I was just askin' because sometimes they just thicken it with starch," said Paco defensively. I guess he used to work at Sizzler.

Lola confirmed blandly, "Yes, there's cream in the cream of wild mushroom soup." She went on to present the dinner special in the same lifeless monotone she always used. "The special tonight is pan roasted Chilean sea bass with a mirin miso crust, stir-fried Chinese broccoli and shiitake sticky rice ..." That sounded fabulous but the way she described it, she might as well have been saying, "The special tonight is shit on a shingle with peanut butter garnish, topped with a raw egg." She droned on, "...served with lobster froth."

Yuck, everything sounded fine up until the lobster froth, I thought. The chef Ferran Adria probably got his cappuccino mixed up with his paella when he invented that one. It doesn't look appetizing on food, kind of like the ick you see at the edge of the ocean now and then. During all of this, the phone had been ringing non-stop in the kitchen. It was one of the hostesses calling to tell us we had tables being seated. One by one all the waiters were sent out onto the floor.

For those of us remaining in the kitchen, Patzo the Clown peeked out from his hidden station to present the dessert special for the evening. Patzo who has to wear that stupid, tall paper chef's hat, often misreads his tickets, causing us all unnecessary stress and making us look like idiots to the customers.

"Tonight we have warm blueberry cobbler with a scoop of French vanilla bean frozen yogurt."

We all just nodded to acknowledge him and then the rest of us waiters stared at the sample specials as if we'd never seen food before. We wrestled and elbowed each other to get a taste of it all, like hungry orphans in a soup kitchen. It was an ugly sight.

All of a sudden, Ariella, our beautiful Betty Boop vixen, popped up. As usual, she was wearing natural nylons, a black gabardine skirt hiked up above her knees and an off-white rayon blouse whose over-stressed buttons were threatening to blow at any moment.

Hey, those could put an eye out!

"What are you guys eating? I want some!" All the guys separated and let her eat what was left, while some of us playfully groped her and took advantage of the starving sex kitten. Ariella's attitude toward sex was as casual as any guy's, and since she was accustomed to this ritual, she paid us no attention. I could swear she was a guy trapped in a sexy girl's body.

"Mmmmmm, what IS this?" she asked with an *ohmygod* California mall rat accent as she enjoyed the leftovers. We didn't answer; we just kept fondling her and pulling at her clothing like the perverts we were. "You guys are sick." She walked away in her five-inch black heels, licking her fingers and swatting us perverts off her like flies. *Hey, I'm a soldier about to go into battle,* I beg her mentally. But she never even slowed down.

Mr. P walks in and states, "Polli, jew 'ave a full station tonight, be careful."

"What! What happened to my training?" *I'm still in boot camp, dammit.*

"I need jew, jew ready anyway, let me know if jew need something."

Well, he's right. I am ready and it's time to raise the curtain on this evening's dinnertime dramas. It was a busy night in July and as usual, Mr. P was running the room short-handed because some idiot executive in the London office sets the labor budget too low.

Keep in mind, this international conglomerate owns more than ten upscale properties and not many of them are in the US. They have a completely different idea of organizational culture than did the previous owners of the Cricket Room – the people who had designed it and built it from nothing. A nameless, faceless corporation was turning a unique and iconic eatery into a commodity.

I was given a five-table station in the garden and as luck would have it, my first table was our GM who was entertaining two women who seemed like his close friends. *No pressure, Kid,* I think to myself. As I walked up to the table I smiled and bowed, then held eye contact with him and said, "Good evening, Mr. Cervantes. My name is Pauli. Welcome to the Cricket Room."

I made eye contact with the women at the table and asked, "Ladies, may I offer you a cocktail or a glass of champagne this evening, perhaps a cosmopolitan martini or a glass of Veuve Clicquot?" One of them ordered an apple martini, surprise, surprise. I immediately offered Grey Goose for her martini and she agreed, and the other woman asked for a glass of rosé champagne. I then offered Mr. Cervantes the option to order a bottle of Moet Chandon Rosé. He looked around the table and asked his guests if they would like that and they all nodded sheepishly.

"Thank you; please bring us a bottle with glasses for everyone."

"May I bring you some flat or sparkling water this evening, sir?"

"Flat, please."

"Fiji water or Evian, sir?"

"Fiji would be just fine, I don't like that French stuff; it tastes muddy somehow," he complained.

I repeated the beverage order back to him, then smiled and bowed and assured them that I'd be right back with their beverages. *"French stuff," huh? Douche alert.* I detected an over-developed sense of entitlement and arrogance. *Better be careful with this dude.*

I entered the order on our computer and picked up everything at the service bar, except the champagne bottle. On my polished silver tray, I carried out two bottles of Fiji set inside special silver sleeves, the apple martini, and the stemware for the table. As I passed by Vino, our quirky sommelier, I told him that the GM was at my table and his champagne was waiting at the bar. He understood the urgency and hurried to the bar. By the time I'd served one lady her martini, poured the water (label facing the guest) and put down their stemware for the champagne, Vincent showed up with the bottle of Moet Rosé. He presented the label to Mr. Cervantes, who gave him the nod to open the bottle.

Vino held the bottle at a 45-degree angle and opened the bottle without much of a struggle – just a hiss was heard when he popped the cork. He followed the protocol and poured a sample for Mr. Cervantes, then got the nod to pour for the table. Vino started with the ladies and finished with the host just as it is supposed to be done. He gently fitted the bottle into a silver wine bucket that he had placed near the table and ceremoniously laid the white cloth wine napkin across the top of the bucket with the neck of the bottle sticking up and resting against the back of the wine bucket.

I'd been watching from a short distance away just to see if Vino would need any help and I gave them a moment to drink a toast and enjoy their drinks. A few minutes later, I again approached the table to address the host and his guests and let them know what the chef's specials were for the evening. Since I could tell that they were not ready to order yet, I said, "Thank you, I'll return to take your order in a few minutes."

Mr. P came over to see if everything was going okay and I wondered if this was my test table. "Don't worry, Baby, jos stick to de Rule of Service and jew'll be fine," he said. "Jos let me know if jew need anything, Baby, okay?"

Somehow when Mr. P calls you Baby, it's not in a derogatory way, it's just his way of speaking. I nodded a bit nervously. Another table of four sat down in my section and as I approached them, I threw a suspicious glance towards Mr. Cervantes and his guests. They were just starting to pick up their menus. I cautiously returned to Mr. Cervantes' table after serving drinks at my new table. As I looked around the table, I asked if they had any questions about the menu and if they would like me to take their orders. Mr. Cervantes said, "I think we're ready, eh, Rita? What would you like?"

He gestured to the woman who had ordered the apple martini. Vino had returned to the table and begun pouring champagne for Rita, who was already getting a little giggly. Rita had short blonde hair, blue eyes, and was about fifty years old; attractive and classy but not in a sexy way. She wore a navy blue, belted cotton shirtdress with a white collar, probably Burberry, and a creamy pearl necklace that probably cost more than all my furniture.

Mr. Cervantes wore a sturdy, well-made charcoal suit, blue and white striped shirt with white collar, and what looked like a Brooks Brothers necktie in maroon with thin gold and navy stripes. He also had on his infamous tinted oversized '70s glasses. His hair was a perfect, evenly shaded brown, which lead me to believe he was hiding a full head of gray underneath. It just didn't look natural.

It had been a hot day but not unbearably so, and by seven o'clock it was starting to cool off. It was actually quite nice out in the garden. I really liked working in this section above all others. All of the candles on my tables had been lit and the garden's lushness, along with the candlelight, brought a pleasant intimacy to my section and I couldn't see why it wouldn't be full of diners within an hour. Even an ordinary drink or dish would seem special in this fairytale setting.

"Yes, ma'am, what can I bring you this evening?" Rita ordered and then I took the other woman's order and finally the host's. Since Rita had requested the gazpacho as appetizer, I recommended some nice ahi tuna carpaccio and an order of house-cured Balik salmon to share for appetizers. I also let them know about our famous chocolate soufflé dessert.

The ladies perked up when they heard about the soufflé and Mr. Cervantes said, "Thank you, eh, what's your name again, son?"

"Pauli, sir."

"Thank you, Pauli, we'll take your suggestions on the appetizers and bring two soufflés for us to share at dessert."

"With pleasure, sir," I said. I read back the orders to each of them as quickly as I could, and once I had my nod from them I knew I could enter the order. I told Mr. Cervantes that I would send Vincent over to suggest some nice wines for these dishes. I thanked them all and went to my other table to see if they were ready to order.

Shortly, I returned to the GM's table to pour more water and reset their setup according to what they'd be eating: soupspoons for gazpacho, steak knives for red meat dishes, etc. Then all I had to do was time their courses correctly so that they didn't have to wait long between them. It's important to keep an eye on the guest's pace of consumption, as I want the food to arrive fresh off the line to avoid any unnecessary time under a heat lamp. To do this you need to know how long it takes to cook the different dishes in our kitchen and how to figure in the soufflé course, which will usually take 20-25 minutes from the time you fire the order. That's if Patzo remembers to put it in the oven, which was never a sure thing. I silently plead, *Fool, don't fail me now.*

The way things worked, I needed to input my entire food order at the same time, including soufflés and correct seat position numbers as well. I split them up by pushing a button called first course and entered all the appetizers and first course items, then pressed the second course button and added all main course items, then the dessert button to order the soufflés.

Every course had to include corresponding table position numbers so that the food-runners would know exactly which guest received which plate. My order would then print out in the four respective food stations (cold, grill, sauté, and dessert), and it would also show all the different courses to all the stations. Once those tickets are picked up and posted in their respective stations, all I had to do to activate them was to press the FIRE or Pick Up button on the computer screen for each course. By keeping a close eye on my guests and judging the guests' eating pace, as well as judging how busy the kitchen was, I knew when to confidently FIRE their order. All this plus the Rules of Service was what I was responsible for at every one of my tables. *No problem, it's a lot of pressure, but I got this.*

My perspective changed as I began to notice how crazy it got when my station was full that night and I had to skip several Rules of Service because there simply was no way that I could perform all of them. The hostesses consistently seated multiple tables without any real concern for whose station she was seating. It is not uncommon to be inundated with four tables within a 15-minute period. That wouldn't have been a problem at a regular restaurant, but here with the timed Rules and the serious importance placed on maintaining a calm demeanor, it became a real challenge, especially when I usually had a six-table station to manage. That could mean coordinating upwards of twenty-four multi-course dinner orders in a very short span.

Luckily, the GM and his guests were finished eating by 8:30 pm and he went on his way to his comfortable home in Santa Monica Canyon. On their way out, I held the door open as he and his guests exited the garden. I very calmly thanked him and he smiled and winked at me. As soon as they left, I race-walked back to my station, trying not to grit my teeth, where I was buried in work for the rest of the evening.

Among many others, I served Kate Hudson who was an absolute joy. She drank a vodka martini and had a glass of Phelps cabernet with her dinner. Next to her at the neighboring booth was Martin Short (and he is, very) who was dining with Carrie Brillstein, philanthropist and widow of producer/manager Bernie Brillstein. Short was in rare form, assuming his frenetic Jiminy Glick persona, bouncing up and down and full of life. We are not allowed to react or interact with celebrity guests, and it was a challenge to not laugh out loud. Short is fucking hilarious. After Brillstein left, he crashed Kate Hudson's table for a while. He was a gas, a regular Chatty Cathy. When Hudson stood up to go to the restroom, Short bowed and kissed her hand. As she stood tall in her heels, reaching about five-ten and towering over Short, she was a statuesque beauty with a butt that would make J-Lo jealous. With her radiant smile, golden hair, fitted yellow top and snug jeans, she was workin' the room without even trying. I felt myself falling in lust again.

A bit later into the evening, I checked in at Penelope Cruz's booth to see what I could help with there. Although it wasn't my table, I was new to this celebrity thing and I couldn't help doing a flyby. She was in a deep conversation with her brother and a lawyer or agent.

Their conversation seemed to revolve around her brother's contract to compose the musical score for a film she was starring in. As it happened, they were ready to order and I took the order. Only her brother Eduardo spoke, and he asked for our special ($48) buttermilk fried chicken with mashed potatoes and gravy. Penelope joked that he liked everything fried. She was right because later he asked for fried calamari too. As I entered the order I saw that she was drinking a soy iced latte and I thought, *How healthy*. The film was eventually released with Eduardo Cruz credited as the film's composer. Lucky little shit. Why isn't my sister Gwen Stefani?

At the end of the night, while doing my closing side work at around midnight, I asked Daniel, "Wow! Is it always crazy like this?"

"Yeah, it's pretty tough sometimes but you'll get used to it."

"How do you guys keep up with those Rules of Service?"

"We don't, I mean, you try to, but they're not really designed for a restaurant where the waiter has this much responsibility, you know?"

It didn't sound like a warning when he said it, but the weight of those words would resonate later on in my career.

"Yeah, I got seated almost all at once around eight-thirty and I was instantly slammed. I couldn't find my busboy, couldn't find Vino to offer wine; it was a total goddamn nightmare and you guys had one more table than I did. How do you handle it?"

"Oh, you know," he said in his sing-songy voice. "You adjust, you just do your best, that's all." I appreciated his comforting tone, but somehow I wasn't convinced. *Really? Here? At the best place in town?*

"But why don't they have more staff, I mean we only cost eight bucks an hour?"

"Ah, it's all fucked up, Pauli!" said Jens who had been eavesdropping on our conversation. "I've worked in fancy restaurants all over the world and never seen anything like the way they've been running this place lately, man!" Jens was so passionate he was talking with his hands and spit was flying. The last time I'd seen Jens that angry he'd been yelling obscenities at Christie over the phone.

Daniel laughed and gave me that knowing gay look and then he said, "I'm going to drive myself home, pour myself a couple of nice single malt scotches, and listen to *My Fair Lady*. Ta ta, see you tomorrow, Newbie." He giggled as he left me standing there. I stopped for a moment, sort of taking in the evening and wondering what I had gotten myself into. Jens had finished and headed to the changing room, not even saying goodnight. Despite his fit of anger, he'd probably made at least five-hundred bucks in tips alone.

When I got home that night, I counted my cash again: $312. Not bad for my first night, but I was exhausted and my feet were aching. I couldn't remember ever working that hard before, but I also never felt as essential or validated. I knew I had done a good job and I'd impressed some important people, primarily the GM, which could ensure a good career at one of the most notable eateries on Earth.

Those are some long-ass shifts, I thought to myself and passed out on the couch. I woke up at four in the morning, stripped naked, and crawled into bed. I slept until eleven for the first time in a year and when I got up I felt completely refreshed and ready to take on the world again.

CHAPTER 8
THE LIVES OF OTHERS

For the next several months my bank account grew nicely and although service was repetitious, every night offered something new. I felt we were always working short-handed but I tried my damnedest to give great service so I could make the big tips and be a credit to the legacy of the Cricket Room. I ended up having to work in the garden area almost every night and since it was such a warm summer, that area was always packed with lively guests. They even put the musicians outside in the garden every evening all the way into the middle of September. The music carried through the open doors and sliding windows so you could hear it throughout the main restaurant. It made the dining room feel even more elegant and old-Hollywood grand than it was. Hard to imagine how you could class up a joint that was already known for its class, but live music can do it. Especially when it's more than just a standard piano player.

There were times, though, when it felt like we were on the Titanic, listening to our swan song as I drowned in sparkling water, wine, and au jus. I race-walked everywhere from seven to midnight and when I got home at night, my legs ached and my feet were on fire. Boo hoo, right? I was making great money so I should shut up.

During this period, I served many celebrities including Jennifer Aniston, Vince Vaughn, Gary Oldman, Leonardo Di Caprio, Juliette Lewis, Rob Lowe, Colin Farrell, Tom Selleck, David Spade, Thomas Hayden Church, Sharon Osbourne, Brad Pitt, John Malkovich, Tara Reid, Toby Maguire, and Diane Keaton. You know all of them so no explanation needed.

The hardest thing about serving such famous Hollywood icons, at least for the first time, is trying not to stare at them. It's so other-worldly to see someone like Selleck, who's not just huge, he's bigger than life, and who you've watched on big screen and small for years. They are invariably taller or shorter than you'd imagined, and the women are either spectacularly beautiful or very ordinary without screen makeup. But you can't stare. It's *verboten* by ownership.

Brad Pitt was cool and very humble. He had a few Pyramid

beers with a producer friend and then he took off on his motorcycle down Sunset Boulevard heading west towards the Palisades. Am I saying that he was driving drunk? No, he was there for two hours and had two beers so he wasn't breaking the law, at least not with my assistance. He had been there many times before; I just hadn't been the one serving him.

I remember when he came in during his filming of *Troy*, he had long hair and a cast on his leg. Ironically, he had torn his Achilles tendon while playing Achilles in the epic film. I remember Jens helping him to the restroom so he wouldn't need his crutch, instead just leaning on Jens and limping a bit. Quite honestly, I think that made Jens's whole year.

Diane Keaton was interviewing assistants and using one of my tables as her office. I think she interviewed four different girls. When I finally gave her the bill, she signed it without giving me her credit card. I then asked her a question that I already knew the answer to: "Ms. Keaton, do you have a house account with us?"

"No," she answered.

So I looked at the bill folder again as to give her a hint. "Oh, did I? Yeah, oh my God, I'm sorry." She threw her hands in the air and laughed at herself in that endearing, exasperated way that only she can. "It's just been a long day, that's all," she said while handing me her platinum Amex card.

"Thank you, Ms. Keaton, I understand," I said. She wore one of her famous yuppie hippie outfits with the vest, slacks and a hat that reminded me of her look for the film *Annie Hall*. She's charming, like the eccentric aunt you always wanted to spend time with.

Colin Farrell was friendly. He kept calling me Bud, chose a bottle of inexpensive French red wine and a New York steak, entertained himself for a while, then paid and left. No one really bothered him too much, maybe because in his roles he's always super-macho and usually snarling. The tip was very "European," by the way. I think it spoke Gaelic.

Bill Maher showed up with a lovely African girl who was so dark-skinned I could hardly see her that night. At first, I thought he was alone. It didn't help that the booth in the garden was only lit by candlelight. I don't know for sure but I have a hunch she was an escort. He is, shall we say, looks-challenged and very small although in this town success speaks louder than anything. She was stunning and well put together; she looked professional.

The late Gore Vidal was a regular and shared a lot of history with the restaurant, as he'd been coming here for decades. Mr. Vidal, who usually never sat in a booth because of his wheelchair, would always take his regular table, number 48. Gore was one of the more interesting people who frequented this establishment. He was a cerebral man with no need for a suntan, unlike his old Hollywood counterparts, Robert Evans and Gorgeous George Hamilton, who always look deep-fried to a crisp. Vidal traveled with his male nurse who usually requested me as their server. One night, I commented on how interesting it had been to see him talking to Robert Evans the night before. In his signature droll style, he said, "Yes, well, he started to tell us a story about this woman he met in San Francisco and the story went on and on. He wouldn't stop! As a matter of fact I think he's still telling it." I laughed; he was a character even by Hollywood's standards and had a rapier wit.

In his usual fashion, he ordered his martini from the hostess, so that it would be ready by the time he was seated. He definitely has his priorities straight and getting his Grey Goose Gibson as quickly as possible was of great consequence. He also asked me for a ham sandwich on white bread with a side of Dijon and mayo, but not before taking a long slug of his martini while his eyelids fluttered in sweet delight.

Since I hadn't had the time and pleasure of talking to him for a while, I took the opportunity to do so on this particular evening. It was still a bit slow in the main dining room, so before his food arrived I took a moment to ask him how he was doing.

"Better now, looking at you, young man," he said in a saucy, flirtatious way. I asked him if he'd had a nice day, and he told me that he had been to the Huntington Library in Pasadena. Mr. Vidal commented on what a remarkably beautiful place it was, and then quickly segued into a rant about how LA was such an ugly city full of ugly people, "Except for you, of course," he said, nodding to me. These mischievous tidbits of naughtiness were nothing new from Gore, though I never quite knew how to react to them. I chose to see them as an endearing quirk, and I usually tried to acknowledge his flirtations without encouraging them; I just responded with a quick, polite smile. I hastily mentioned how enchanting I think the gardens are at the museum, and he praised the Japanese and botanical gardens. Eager to keep the conversation going, I described how, during my last visit, I had felt that the *Blue Boy* painting by Gainsborough and the painting of

Pinkie by T. Lawrence stood out in particular. He proudly mentioned that he owned one of the largest private collections of Neapolitan paintings and that he would donate his art collection to the Huntington Museum when his time to leave the Earth arrived, which he said he felt would be sooner rather than later. Then his face turned angry and he suddenly said, "Because I can't stand my family! I hate them all! I'll be damned if I leave them any of my art collection!"

I really wasn't ready for that outburst so I changed the subject and I asked if he needed anything else at the moment. He took a breath, and then said loudly: "Bring me the head of John the Baptist!" I held in a snicker and told him we were all out of that item, and he said, "Well, then, I'll have some oysters, please." And from there he went right to ordering dessert – vanilla ice cream with chocolate sauce. He usually didn't sign his own check, but on that night he did the math himself. Even though it was an odd amount he managed to figure twenty percent exactly to the penny. He was still a sharp man up 'til the end. That is, until that second drink kicked in and he was either singing along to the oldies by the piano or falling asleep in his wheelchair. But mind you, he never lost that grip on his martini.

As a side note: when he ordered the head of John the Baptist, I seriously thought about offering up the head of my busser as a sub-stitute, but censored myself before I could horrify Vidal. On second thought, however, anyone who would come into the legendary Cricket Room and order a plain ham sandwich might have a high threshold for horror.

Tom Selleck, always low-key and pensive, would come in solo at first and spend an hour making notes regarding his crime drama show, *Jesse Stone*. Later his friend Tony would join him for a couple of scotches as an appetizer, then a juicy NY steak with a couple of glasses of red wine. For dessert, they would skip the sweet stuff and go right for a great cigar afterwards. I even sold them a couple of Davidoffs from our house selection. Beverly Hills hadn't yet enforced the no-smoking rule for outdoor dining areas. He's a gentleman and a class act all the way, imposing and impressive. No chit chat from him.

John Malkovich came by for a couple of evenings with his family. It was strange watching the androgynous-looking Malkovich speaking French with his wife and two kids. They seemed very tight as a family, with beverages all around as appetizers while they played cards together. On the other hand it was strange, looking into his eyes. When he speaks, he seems to stare directly into your naked soul in a sinister sexual way. I can't explain it but he ain't no regular Joe, that's for sure. That's probably why he's so good at playing weirdoes and monsters; might be a little bit of typecasting. I felt like he imagined a section on the menu under which Filet of Pauli were listed.

When Jennifer Aniston and Vince Vaughn came in, it would actually cause quite a stir. He's a huge handsome guy and she's gorgeous, so of course people gawked. Many of our guests would try to send over drinks, but we wouldn't allow it. People also tried to take pictures with their phones and we had to have security confiscate their phones and delete the pictures. We were actually glad when they broke up and stopped coming in together.

One quiet Tuesday night I got an unannounced visit. As I gazed toward the front door I saw a couple of tall guys walking in, casually dressed, and a skinny guy behind them walking in holding a little girl's hand. In a moment, I made out Johnny Depp and his daughter. He wore a tan fedora, a dark chocolate-brown fitted T-shirt, a short, light, beige cotton traveler jacket, and comfortable, roomy blue jeans; I didn't make it to the shoes. Depp's then-ten year-old daughter, Lily Rose, is the spitting image of her lovely mother, and is adorable with her golden blonde locks.

This was my first time serving Depp. "Good evening, Mr. Depp, Miss Depp, good evening, gentlemen." I assisted Mr. Depp into his booth where he sat alone with Lily Rose. His two assistants and his security guard sat at a nearby round table more or less blocking the view from googly-eyed onlookers.

"How are you this evening, sir?"

"Doin' great, thanks. It's nice to be here," said Depp pleasantly. He's played such famously weird over-the-top characters I wasn't sure what to expect, but he seemed entirely normal.

"Sparkling or still water for the two of you?" Johnny looked at his daughter who whispered something, then said, "Still, please." As I looked into his kind eyes I instantly felt as if I'd known him for a while; he seemed so open and friendly. I almost felt like striking up a conversation about knowing a musician friend of his who runs a music studio in Hollywood, but I decided it was best to keep things professional, for now, anyway. Our sommelier Vino popped up at the table out of nowhere with an almost inappropriately eager and intense energy.

"Good evening, Mr. Depp!" he chirped. "My name is Vincent, I'm the somm here at the Cricket Room and I'll be happy to assist you with any wine choices you'd like to make!" He sounded nervous and his energy was the polar opposite of Depp's. I looked at him and then at Depp. Depp was still smiling and looking at Vino with his calm eyes as though he were being entertained. His lips twitched in that signature almost-smile you must know.

I left the table to approach Depp's assistants and take their beverage orders with my ears still tuned in to the conversation behind me. I was terrified Vino was going to make a fool of himself.

"What's your taste, Mr. Depp?" said Vino.

"Well, I normally go for French wines, La Mission, Haut Brion, but even a really well-made Margaux might be okay."

"Let me suggest two wines that will absolutely knock your socks off. They are both the biggest cult names coming out of Napa right now." *Oh my fucking God, how inappropriately casual. A sommelier is supposed to be very professional and aloof, not a sports buddy.*

"Sure," said Depp.

As I turned around to go to the kitchen, I saw Vino leaning in and pointing at the menu and I heard Depp saying, "I've heard of them but I've never really tried them." Next thing I knew, Vino was decanting a 1997 Screaming Eagle, a highly regarded Napa Cabernet, rated at 100 points by Robert Parker. Depp asked me to bring glasses to his crew as well. A bit later, Vino asked Depp if he would like to have him open the 1991 Harlan Estate so he could decant it for a while, and Depp concurred. Unfortunately, Johnny was not too fond of the Screaming Eagle and his exact words were: "It's not desirable to my palate." So he only finished one glass and his crew drank the rest. Later on he admitted to liking the Harlan Estate a lot better, though "It's still not really what I like in a wine but I do like it a whole lot better than the Eagle. Probably because it has some age on it, you know?" he explained to Vino. The guy seemed to know his wines, probably from living in France.

By then the "Pirate" movies must have grossed around three billion dollars worldwide, so hopefully the studios were picking up the tab because the Eagle was priced at almost $7,000 and the Harlan near $4,000 per bottle. That's a lot of cash to drop on wine you don't like.

I told Vino later before Depp left, "Hey, man," eyeing Johnny's feet, "His socks are still on. WTF?" I was disappointed that Depp's assistant left a very modest tip, though I can't say I blamed him considering he didn't fancy the wine that cost him a more than a pretty penny. I felt bad about that. But not that bad.

Ironically, after a while, it all started to look normal. It's easy to lose your perspective in these circumstances. Somehow I managed to tell myself that I fit in with these high-profile people, as if we were cut from the same cloth. It was giving me a great feeling of importance to serve and be around these types of guests. I was getting high on it – their influence became addicting and I craved it. It didn't register at first that the silver tray I held between us not only connected us but drew an impenetrable barrier between us. It was easy to forget that the title of "server" was my raison d'être.

As that summer slowly faded away The Cricket Room entered its slower period, which is usually from Labor Day until November. The dip in business is mainly because most of the rich tourists leave town. During that period, we had a chance to take a deep breath and work on things that we didn't have time to work on during the rest of the year.

It was early on one of those warm, almost sultry, nights and I was again working in the garden section. My guest, Mr. BJ Tyler, had been meeting with several music-business people, and since I wasn't very busy I was able to eavesdrop on his meetings a bit. They were putting together a company to sell music to television. Apparently, they all had connections with music supervisors for different networks and shows; there were well known names being thrown about with abandon. The air was bubbling with positive energy and there were ideas flying around that were being knocked down then altered and customized, and then finally being accepted. Though I couldn't really hear all the details, I have to admit that my ears perked up as I thought to myself, *Hmmm…television music…I could do that!* They were on to something: the demand for original music had grown tremendously with all the new cable channels pumping out comedy shows, cheesy movies, and dramas 24/7.

After Mr. Tyler and his friends had finished their $36 burgers, their pedestrian red wine and mojitos, I went back to the table to clear their dinner plates and present a dessert menu. I told Mr. Tyler that if he had the time he should order a chocolate soufflé. "They are definitely worth the wait." He agreed enthusiastically. His friends said goodbye to him and he said he was going to stay for a bit and finish up some work. I offered him some coffee and he smiled, "I'm gonna need it, thank you." *Great, my scheme to keep him there was working.*

After I brought him his French press coffee, I asked cautiously, "Are you in the music business?"

"Yeah, we're expanding our company right now, it's really

exciting"

"Oh really, what do you do? I hope you don't mind me asking, sir?"

"No, no, not at all, we're gonna be focusing on licensing music to television productions."

I think he noticed the split-second delay as I fought to stay professional. I had been longing to meet someone like him for years. "Wow, yeah that does sound exciting! Well, good luck, I'm sure you'll do well." And then with a wan smile I turned around to walk away, literally biting my lip to keep quiet.

"Why, are you a musician?" I froze with my back turned. It took another split second to recognize that the moment wasn't lost. I thought to myself, *This is my opportunity to see if I've still got what it takes.* I turned back around to face him. "Yeah, how did you know?"

"I didn't, just thought you might be, that's all."

I gave him the short version of my history in the music business and he offered me his card and said they were looking for songs by unsigned artists that they could place in television shows, either as background or theme music. He also told me to make sure that all performances on the recordings were cleared before sending them to him. "Thank you, Mr. Tyler, I really appreciate this opportunity."

"Just call me Tyler, and you're Pauli, right?"

"Yeah, good memory, sir. I mean Tyler, sorry, they want us to be so formal here." He laughed then he said to call him or send the material to the address on the card.

"Thank you, I will, Tyler, thanks."

I was excited! I had been dying to start writing music again and suddenly the opportunity was before me. Tyler's chocolate soufflé arrived a few minutes later, and he loved it. He asked me for a side of Crème Anglaise – imagine that, a music-business dude who knew about Crème Anglaise. That soufflé really did look good, though. I thought I just might ask Patzo to make me one with Crème Anglaise later. Treat myself for uncovering this great opportunity and having the balls to pursue it.

Tyler left a nice tip and gave me another card to give to any of my songwriter friends that might "fit the bill" as he put it. So Tyler was obviously building a music library. It was probably a cattle call like everything in this town. Well, at least I wouldn't have to audition in his office with a ukulele and tap shoes.

After saying goodbye to my new best friend Tyler by the front door, I broke down the garden dining area, collected all the silver candles and linen from the tables, and turned off the glowing heating lamps. I found out later what he meant about performance clearance. Anyone who performed on a musical piece must provide a signed clearance form specifying that they have been paid for their perform- ance and do not wish to claim any further interest in the recording. You need a specific contract for that kind of clearance. So I decided to send him songs I had recorded with only one other person just to keep it simple, stupid, as someone famously said.

And so went another typical night at the Cricket Room, I thought as I rode my scooter home down a quiet and dark Sunset Boulevard. It always seemed to take twice as long to get home as it had to come to work, but I enjoyed it. It gave me time to reflect on the events of the evening. Where else in the world would I be serving Gore Vidal, Diane Keaton, and Johnny Depp? I was learning valuable lessons in my new role as server in the Cricket Room, such as the rules of five- star service, the caliber of guests we serve, and their particular "handle with care" instructions. I also learned that in this high-society world, even a stingy tip on a huge check is still pretty damn good. And it didn't hurt to see firsthand the results of all the hard work, training, and luck that went into making these people stars. Most of them had all come from humble backgrounds and had made it big. Maybe I could too. All in all I felt I was in the right place, for me, at the right time, as my meeting with Tyler seemed to prove.

CHAPTER 9
RUTHLESS PEOPLE

We called them the Brat Pack, a collection of highly competitive trust fund kids who were just becoming legal and could finally throw away that fake ID they'd been handing out all over town. I'm not sure what Beverly Hills trend brought those kids to the Cricket Room, but they visited quite often and generally ordered crap food and hung out for hours. I guess it made them feel like grown-up ballers on a Beverly Hills level but they didn't fit in at all and frankly hurt the rep of the place. Their nickname was apt. Unlike the renowned Rat Pack (Sinatra and pals), they had no class, no manners, no talent, and were completely socially inept. They obviously knew the restaurant is famous (everyone does) and that's all the excuse they needed to assault us. You could almost hear the place sigh whenever they slouched in, and it seemed that even the ghosts stayed away on those nights.

I couldn't stand serving these rude, over-indulged children of the rich and shameless. They were shameless yet they played no part in becoming rich. They were a terrible waste of time and energy when I had educated, refined guests who were eager to spend top dollar for the fine experience of dining at the Cricket Room. It was a pain in the ass because they would all show up one by one, then order one drink each and sit for hours. When they were finally ready to leave, they'd give us ten of their parents' credit cards, each requesting that a different total be charged to their card. Many restaurants have policies against such nonsense but unfortunately the Cricket Room had no such policy; we were trained to be guest-centric, so if that's what the little beasts wanted, that's what they got.

Even though I had worked hard to clean up my language when working at the Cricket Room, no one could control my inner monologue: *Fuck you, you fucking fucks! Rude little fuck-faced fuckers. Eat shit and die, fuckers.* That had sort of become my mantra and helped me deal.

Holding court were the infamous baby billionaire brothers, Gummi Bear and Greasy Bear. Gummi was notoriously rude and fat and Greasy much more discreet but doubly arrogant. Gummi Bear would always spend a bundle in less than thirty minutes for several drinks and all his food. He was by far the most unpopular patron with the staff. I was near the door when Ariella greeted him, and he kept walking towards his table, shouting out his food and beverage orders to me like I was fucking deaf, without ever looking at me or acknowledging me as a person. He was enormously heavy back then and his thighs rubbed together as he struggled up the few stairs that led up to his favorite table in the garden. He just expected me to run – or waddle – after him and write down his order as he oozed his way to his table. Fortunately, the patterned carpeting didn't reveal the slime trail he left.

It was evident that we were not people to him; we were just servants unworthy of eye contact. Or human courtesy. Gummi and Greasy were on the payroll of their tremendously wealthy grandmother who had inherited nearly $2.5 billion from her husband, a Los Angeles oil tycoon who had passed away in 2004. The two bears had accomplished nothing in their lives and didn't seem to be trying. There wasn't a Goldilocks in sight to set them straight. To say I despised them doesn't even come close.

Then there was the good-looking Marciano kid, son of a Guess® co-founder, and his bestest little buddy Lucas. Marciano was the first dude to wear tight European-style jeans low on his hips to show off his underwear. He took the "ghetto" style to a whole new demographic. *Thanks, buddy. I was dying to know whether you liked tightie whities or designer boxers.*

There was also another twit named Brian. Brian came from Arkansas and spoke in a heavy Southern accent. He was a bucktoothed boy, the son of wealthy parents who held high hopes for him in spite of investing nothing in his appearance. He was barely of drinking age when I first met him and he wanted badly to fit in with the likes of the Marciano kid, Gummi and Greasy Bear, and all the other pseudo-cool Beverly Hills slacker kids. He quickly bought his way into the crowd by paying for drinks and food. It's called lobbying in the real world; really, it's no different here. And if Washington is Hollywood for ugly people, why are these kids here? They were the pimples on Hollywood's well-toned ass.

Brian obviously wasn't quite sure if he was gay or straight but in the openly bisexual climate of these exploring young Beverly Hills kids, he found out that indeed boys were his preference. He ended up having an intimate dalliance with one of Marciano's buddies that would clear up his ambiguity regarding the matter. Always good to pick a side and stick with it. Brian was supposed to keep it to himself but he was way too excited to do so. He just couldn't help spilling his guts to Daniel, his waiter. Little did he know how well voices carry out there in the garden. The only thing that was endearing about Brian was his willingness to accept most of us at an equal level. He never swore or talked dirty; he was definitely a well-mannered young man. He wanted so badly to be important and have friends that he would ask our opinions of certain people and always introduced us to his new friends. Now mind you, these kids always came in after regular dining hours when we could have been closing up and finishing our side work, but instead we had to keep serving these brats for an extra two hours. Every time we turned around there were new adolescents pulling up a chair from an empty table to seat themselves. Orders for food and drinks would trickle in at an ever so slow pace that it became their own little cafeteria for the rich and shameless juniors, and a nightmare for us. Nothing says douche like being inconsiderate to people you think have no power.

Nearby was J. Pole, who'd made more money in real estate by the time he had reached twenty than most people do in an entire career. You've probably seen him on TV, a tycoon at all of twenty-two years of age. I remember approaching him at a table as he was describing to his girlfriend how he had licked some guy's ass and liked it. Unfortunately for me, he finished that sentence while I was standing at his table trying to take his order. *Traumatizing.* I had witnessed a startlingly fast transformation in J. Pole's life. When he began dropping by, he was a young, clean-shaven, twenty-one-year-old shy boy who wouldn't drink more than one drink and ate and managed his money very frugally. He had dressed in average off-the-rack clothes and looked very innocent. His attitude in the beginning had been respectful and genuine. He had just been featured in a local magazine as the biggest sales agent in Beverly Hills. Within two years' time, he was on television regularly and his attitude had become that of a much more arrogant and unbridled person.

He was always unshaven and sported designer clothes that were a better fit for Russell Brand, but that was the Hollywood norm and I'm afraid he fell head first into it. Next stop would be the overpriced shrink's couch. At his core, I know J. Pole will always be a great guy and I think by now he's probably grown into a fine man. But he still dressed like a twat. Or twit. With him, I was never sure.

After a while, the Brats got the hint that they were out of their league at the Cricket Room and only came in once or twice a year just to prove they could. The Beverly Hills smoking ban certainly helped make that happen for us.

One co-worker who benefited from the Brat Pack's infatuation with the Cricket Room was Ariella. She managed to impress both me and Jens, not only with her looks, but with the number of guests she dated then quickly threw to the side. There was one Dole family heir (think pineapples, not politics) whom she used as a booty call until his skinny ass began to bore her like a bad reality TV show. She soon took up with a millionaire kid her own age who couldn't handle her at all. He was constantly suspicious and jealous. She ended it after he came in one day making accusations of infidelity and getting so angry that he spit on her shiny black high-heeled designer pumps. A famous actress had worn those exact shoes in a movie and Ariella loved them. He should've known better than that – those heels were her everything. She probably slept in them. We didn't see that guy at the Cricket Room for at least a year and even then with several months between visits. I think he had to get therapy to heal. Finally, it was the Dorfmeister as I called him, a celebrity actor who courted her for months right in front of us before she finally let him at it. That lasted a while – almost six months – before she fired him, too. Ariella was demanding and not many could "measure up" to her expectations.

Most important to Jens and me was that Ariella had impressed us with her regal bearing, paradoxically tinged with slutty overtones. We summoned her to our bad boy club to hang out with us, drink our booze, and toot our toot. And she didn't disappoint in the least. One night after an especially stressful night, Ariella, Jens and I headed over to Jens' girlfriend's condo for a raucous party that brought out the "breast" in all of us, when she finally opened that bursting blouse of hers. Thank you, Ariella. Even Jens' girlfriend was impressed with her. I would share more juicy details, but Ariella would find me and kill me. I love you, dear reader, but you're not worth dying for.

The Cricket Room attracted some of the most bizarre people I've ever seen in action. So many Beverly Hills wanna-be MILFs have the reconstructed bodies of girls in their twenties, and enough plastic surgery to actually scare people. It's cool to be skinny but when you're wearing a sleeveless dress that ends above the knees, there is very little excuse for exhibiting all the extra skin that's dangling from your arms and legs. It's actually quite shocking. Who told them that that dress looked good on them? Some salesperson on commission, no doubt. Just because you can fit into your grandkids' outfits doesn't mean that you should wear them. We served them every single night and it could be traumatizing. You've probably seen them on TV and thought "that's horrifying." Imagine it up close. It's even worse. You feel like if they turned around you'd see all the mechanisms that held them together and made them look human, like one-sided creatures full of stitches, scars, pins, clips, and botox.

Usually they bleach their hair blonde and paint on their eyebrows because their real brows are somewhere up around their hairline from all the facelifts. They dress like teenagers going to a ritzy nightclub and wear very expensive trendy Gucci jewelry. Their orders were always the same: I'll have this with no that and no that and no that. I end up writing a frickin' book chapter just to take an order whereas they could have just as well said, "I'll have some lettuce with plain grilled salmon and a side of unsalted air." They prefer to take all of their calories from the expensive wine or Champagne they guzzle, and oooh how they love their Champagne.

It's a laugh to watch these mannequins desperately trying to forge a new identity after their shallow husbands dump them for younger girls half their age. Even the ones who are still married mess up their boobs and faces with plastic surgery. I think it's just the Beverly Hills "look." If you want to see someone who embodies the look, check out the over-botoxed Christine Peters, the ex-flame of Sumner Redstone. I think they both have the same surgeon because he's ninety going on sixty. And sorry, Joan (Rivers), you were funny and talented, but you looked creepy. Ditto Kenny Rogers and Mary Tyler Moore. Just say no to any more facelifts. Put down the scalpel and pick up a cheeseburger for Christ's sake.

Beyond the phantasmagorical parade of plastic women, we were having a strange night. First a Mrs. Kangis called ahead to have us prepare pureed stewed apples and pears as well as steamed broccoli and carrots, all very soft. When she and her husband arrived, they sat down for twenty minutes and fed their nine-month old a hundred bucks' worth of mashed up vegetables and fruit, and drank a few Diet Cokes. That's how the rich roll, hundred-dollar baby food. It's insane. For some reason it struck me in a strange way. I've watched people order thousand-dollar wines almost every night but this seemed even more pointlessly extravagant. That fat baby didn't know from shit what it was eating. It made me sad somehow. His innocence just didn't fit in with this den of iniquity and fakery, like they were trying to prove their love for the kid by spending a ridiculous amount of money. In a couple of decades he'd probably be a member of a brand new Brat Pack thanks to Mommy Dearest.

A typical story of entitled Beverly Hills locals starts like this: Mr. and Mrs. Haig brought two guests with them, and the first thing they tell me is that they are regulars. That's funny because I've never seen them before and when we checked the computer, we saw they had only dined with us once in the past year. They obviously thought we were all naive or there's high-enough turnover that no one would know the truth. Wrong on both counts. However, they ordered their martinis up with a whole plate full of cocktail onions and olives on the side so that we wouldn't compromise the amount of vodka in the glass. That's a trick I use when I'm drinking, but of course I don't live in a seven-million dollar mansion. So the night's just begun and these "regulars" are already down one lie and one cheap trick.

As the night continued, the husband used more vulgarity than a sailor on San Diego shore leave, swearing the whole time he was talking to his wife and guests. Meanwhile there was a gentleman at the next table visiting from out of town with his ten-year-old daughter. When I asked the gentleman if his dinner was to his liking, he said, "Yes, but who is this man next to me? I wish he wouldn't use such foul language, since my daughter is here with me."

I nod, "I understand, sir."

I approached Mr. Haig to tell him discreetly that the young girl at the next table could hear everything they were saying. This was all that I said, nothing more. I thought that if he were a decent guy, he'd realize that he was compromising someone else's fine dining experience and adjust his vocabulary. He said, "Okay," but later when I came back to help José clear the table, Mrs. Haig said with a serious pout on her face, "I can appreciate what you told my husband but we are in a free country and we should be able to say whatever we want to say."

I smiled and said, "I'm just trying to keep everyone happy, that's all." *Bitch. Rich and shameless to the bone.*

Mrs. Haig turned to her friends and said, "I can't believe no one is backing me up here! Children should be in bed by ten anyway!"

It was 9:45 pm and the gentleman and his daughter had arrived at 9:00. Finally, one of the couple's guests said, "We are frequent guests and should be treated as such. I'm going to save my comments for later." He said "comments" in a way that meant he was going to leave me a shitty tip – as if I had been rude to them. Riddled with guilt and entitlement, they struggled to make sense of their own bad behavior, working it out so that someone else was to blame for their immodesty. I immediately fetched Mr. P and explained the situation in case it escalated. When he came over to talk to them, they said everything was fine. We politely bade them farewell as they departed but secretly we were holding our middle fingers high behind our backs as we bowed our heads in an act of faux respect. I was surprised to find that they actually left a decent tip; maybe their consciences kicked in.

One night I make a quick stop at Robert De Niro's table unaware that the simpering, star-struck idiot who's been filling in on Mr. P's night off had been checking on him constantly. That particular night, my favorite actor ever had requested a table in the Cove and specifically paid the annoying Maître d' a hefty sum to keep the booths next to him empty because he was entertaining a young black girl and obviously didn't want to be bothered. I wouldn't normally check in on a guest who isn't in my station, but I took this rare opportunity to interact with one of the greatest actors in the world. As I approached the table to make sure all is well, I asked with a happy face, "Is everything alright here, Mr. De Niro?" Sneering at me with that "You talkin' to me?" face, he practically yells at me, "Why? Did I say something was wrong!?" Whoa. Apparently the world's best actor also has the biggest balls in Hollywood. Later, as De Niro's leaving, Dumdum asks for his mini flashlight back which he had loaned to De Niro to read the menu. De Niro scoffed and told him to buy a new one. First time in my experience that a guest reacted negatively to too much attention from the staff. Who knows, maybe his lady friend wasn't in a generous mood that night.

On that same night, I heard that Sir Elton John along with his husband David Furnish, and Nicholas Cage all gave bad tips to their servers. And when I say bad, I mean 10% and less. Though I wasn't their waiter, I couldn't help but think, "That shit stinks." But some celebrities think it's an honor to serve them so you should be grateful they leave you anything. It's arrogance on steroids, like their bodies. If you can't afford the full experience, including leaving a decent tip, then stay the fuck home. Order pizza with a side of human growth hormone.

Unless the service sucked, which perhaps it did, but then why didn't we hear about it later? It's just unforgivable to be a regular celebrity customer and pretend that you don't know the drill. Yes, even Cage, an American who's married to a former waitress, gave a crappy tip to one of my co-workers. I remember overhearing him at the bar telling the bartender that he was a bit upset because his wife made him spend too much money on real estate and now he was being forced into foreclosure on several properties. This was no secret, because he was willingly dishing out this confession to several listeners at the bar, and it was all over the news that he'd had tremendous financial troubles involving the IRS and his real estate holdings. I mean here's a guy who earned an average of $20 million dollars a year or more. Do I really want to feel sorry for him? Still, celebrities are human beings (most of them, anyway) and they have problems just like the rest of us. Making millions doesn't give them instant wisdom or morals.

I remember serving Mr. Cage myself a while back. He came in with his wife Kim and his twenty-one year old heavy metal son Weston, and Weston's girlfriend. Cage didn't drink very much – just a couple of glasses of Turley Zinfandel. Prior to Weston showing up, he had ordered three appetizers, a tortilla soup (which was our most popular soup), a jumbo shrimp cocktail and a chicken quesadilla made with roasted corn and Monterey jack cheese, served with salsa fresca and sour cream. When his son, looking very Ozzy-like, and his girlfriend showed up, they each ordered Ahi tuna tartare topped with chopped yellow heirloom tomato, and seaweed salad with fresh mashed avocado on the side, as well as two mixed juices made with pineapple, cranberry, and orange. When Cage saw their tuna, he ordered an Ahi tuna tartare for himself and one ounce of Siberian caviar. I guess that's what guys like him eat when they have the munchies – three-hundred bucks' worth of appetizers.

For their main courses, Weston's girlfriend ordered the juicy rotisserie chicken with watercress salad and roasted fingerling potatoes, and for Weston it was even more tuna: the rare grilled Ahi steak with sautéed sea-beans, rapini, roasted peewee potatoes, and a fresh ginger-red chili ponzu sauce on the side. Cage had Spaghetti Vongole, sort of a joke version of this classic dish if you're from the Mediterranean, and for the Mrs., a chopped salad with everything on it except bacon.

The overall mood among them was a bit tense. Cage seemed uncomfortable as they discussed Weston's recordings with his band, Eyes of Noctum. Weston complained about the long hours in the studio and the tedious recording process. Cage trumped it by saying, "The movie-making process is so slow, it drives me crazy sometimes.

They keep you there all day and much of the night waiting to act out a few lines."

Oh, boo hoo. We all started crying for him; I swear I could hear violins playing a lonely, sad song in the background. WTF, schmuck! You make millions on every movie while "waiting around to say a few lines" – is that worth waiting for? I guess our complaints about life are all relative, aren't they? Many celebrities are incredibly generous and thoughtful, and support huge charities and foundations. Others seem to have no perspective on life beyond Beverly Hills and Hollywood, and the rest of the world might as well not exist.

Though Mr. Cage was a bit arrogant and avoided eye contact with me most of the night, I managed at last to catch his eye when I gave him his check. I thought it'd be important for him to look up and actually see me, so that he would see who had been busting his ass to serve him for the past hour and a half. He tipped me one-twenty on a five-eighty tab – that's 20%. In my experience, Cage is a good tipper when he gets good service, even if he does whine like a bitch about his job.

Now, regarding David Furnish, Sir Elton's man toy: I had served him during a previous visit around the same time as Cage's earlier visit. That night he came in with his parents, as he often does right around the holidays. Obviously, he is used to impeccable service as he is married to Sir Elton John. The two of them employ several full-time butlers and servants. I know this because they travel with Elton and his bride everywhere, and the butlers dine with us all the time and actually leave generous tips for those lucky enough to serve them. On this evening, Mr. Furnish and his distinguished parents had a bottle of Ruinart Champagne (a terribly overlooked wine in America). My first impression of his parents was a lasting one. What absolutely sweet people Jack and Gladys were – so down to earth and yet dignified at the same time. They seem like typical good salt-of-the-earth English folk. Furnish always looks impeccable, like a Wall Street banker, certainly the opposite of his flamboyant partner.

They ordered a bottle of Peter Michael La Caprice Pinot Noir along with their main course, per Vino's suggestion. Of course, Furnish had to change the menu – that's just what people like him do to declare their wealth and superiority. He had the caramelized scallops with steamed broccoli and truffle parsnip puree, without the risotto base, garnished with lemon on the side. It looked absolutely terrible without the risotto when it came out, but he said it was "Wonderful!" It seemed like it was missing something to me. In the end, Furnish left me over 20% for a gratuity: one-thirty on a six-hundred buck tab.

I remember that night quite clearly because I was also serving Gina Gershon and writer-director Brooks Branch at the adjacent table. She's seriously cool – I like her style, but she's another Hollywoody who can't leave well enough alone and always makes up her own dishes. She has a sort of New York artsy air about her, though she was brought up in Beverly Hills. Brooks directed and co-wrote a Woody Allen-type movie titled *Multiple Sarcasms* starring Timothy Hutton. They enjoyed four Chopin vodkas with a dash of bitters and soda, and Brooks took his with a lime.

Big Lips Gershon asked: "Can they make me a rigatoni Bolognese?" which is not on the menu. Brooks had the halibut special. Brooks talked a lot about his trip to China and his experiences there. I assume that his next project will reflect this. They finished up with two fresh mint teas and another nice tip for me.

Anyway, my point at the beginning of this Cage/Furnish rant was that they both left me good tips for good service during their previous visits. So I'm going to have to assume that on the night they didn't tip their servers well, their service must have sucked. Well, that's just too bad for Germaine and Daniel. I guess we all have bad nights, though I can't say I've ever had one quite as bad as that.

When you sign on to serve ruthless people, a/k/a the rich and shameless, you have to take the bad with the bad.

CHAPTER 10
THE MAN WHO WOULD BE KING

Sometimes the good does outweigh the bad. Late one night around nine-thirty we got a call letting us know that Russell Crowe and eight guests would be dining in the garden. The manager asked me if I would handle the table even though it was not in my section. I complied and went outside with the busboys to set up the table and prepare for a good time. I love it when Crowe comes in – it's amusing to watch him hold court as if he were a medieval king surrounded by his courtiers. Just like you'd expect from watching him portray a gladiator and Robin Hood, he's a very take-charge New Zealander and "owns the room." I think what really impressed me about him, though, was that he's also a rocker. His band is called Thirty Odd Foot of Grunts, a cool name but I've heard it also has real meaning. Apparently he had to re-record some dialogue for a movie scene in which his character is beaten up and kicked down an alleyway for thirty feet.

At this point in time Beverly Hills, as in much of the country, didn't allow smoking anywhere near a dining area, but if you're Russell Crowe we'd bend the rules. A lot. I prepared fifteen polished ashtrays and placed several on the table, with the rest set aside for backup. It was a cold night and no one else was sitting outside. So we turned on the heaters and I set the table with a thick vinyl liner under double tablecloths to cushion the cheap glass-top table, two candles, two courses of silverware and white and red wine glasses (yes, there's a difference).

By the time bad boy Crowe showed up an hour later at ten-thirty, all of my other tables had cashed out and gone home. I grabbed Vino and said: "I've got a feeling he's really gonna be worth our time tonight; let's make his night a memorable one! For us!"

"Ha! You got it, buddy," says Vino. *Woo hoo* – Crowe was in town and his hangers-on had been summoned! Forget *Entourage* – this was the real thing. He was flying solo with no wife, Danielle, and no kids on this trip. It was party time!

Crowe sat at the head of the table, of course, and his eight acolytes showed up a minute later. Red, his main yes-man, was there with his hot girlfriend whom Crowe was eyeing big time – she was the only girl in the company of eight men and must have felt like a minnow in a shark tank. There was a lot of loud chatter at the table, most of it coming from Red, whom I frankly couldn't stand. This guy was so impressed with Crowe that he probably signed on to lick his underwear clean and spit-shine his shoes every morning. Crowe eats it all up as if he's the Messiah and these young admirers are all his disciples who will carry on his great prophecies one day. Sycophants should be spelled sick-o-fants.

I approach the table. "Good evening, Mr. Crowe, it's nice to see you again. Welcome back."

Red, who sat nearest to Crowe, chuckled and mimicked me, "Good evening, Mr. Crowe."

Crowe said quietly, "Shut up, Red." Then, to me, "Good evening to you, my friend, bring us a round of Belvedere on the rocks with lemons."

"Nine, then, Mr. Crowe?"

"Yes, nine."

As always, excitable Vino showed up a little before his cue and jumped in with: "Would you like me to bring out some wine for you, sir?"

"Yes, bring us three bottles of Cloudy Bay."

"Right away, sir."

Red chuckled and said, "Oh, yes, right away Mr. Crowe, sir!"

"Shut it, Red."

Red had one of those high-pitched annoying voices and he often becomes over-excited very quickly, which makes his voice even more unbearable. Other than his ability to suck up to Crowe like a turbo-charged Hoover, I don't know what Crowe sees in him

By the time I'd brought their first round of drinks, they were already smoking like a row of chimneys. Crowe downed his drink quickly and headed out to make a call. My buddy Red called me over and ordered a new round for everyone, but he instructed me to make sure to bring a glass of Grey Goose to Mr. Crowe, not Belvedere. "We're doing an experiment!" he said, chuckling again in his annoying voice. I did so and returned with the drinks and Mr. Crowe's mystery vodka. The Crowe was still out on a call.

I put down clean ashtrays and noticed most of the cigarettes had been smoked right down to the filter. Crowe returned and I watched from a distance as he made a toast with his wine and welcomed everyone. I finally grasped the obvious: Red and some of the guys were actors from the *Robin Hood* set. I could only hope the Robin Hood spirit would prevail when it came to paying the check.

There was more loud talking and they all listened intently as the king regaled his minions with stories about football, music, rugby, the farm back home and his kids. Red piped in every now and then, shouting (or squealing), "Russell! Russell! Remember when we blah blah blah!" Guess he was playing the part of the court jester, he just didn't know it.

Crowe The Great smiled, obviously feeling important in this setting. He was the center of attention as he always is when surrounded by his subjects. He lifted his vodka glass. I watched from a distance where I could have eye contact with him without anyone at the table seeing my face. Red, still chuckling in his annoying way, said, "How is it? Tell me if it's Belvedere or something else!" I thought: *Judas is trying to discredit the boss.* Where I come from people will bury you in a cement block and dump you in a river for that kind of shit. Hell, if this was *Goodfellas*, Joe Pesci would have shot that screeching hyena a long time ago and put his bullet-ridden body in the trunk of a Buick where it belonged. Trouble with today's cars is size; no room for a body in the pathetic excuse for a trunk anymore. Sad.

The Great Crowe threw a serious look toward the glass, as if he'd been caught by surprise. He tasted the Grey Goose and looked around pensively. Then he threw me a quick glance and our eyes met. I held his gaze for an instant and then quickly, subtly, I shook my head, "No." It all took only about one second but it had seemed like time stood still for at least a minute. Everyone was dead silent, except for Judas who was chuckling in a more nervous tone now. He's probably realized that if Crowe got it wrong, he'd be revealed as the Betrayer, having undermined the illustrious host of this sweet little party. Oops. But fortunately for Crowe, thanks to yours truly, he didn't have to eat any.

Crowe said, "I don't know what this is but it's not Belvedere, that's for sure."

Red Judas responded, "No way! How can you tell?"

Crowe, feeling quite sure of himself after my clue, said, "I just know my vodka, that's all."

Red squawked: "Wow! No way! You can't! Wow! That's amazing – you got it right, man. That's amazing! The waiter switched it out for a Grey Goose or something."

The Crowe shot me a look with a completely straight face. I gave him a swift, subtle nod.

Red continued sheepishly, "Well, we told him to bring you something else."

Someone else at the table said, "Whaddaya mean 'we?' You told him to switch it out!"

"Well yeah, but we were all kind of in on it, right?" No one answered.

Crowe looked at Red, then said with a smile as he rubbed Red's head and eyed his girl, "You just don't know who you're dealing with here, Red, do you?" Everyone laughed, following The Great One's lead.

Crowe called me over. Taking charge and savoring his triumph, he looked like the Master and Commander of the Cricket Room tables, having put down an inconsequential mutiny.

"Yes, Mr. Crowe?"

"Why don't you bring us all a petit filet with mashed potatoes and some sautéed spinach?"

"Would you like me to bring a nice market green salad with a white balsamic dressing to start you all off, sir?"

"Yes." He gazed around the table with a powerful look of contentment on his strong, handsome face, practically daring anyone to disagree. "That will be fine."

As I went around to each guest to take cooking instructions, one person quietly asked for a spaghetti pomodoro instead of steak. He was probably a vegetarian or vegan but wanted to keep it quiet. You wouldn't want to offend this meat-eating man's man, the mighty Crowe, the great Gladiator!

Crowe: "And you! What's your name?" he gestured with his regal head towards Vino.

"My name is Vincent but everybody calls me Vino."

Red chuckled. "Ha ha! Vino!"

Crowe, ignoring Red the Buffoon, said, "Well, I suppose that's an appropriate name for you, Vino." Everybody giggled at the table until his Majesty puts his fist down, loudly commanding silence. Crowe turned back towards Vino. "Bring us three bottles of Hill of Grace, my friend."

Vino responded nervously. "I only have two bottles, sir, a '98 and an '04."

Crowe: "What? But it's on your list!"

Vino flinched at the rebuke. "I can order more for your next visit, Mr. Crowe."

"The Russians would have fun with you, my friend, they'd skin you alive," Crowe said, commanding great laughter from his audience. He continued: "Order me a case – I'll drink it all next time I'm here. Now go ahead and bring us what you have and we'll figure it out from there, son." He must have had a deal go bad with some Russian producers, I imagined.

Vino nervously replied. "Yes, Mr. Crowe, sir, right away."

Red chuckled at Vino's awkwardness: "Yes, sir, Mr. Crowe, sir!"

I myself am chuckling now at the whole thing. The thing about Russell Crowe is that you can't be a pussy in his presence. He'll drive over you like a twenty-ton bulldozer. Several of the other waiters here don't like him because they say he doesn't tip well, he's rude to them, he's bossy, etc. They are a bunch of pushovers who are afraid to look him in the eye and command their position. If you don't have any confidence in who you are and your ability to give great service to Mr. Crowe, he'll run you like a dog and tip you like a bitch. He wants your undivided attention. He wants good service, but he also wants to be able to understand you and be understood without repeating himself. Is that too much to ask? No matter, he expects it and if you serve him, you had better know it.

Paco brought out the salads, which looked fresh, plump and perfectly tossed with just the right amount of our house-made dressing. I assisted him in setting them down and offering fresh ground pepper, the lady first then everyone else, and the host, Mr. Crowe, last.

Man, I can't believe it, they're smoking those ciggies right down to the filter, I thought as I noticed the full ashtrays. I poured more bottled water and asked if anyone wanted more of the Cloudy Bay. There were a few takers. Mr. Crowe ordered another cocktail round. I asked him if he wanted to order some dessert soufflé this evening.

"Great idea, mate, what do you have?"

"Chocolate or raspberry tonight, sir."

"Thanks, give us four and four."

"Yes, sir."

Vino was finally on his way out with the Hill of Grace, a spectacular single vineyard Aussie Shiraz, just over eleven-hundred a bottle on our list. I exchanged all the ashtrays for clean ones and walked to the bar to pick up Mr. Crowe & Co.'s drink orders. *Wow, these guys are smoke fiends*, I thought, *who knew?*

I delivered the drinks and by now, most of them were almost finished with their salads. I set up a large service tray to the side, out of sight, and started clearing all the salad plates. Then I made sure everyone had a proper fork and steak knife, except for the guy who was having spaghetti – he got a spoon for rolling his noodles.

Carlos picked up the tray full of dishes and took it to the kitchen, nearly colliding with Paco who had nine plates with silver covers piled high on one very big tray, rushing towards the Crowe table. Each lid had the table position number on it so that Paco could keep track of the differing meat temperatures. The plates looked beautiful with the steaks perfectly roasted on the outside and the crème fraiche mashed potatoes lightly sprinkled with fresh chives as garnish. The spinach was sautéed with chopped, lightly roasted garlic and it wasn't too oily.

Wonderful, I thought, as I was finally serving Mr. Crowe, who had a bit of a humbled look in his eyes. He gazed at me like he wanted to say something, but he didn't.

Vino quickly commanded his attention as he formally introduced the first taste of the Hill of Grace Shiraz to Mr. Crowe's waiting glass. Crowe turned away from me and toward Vino. He held up the glass, looked at the color, tasted it quietly, and gave an approving nod.

Red, in his awkward, tasteless, chuckle-talking voice, asked Vino, "What? What? What is he drinking?"

And I don't know where the hell Vino got this from, but he replied in his rather high, androgynous voice, "Your Graceness is drinking the Henshke Hill of Grace Shiraz, a very noble choice, if you don't mind me saying so, sir."

Your Graceness gave another approving nod. Instead of laughing, everyone just became very quiet for a second. Mr. Crowe was just eating it up, the comment, the wine, and all the attention from his friends and the service staff.

"You should all have some of this. This is my most favorite wine, and it's Australian, of course." Everyone laughed and smiled, and we quickly filled their glasses so they could all toast together with the Crowe. No one seemed to repeat the comment regarding His Graceness; it was either forgotten or too far out to deal with.

I told Vino to approach His Graceness to offer him some other great Australian wine that we carry. Regarding his "Your Graceness" comment, Vino asked me, "Did you like that one?"

"Like it? I loved it! He loved it! You didn't see what happened earlier with his vodka but we're good with him tonight, my friend, just go over there and offer him something else that he'll like."

"I will!" he said confidently. I was just hoping he'd call him Mr. Crowe this time. He didn't fail me.

"Mr. Crowe, would you like me to bring out the '98 Penfolds Grange and decant it for you and your guests?"

"That'd be nice, mate, bring two. Wait a minute! You do have two, don't you?"

"I do, sir, I've already checked," Vino replied gravely.

"Very well, then. Let's open one and keep the other as backup."

Vino bowed and rushed away from the table as he always does when he's excited about a good sale. This one was nine-hundred a bottle. Like me, he could see dollar signs floating from the check into his pocket. Money is not all we care about, but it's near the top of the hit parade.

Vincent was an amazing sommelier. He had memorized every bin number and price on our wine list and that meant close to fifteen hundred vintages. He was passionate about wine, he knew the vintners of most of the wines he sold and also knew what region they were from, the percentages of blends, and every other bit of arcane wine data. Though Vino was a bit obsessive-compulsive, when he applied it to his wine business, it really worked for him. I loved listening to him talk about wine – he's so passionate, it's like grape porn.

Vino and I returned to the table with nine sparkling clean wine goblets, two decanters and the two bottles of '98 Grange. I asked Crowe, "Is everything to your liking? How is the filet, sir?"

"Very nice, thank you," he said, leaning back with a pleased look on his face and a small piece of steak in his mouth. Vino opened the Grange as if it were the last great wine left in the cellar and asked Crowe to taste it.

"Mmm…lovely," said Crowe. "Go ahead and pour a little for everyone, I want them all to taste it."

"Very good. I will, sir, thank you."

When I came around to Mr. Crowe's left side, Red was engaged in a conversation with his girl on Mr. Crowe's right side, and the guy who had been sitting on Mr. Crowe's left side was gone, possibly making a call or answering one in the bathroom. Crowe looked up at me humbly and said, "Nice work earlier, mate," as if I were the quarterback who set up his winning touchdown.

I gave him a knowing smile and nodded. He continued, "You'll be mentioned in the will." We both smiled because we both knew that I saved his ass on the vodka prank and now his buddy Red was even more impressed with him, as if that were possible. I think at that point Red would have given him a blow job under the table if Crowe had deigned to offer up the family jewels.

A few minutes later Crowe made a toast with the Grange, and then everyone leaned back, satisfied, and looked ready to call it a night. This was usually my cue to start cleaning off the table. Carlos and I removed the dishes and crumbed the table until it was ready for the next expensive course. Well, it wasn't completely clean because the King and his men had gorged, as real men should.

A strange thing happened while I was clearing the Crowe table. While Red was in the restroom I picked up Red's dinner plate and just underneath the edge of the plate was a Marlboro cigarette that had not been smoked but was trimmed off only an inch from the filter and twisted at the end. I looked at it, clueless.

Crowe looked at me, I looked at the Crowe, our eyes met, but nothing was said. He looked back down at the cigarette but didn't touch it. I hurried to reset the table with small dessert plates, clean napkins, and spoons for the soufflés. Crowe said he wanted an espresso, and I took a few more orders for cappuccino and tea. When I returned with their coffees, I noticed a strange odor. It was something like a burnt-out light bulb or some kind of weird smell from an electrical fire. Hmm, maybe a huge bug had gotten stuck in the insect zapper and was just frying in the heat. I remembered noting that same chemical-like smell earlier in the evening just after they had all arrived and were drinking their vodkas. I had forgotten about the smell because it only seemed to hit me when I approached the table from the bar or kitchen. With so much else to think about, I hadn't focused on it.

The coffees were down, Vino was pouring wine but used discretion regarding whom he poured for because he knew Mr. Crowe did not like to waste good stuff on people who weren't going to drink it. At that moment, Paco showed up with the soufflés and everyone at the table tried them. I heard some of them begin to groan with *Harry Met Sally* pleasure. They stayed at the table and talked for another twenty minutes or so, and then Russell gave the word, and everyone rose from the table.

Some of them said goodbye and started walking towards the exit. Mr. Crowe was the last in line to leave. I handed him the bill as he stood up. He never really asked for the check, never does, that's just how he rolls. The total for their royal feast was $4,800 and change. He signed the bill to his account and left me a $1,000 tip on paper. Then he took out a huge wad of $100 bills and counted out ten of them, looked up at me and tried to stuff them in my faux breast pocket. I helped him out by putting my hand near the pocket. As the bills reached my palm he looked at me and said, "Nice work tonight, mate. This is for you to do what you want with. You can share it or not share it."

He turned in his suave, macho way and I said, "Thank you, Mr. Crowe, it was a pleasure serving you tonight." I really couldn't come up with anything better and still stay within the rules of service. Crowe was already walking away. "Cheers, mate," he said with one final crooked grin. And out walked a true acting legend. It was all I could do not to kiss him, and I suddenly understood how Red felt. Except I'm not a suck-ass.

Though I'd served Crowe many times before and he'd always tipped me well, that night was beyond all of my expectations. Perhaps it was because I had been able to tend to his table all night without having to serve other guests. Or maybe it was just that we'd connected somehow in some perhaps meaningless way to him but an unforgettable way to me. As I stood there looking over their table with all the half-drunk glasses of wine and the half-eaten soufflés, chocolate-laden spoons and dirty napkins and ashtrays, somehow I felt as if I'd been watching a film in which Mr. Crowe had played King Henry the Eighth entertaining his advisors, closest friends, and court jesters. But in this movie, there had been only one memorable star. Let's just say I'm a big fan of King Crowe. Long live the king.

Later, talking to Paco, we figured out what that cigarette had been and it all came together in my mind. They were smoking "coco puffs" (tobacco cigarettes with powdered cocaine mixed in) and the reason I hadn't seen them do it was because they would send me to the bar to get drinks or coffee and then light up. That's why I had only smelled it when approaching from the bar or the kitchen.

I gave Vino a good chunk of my cash tip and we left to enjoy a nice bottle of wine at his place and then a late-night French dip sandwich at the French Market. Not really my idea of a royal feast but sufficient enough.

To my delight, I checked my messages on my way home and found that my agent had placed some of my music on two CBS television shows to run nationwide. There couldn't have been a better way to end that memorable night. Unless I had turned the festivities over to Jens to coordinate, but I was too damn tired to handle one woman, let alone the two or three he would have arranged. Money, music, and memories would have to suffice.

CHAPTER 11
HOW TO SUCCEED IN BUSINESS WITHOUT REALLY TRYING

The nameless, faceless, godless, mindless, spineless, greedy bastards – not that I don't love them – who had recently purchased the Cricket Room as part of a nameless, faceless, heartless hospitality portfolio, should perhaps have taken How to Run a Business 101 in college, rather than lacrosse or basket weaving. Or even purchased a basic book, such as Business Management for Idiots. But they hadn't and we were now their unwitting victims a/k/a cash cows. Moo.

In past years, the Cricket Room had famously provided five-star service to upscale clientele, charging accordingly. During that time the bottom line had always been top service, not top profits. The place has such a luminous history and reputation for legendary service that guests never really minded that the food is less than five-star. They would pay top dollar for crap food in many cases just to say they'd eaten there. Or had a drink at the bar next to a celebrity. Recently, however, our new corporate overlords acted as if they had adopted Gordon Gekko as a role model. I kept waiting for them to embroider "Greed is Good" on the napkins next to the shield logo.

After the corporate goons started sinking their fangs into our historic restaurant, morale hit rock bottom. They slashed our budget leaving us shorthanded at the most crucial times. They set up speeches for us to perform at every table and made us go through all the ridiculous rules of service, numbers one through twenty, with each guest, even the regulars. That kind of forced, scripted performance took the personality right out of the exchange and made us look like trained monkeys. And then they'd send out anonymous "shoppers" every month to make sure we followed their guidelines. I can't tell you how many times I've heard our managers recite: "Treat every table like it's a shopper, because if a shopper comes in, they will also be judging your performance at the neighboring tables." These little worms always tried their damnedest to make us lose our temper, screw up their order, overcharge them, or they would even try to set us up to pocket cash. Since we had a solid tourist clientele (one-time guests), it was almost impossible to spot the shoppers, adding even more pressure to our jobs. If we messed up on a shopper, it would be documented in our records, upper management would be notified, and it could lead to penalties or even termination. So we had to look at each customer as the ultimate test, and eschew the genuine, warm, human interaction that has long been a hallmark of the Cricket Room. Nothing says trust like spying on your hard-working employees, especially when we were being told our relationship with management was a "partnership." Yeah, like the partnership between a slave and his master.

They made it clear that we are expendable, and that there was someone anxiously waiting around the corner to take our jobs. It's called "Management by FEAR." And I can say from experience that it actually reduces performance and leads to nervous, anxious employees who are more likely to screw up or burn out. Yet all of our special guests came to the Cricket Room for the incomparable, personable service and to see that familiar face ready to serve them. Didn't the suits realize that? There is a distinct value in being served by someone who knows what you like and on whom you know you can rely. That had been the trademark upon which the Cricket Room had built its legacy. We always recognized our many repeat guests, and welcomed them back each time by name. And why did we do that? Not out of fear, but because we'd all been there so long and we genuinely felt privileged to be serving not just celebrities, but all of our valued regulars. In my not-so-humble opinion, the suits ruined the experience for the staff who genuinely loved their jobs, and destroyed the uniqueness of the experience for the guests. But try telling that to a bunch of businessmen who have never waited tables in their lives and are under so much pressure from their corporate bosses to perform that they lose sight of the most fundamental reasons a restaurant is successful.

There we were at the peak of the real estate boom and the chatter you heard at every table was about buying and selling real estate. One of my customers was a local named Perry. He told me that he had bought his four-bedroom house in Beverly Hills for $1.3 mil in the mid-nineties and he had sold it that day, just over ten years later, for $3.4 mil. His story was typical and I'd been hearing those kinds of things a lot. Beverly Hills 90210 real estate is finite; no one's making any more of it, the locale has cachet, and even in economic downturns, properties here increase in value. Not only California was booming – there was nouveau riche money pouring in from all corners of the globe. New fortunes were being made in stocks all over the world; middle American farmers were selling off their land to oil and gas explorers and collecting a royalty on top of it; and in recent months, there had also been boatloads of tourists from Europe throwing money around in the Cricket Room. As they say, when America sneezes, the rest of the world catches a cold. So when we do well, so does everyone else. Everyone was spending, spending, spending and we had more business than we could handle.

The restaurant grossed around $13 million that year and paid its GM over $500,000 annually. You would think a corporation with those kinds of numbers should have enough cash flow to run the restaurant like a dream. In fact, the budget for staff was so small that we constantly worked the floor of fifty-eight tables with only six or seven waiters and three busboys, one of whom in each category was always on break. Because of California state law every employee had to take a 30-minute break, but not until he or she had been clocked in for two hours minimum. Because we were understaffed, this meant that around seven when the dinner rush was at its height we were always short-staffed by one waiter at a time for three hours straight just to get each break out of the way. That also left us with one busser per 28 tables at the height of dinner service. Ridiculous! The pancake house has more busboys than that. Those guys cost ten bucks an hour and can get a table turned in seconds, seating more guests who spend more money. That's something that the suits forgot to calculate. But of course, their concern was the bottom line and not efficiency, guest satisfaction, or employee well-being. One manager suggested hiring a "break waiter" who would fill in for each waiter while they were on break, allowing us to take back the same tables after our breaks. Great idea. Never fucking happened.

The place was making huge profits, but they distribute the gold at the top levels rather than reinvest it in the face of the business – that is, the staff – and squash us little guys until we make room for the next willing victims. It doesn't make sense. A fine establishment needs plenty of polished, highly trained staff to fawn all over its wealthy patrons and to anticipate their every need. But in the Cricket Room, where we served the biggest names in every industry, we were cut off at the knees while being held to a higher standard. Is greed really that good? No, it's actually counterproductive and destructive. You're killing the golden goose by running the shit out of her.

Because the Cricket Room never had a drastic lull in the late afternoon, management refused to close the restaurant for an hour between afternoon and evening service like most other fine dining establishments do. This prevented both shifts of waiters from accomplishing the side work so important to an organized dining room, and also wreaked havoc on the handover of tables from the lunch shift to the night waiters. And because the economy was booming and guests were constantly streaming in, it only got worse. There were numerous arguments stopping just short of bloodshed.

Management had an unrealistic, or purely ignorant, expectation of how their constantly-open business model should work. Sometimes things that look good on paper, or sound logical around a conference table, don't play out that way with real people in real life.

A typical night at the Cricket Room would go something like this: I would come in at four o'clock with one other server to open the night shift. Our duties were to clean up all the service stations that were invariably left in a mess by the day shift. We had to polish and restock all the specialty silverware, such as steak and fish knives, forks, bouillon spoons and soupspoons. Then we had to clean out and restock the three supply dressers with silverware, folded napkins, sugar caddies, salt and peppershakers, dessert plates and the like. The dressers were strategically placed in the main dining room, another in the garden area, and the third in the front dining section. Once all that was done, we had to stock and refill all the ice water pitchers at all the stations, then polish silverware and glassware and set every table in all the dining areas. All of this would take two waiters approximately forty-five minutes to do.

The day shift was supposed to keep taking tables until five o'clock, giving the night team the time described above to complete our preparations. At that point, they were expected to transfer any remaining tables to us and clock out. In a perfect world, it might work that way, but have I been describing a perfect world? You can understand how that would build animosity, with the day shift having to start tables and sometimes wait on them for hours, only to transfer them over to us as we became available. We would then cash in on their tips, which could be worth an extra $100 a night.

Therefore, the way it really went was that within just ten minutes of the night team's arrival at 4:00 p.m., the day shift would already be trying to pawn off their tables on us so that they could avoid starting any tables that wouldn't garner them tips. Why couldn't they just stay and close out their tables, you ask? Because the corporation didn't want to pay for their overtime, which in essence would amount to about $12 an hour for a few waiters – and one hour was usually all it took to close those tables. So, to save the multi-million dollar corporation about $36 a night, we night waiters were burdened with all the necessary side work at the same time that we were being handed tables in progress, at which, of course, we had to follow all those anal rules of service under strict deadlines. And the day waiters invariably took off without finishing their own side work.

But wasn't side work one of the procedures put in place to allow us the preparation required to provide excellent and efficient service? Apparently, this didn't matter to management when $12 an hour was at stake. I'm sure the higher powers thought they were being clever when they went so far as to change the cut-off time for the day shift to 4:30 pm instead of 5:00 pm to doubly ensure that they didn't go into overtime. This guaranteed the night waiters' collective failure to complete any sidework and solidified the shortcuts that the day waiters were already taking. Shit, I didn't blame them. I don't want to work for free either. The corporation was looking for teamwork but they weren't giving any to us. We needed more staff, not less.

But that anonymous corporate baboon in our foreign headquarters who set the budget for the Cricket Room was happy because the restaurant was coming in way under budget and he was getting a nice bonus because of our hard work. When you stop to think about it, this is how every big or small corporation operates. Some jack-off sits in a corporate office with a suit and a tie setting budgets and rules for a place he has never even set foot in. It would have been so much smarter to make sure the room was staffed properly at all times because our affluent clientele expected to blow wads of money at the Cricket Room, and if the waiters were plentiful and attentive the room could have grossed another million more a year. "A waiter with time is a waiter who will earn you that extra dime." That's fucking novice but not to these idiots. Quite often, the guests would have ordered another glass of wine or another cocktail if I had been able to return to their table in time to offer it to them. Instead, the next time they saw me, they would ask for the check since they were not sure when I'd be back again, and neither was I. Is this really five-star service? Compare and contrast that to the night I served King Crowe and his large royal party. With no other tables to manage, I gave them excellent personable service and we all left shiny and happy. This shortsightedness infuriated me, as I took great pride in my work and was simply not given the tools to succeed.

In the old days, the Maître d' of the Cricket Room sometimes introduced guests to each other who might have similar business interests, or who might need each other's services. It wasn't unusual for a director to find an undiscovered leading man at the next table, thanks to a clever introduction. But new ownership meant that our Maître d' was run ragged taking reservations, setting staff schedules, dealing with guests' complaints, waiting tables, and ringing up tabs due to constant underfunding and therefore short-staffing. He too was spread too thin, wearing two hats as both Maître d' and restaurant manager. Those should be separate positions, and in most establishments of this caliber, they are.

Between lunch and dinner, which was no longer slow, Mr. P had to work out a weekly schedule for forty different employees (runners, busboys and waiters, all with their individual vacation and special schedule requests) but the phone kept ringing and VIPs kept coming in with whom he had to chat amicably and accommodate their special seating requests. He also had to stay on his toes to ensure everyone feels like the most important guest in the world, including working in those clever introductions wherever possible. He didn't have time to worry about what we were doing every minute, so he just tried to make sure that someone – anyone, for all he cared – was serving the guests. The old ambiance was long gone, in deference to the corporate dollar. Fuck those greedy pigs! I came to despise them for ruining a legendary restaurant. It just wasn't necessary, and to me was like turning the Taj Mahal into a food court.

The pay was so inadequate that we also couldn't find competent hostesses to manage the arrivals. In that room, you need someone smart enough to actually recognize the celebrity they are greeting and to know how to deal with the rich and shameless. They needed to be a combination of Vanna White, Attila the Hun, and a U.N. ambassador. They also needed to be able to cull the wannabes from the herd who pretend they are someone in order to scope out the room for victims to con. That level of experienced, discerning professional hostess didn't work cheap. The girls we hired for twelve bucks an hour were never older than twenty-five and so clueless that you could tell them anything and they'd believe it. Most of them wouldn't even have known Michael Jackson if he had walked in the room accompanied by an eight year-old boy and moon-walking backwards. You get what you pay for, and what they paid for were usually idiots who looked good in a tight dress with boobs twice the size of their brains.

When Dennis Quaid walked in one night without a reservation, they made him wait at the hostess stand for fifteen minutes until he walked out and returned with a house account holder who got him a table. The hostess didn't even recognize his name, let alone his famous face. Or how about the time another hostess put a menu in front of Stevie Wonder? Was that our one and only secret Braille menu that only she knew about? But she did smile nicely at him. I'm sure he appreciated that. Ariella was our only competent hostess but unfortunately she only worked three dinner shifts and two lunch shifts a week.

The solution was elementary yet it was beyond our corporate bosses' comprehension: hire and schedule two more waiters on the floor and a fourth busser for each shift. But they never did because coming in under budget was always more important than securing truly fine service.

Another way to raise revenue would have been, for example, that since our refined guests enjoyed learning about wines, we should have hired a second wine steward to meet that demand. As it was, there was no one to help the guests choose wine on Vino's days off, and on the nights he was working, he couldn't possibly meet every demand. Another talented expert like Vino, passionate and knowledgeable about wine, would ensure that no interested guest ever missed an opportunity to inform his palate. It's obvious to me that the Cricket Room's extensive list of 1,500 wines is another treasure chest that management forgot to open.

The story of the latter day Cricket Room would make a good case study for the Harvard Business Review. Or a classic study of what not to do to increase profits. Our management left a lot of low hanging fruit to rot on the tree. As brilliant as they may have been at business theory, they never bothered to come in and see the results of their decisions first hand. It was paint by numbers, and they were painting with our blood, sweat, and tears.

And to add another level of detail from the Genghis Khan School of Management, the higher ups would try to make up for missed sales opportunities that they lost to under-staffing by pushing us to increase sales in ineffective ways. They forced us to up-sell indiscriminately, even when it wasn't appropriate. Of course, enticing customers to order more expensive food or drink is an important part of any restaurant's operations, but when it comes to the matter of up-selling in the Cricket Room, genuine discretion was, or should have been, of great importance.

Our very sophisticated guests usually knew exactly what they wanted. They are used to choosing the best of everything, so up-selling often creates awkward moments and thoroughly annoyed customers. It looks as though we don't trust the guest's taste or judgment, let alone his or her ability to read a menu. It's embarrassing. And it's even worse when it comes to liquor. For example, people who drink Lagavulin, a "peaty" Scotch whiskey with an almost burnt tar-like flavor do not want to be asked if they'd like a (more expensive) Macallan 18 instead, which is smooth and silky. Although they are both single malt Scotches, people who like Lagavulin do not like smooth and silky, understand? What's more, all of our peaty Scotches were in the same price range, so to direct a customer to a higher-priced alternative, we had to suggest a smooth and silky choice which forced us to look like idiots who had no idea about anything they were serving.

Those of us with any experience knew that you have to understand your guests, quickly get a real read on them, and sell appropriately. You don't serve Gore Vidal the same way you would Paris Hilton. They're from different planets. That's something much more delicate to teach than simple up-selling. But no, rather than teach new staff the art of tailored, suggestive selling, we were punished if we were caught missing any opportunity to do the hard up-sell. We were not allowed to use our own discretion in order to avoid insulting the guests. It's another example of how the company thugs thought their stupid rules of service were appropriate for every situation.

I couldn't understand why they would run the most beautiful and prestigious room in all of Los Angeles with a laughable budget that put so much strain on the staff and affected our ability to sell and serve our guests properly. It was not only unreasonable, it really didn't make good business sense. I always got the impression that our "owners" – and I did feel owned – had never been in the Cricket Room and had no appreciation for its history and reputation.

The restaurant was being run like the proverbial nervous duck – seemingly calm on the surface of the water but paddling frantically underneath. And for no good reason! I'm sure they're not all that way, but it seems many corporations look at staff as the easiest thing to cut to increase profits. Food cost was never an issue, nor superficial things like fresh flowers and linens. Just people got cut or run into the ground. But we, the wait staff were the face of the business and we could make it or break it. They never seemed to realize that. Or they just decided not to respect it.

The stress was taking a huge toll on many of us and I still remember the day that Steven, a fellow waiter, walked out after his break and never came back. Here was a guy who had been sober for ten years, who had suddenly cracked up big time, left the Cricket Room, lost his apartment and was found drunk in a back alley behind Pavilions grocery store in Beverly Hills. He spent a few months like that then picked himself up again and got a job at the Peninsula in Beverly Hills. I spoke to him six months later and he told me the whole sad story. He had started drinking again because of the stress at the Cricket Room. He said that he was much happier at his new job and was back to attending AA meetings. It may sound trivial, but when you really care and want to do a great job, it's frustrating as hell to be blocked at every turn by budget cuts. Especially when there's no need for it. We were raking in the dough.

Another waiter who cracked was Ernesto. He was by far my favorite waiter to work with besides Jens. He was always joking and laughing, but like Steven, he was developing a serious drinking problem. Much to my surprise, I also found out that he had taken a mistress. This was Ernesto, who would show me pictures of his kids and tell me funny stories about their baseball games, and who always talked about the wife he loved so much. But the job was taking its toll and he always got sloshed right at the end of work. One night after work, he went to see his mistress and upon leaving her house somehow ended up on the I-5 freeway headed in the wrong direction. He was hit head on by a Volvo. Ernesto was found dead in the back seat with a broken neck. The woman who'd hit him lived but suffered major injuries. It was a terrible shock to all of us when Mr. P told us right before our shift. Several people burst into tears. Why couldn't he have told us after work? We all attended Ernesto's wake, paid our respects, and pooled three grand to give his wife and kids. It was strange seeing him in the casket. No matter how much make up they'd put on him, he didn't look like Ernesto; he had too many broken facial bones.

That night I wept long and silently on my drive back home. The stress was wearing on me as well. My girlfriend at the time often complained that I'd stay out too late after work and come home smelling of alcohol. You'd think a bartender would know better, but it's quick and readily available numbing medicine. Orajel for the brain. Shit, I even fantasized about snorting the stuff, imagining it might numb my thoughts.

I constantly had this recurring terrifying dream: it started with me serving a table full of friendly guests. I would be greeting the guests and getting to know them, laughing and having a good time. Then I would go to the bar to pick up their drinks and upon my return, I would discover two new tables full of guests and no one around to help me. I would approach the new tables and then as I went to fetch their drink order from the bartender, he would be gone. So I would have to make the drinks myself. When I'd return to the kitchen to check on my food order from the first table there would be no cooks in the kitchen. At this point, I would become short of breath, feeling panicky and totally overwhelmed. As I walked back out to the dining room, more and more people streamed in with no other staff in sight to seat them. Very quickly things would take a turn for the worse, because then I found myself seating people at tables as well as serving them.

Soon these faceless guests had their hands in the air signaling madly for service as I ran around trying to figure out why there were no cooks and no bartenders to be seen and no one but me left to cook, serve, bartend and seat the entire restaurant. I'd start choking and gasping for air because the anxiety was overwhelming. A steady stream of new guests arrived and I experienced a sense of complete terror and was unable to move. I couldn't decide whether I should make a drink order, seat the new guests or try to cook the dinner orders that have been waiting in the kitchen for forty minutes. By now dinner guests are standing up by their tables looking around for help, loud complaints are bombarding me and I am completely helpless but still trying to do whatever I can to keep up with the orders… and by now I'm suddenly naked and everyone is just staring at me. Talk about a nightmare!

I always woke up sweaty and gasping for air every time I had that dream, usually shouting myself awake and frightening my girlfriend du jour. Oh great! I just worked a busy night and had to dream of an even worse night after that. I wouldn't want to go back to sleep in case the dream would continue so I usually went out to the living room and watched TV until daybreak. The only thing worse than having a bad job is having a bad one you really care about.

After this happened several times, my girlfriend walked out because she couldn't stand hearing me complain and act so erratically. I can't say I blame her – I would have left me too.

One morning I woke up crying. Just repeating the words, "I can't take it anymore. I just can't take it!" Me? Mr. Tough Guy? Crying like a baby? Finally, I began seeing a shrink to try to lessen the stress, but it didn't help. He just listened to me rant on for months, then cashed the checks. I finally got sick of hearing my own voice. It was surreal that a waiter was having anxiety attacks because of his stressful job, but this just seemed to get lost on the guy. I tried jogging, too, but since my body was so tired from working it was hard to keep it up. The last thing my knees and ankles needed was more pounding. If only there were a way to send my mind out jogging and leave my body home in the recliner.

After a few years, I was asked to join the management staff. I was smart, a hard worker and requested by guests so often that they obviously knew I was an asset and didn't want to lose me. Perhaps even they could read the flashing "Burnout" sign on my forehead. I reluctantly declined, though I felt I could have made real improvements to the way the place was managed. But why would I want to work twice the hours with half the pay? I'd be getting a salary but losing the gratuities. Because the restaurant's name would secure my future as a manager? That's probably true, but that's not the future I wanted.

I was disappointed with the reality versus the myth, but not unhappy enough to join the enemy ranks, which is what I considered management. I knew they would never really revert to the standards of days gone by, so why bleed myself any further? It would be too heartbreaking to watch; like witnessing a beautiful and gracious lady turn into a meth addict right before my eyes. No thanks. Check please.

My bottom line was this: I had been drawn to a very special place, one with an instantly recognizable name worldwide, and synonymous with class and elite service. But that dream was dying, giving way to fatter profit margins. New corporate management didn't care how the money came in, just so it did. I still clung to the dream but it was getting harder and harder to stay asleep since the dream had become a recurring nightmare.

I even thought about arranging a séance during which I could get some advice from Frank Sinatra and former luminaries who had built the Cricket Room and whose legends were the foundation of the business. Maybe he could whack somebody and we could get back to serving with style. We cash cows were sick of the bullshit.

CHAPTER 12
THE HANGOVER

One good thing about a restaurant being run by a bunch of penny-pinching schmucks who won't pay overtime is that you can always count on getting two days off every week. They do that not out of consideration, but solely to avoid paying time and a half. Mr. P was always thoughtful about scheduling our two days off in a row. And with all the pent-up stress we'd been accumulating, Jens and I try to make the most of our weekly vacations.

Jens contacted the Maloof brothers, whom he had served many times, and booked us into their hotel in Vegas, the Palms. They gave us a great deal on a suite. It was the week of the Nightclub and Bar convention and we procured tickets to the trade show through our liquor suppliers. We ended up being invited to every sponsored party having to do with the show. When we arrived, we found the convention center set up as a playground for sinners and we promptly deployed ourselves. With free booze everywhere, extreme bartending shows, and gorgeous brand models like Victoria Silvstedt at the Patron booth, we could hardly contain ourselves. Speaking to her in my best Swedish, I tried to scam my way into hooking up with her but all I ended up with was a Patron business card. The place was like a great big orgy of tasting booths featuring different kinds of booze and wine, lighting systems, DJ and karaoke set ups, plastic ice cubes that blink inside your glass; you name it, it was there. Anything to lure you into this great escape from reality, and we were all in. To say we were like sailors on shore leave would be an insult to sailors. We were more like pit bulls let off the chain, hungry for whatever Las Vegas had to offer.

After the convention center closed for the night, we headed over to the Hard Rock Hotel and Casino for the Bacardi brand party. Bacardi owns Dewar's, Grey Goose, and seventeen other brands, and what a party it was! I think Lynyrd Skynyrd played in a new lineup but I can't remember. Tons of free booze and gift bags filled with swag at every table. Jens and I were already buzzed and completely electrified by the crazy level of adrenaline in the air. The Cricket Room's classic elegance was a world away from the raucous Wild West atmosphere of

Vegas — exactly what we wanted — and not a word about work had been mentioned since the previous night. We needed the escape desperately. We sure as hell work hard, so we took the opportunity to play as hard as hell. It was the only way we could let out all the accumulated stress, tension, and frustration that the Cricket Room laid on us day after day. I considered it a key to my survival.

My confidence soared as my eyes fixated on a vivacious long-haired blonde in a tight, full-length, burnt orange dress. I walked right up to her, dropped some cheesy line on her that would only work in Vegas, and kaboom! She's mine! An hour later, the three of us ended up leaving the party in a cab. Linda said her sister was staying in the room next to hers, so we headed to her hotel. As soon as we get into her modest room, Jens gets the coke ready, she calls room service for a bottle of Veuve Clicquot, and the party is on. It was only eleven o'clock and we were already cutting to the chase. My radar had been spot on when I'd honed in on Linda at the party. She was apparently up for anything, and, um, so was I.

Once the Champagne and the coke took effect, Jens docked his iPhone and started blasting some monotonous dance music that seemed terribly fitting at the moment, even though it wasn't something I would normally ever listen to. One minute we were all dancing and bumping and grinding against each other like a scene from *Dirty Dancing*, then all of a sudden Linda began bawling.

Surprised, we stopped the music and turned the lights a little higher so we could see what was wrong. Jens turned to Linda and said, "What's the matter, honey?"

I added, "Why are you sad?"

Linda said, "You don't understand! I don't do this, this isn't like me at all to hook up with total strangers like this! I'm a Sunday school teacher!"

Well, Pauli, so much for your fucking radar, I scolded myself.

Jens almost choked on his drink and strained not to crack up. If you're a man anywhere near your late thirties you've probably heard this kind of thing before. Women are only human — they have desires just like we do — but when they act on them they are considered sluts or tramps or whatever. Meanwhile men who score look like heroes to each other. It's totally unfair but there has always been a double standard and probably always will be. But that was the brilliance of the Vegas line "What happens in Vegas stays in Vegas." It acknowledges that adults need some secrecy in their lives and everyone needs to let off steam now and then. A little walk on the wild side.

So she was going through the guilt stage which to me meant that she was probably gonna go through with at least part of the evening's festivities, but we just needed to be understanding at this point, comfort and reassure her. I for one was not willing to just let this one off the hook. I have a "no catch and release" policy.

I said, "What are you talking about? We're just having a good time right now, that's all. Nothing bad has happened. You're fine." I sat down next to her and rubbed her arms, and I'll tell you honestly the more I touched her, the hotter I got, but I contained myself.

"Would you guys mind if I read from the Bible for a while? Can I read out loud? I think it will comfort me."

It's been said – certainly not by me – that men are walking peckers, like heat seeking missiles always waving around in search of a likely target. So the next voice that spoke was my dick. His voice was deeper than mine, and much more authoritative. He sounded like the devil in *South Park*.

"Of course! We would love that, wouldn't we, Jens?" I nodded enthusiastically to encourage Jens. I could see him eyeing the door, thinking about escaping. But I knew we could salvage this party and I – read Little Pauli – was not giving up.

"Yeah, yeah, of course, that would be nice," he said, holding back his laughter, probably stunned that my pecker could talk.

She opened up her Bible, which she pulled from her huge purse, and read a passage about forgiveness in John 1. As she read she began writhing and the further she got into the passage, the more she writhed and wriggled. At this point we really didn't know what to do, because it was a very weird and awkward situation. I wanted to rip her clothes off and eat her up but I sat there quietly pretending I was moved by the words she was spilling out. Once she was finished she carefully put her Bible away and lit a scented candle she had brought.

"Thank you guys for listening. I knew you were good guys, I could just feel it. You're different, not like the rest of those other bad boys out there." She said it teasingly and I wondered if maybe this was some act she liked to put on. Yet she had seemed sincere and really into the Bible verses.

She asked Jens to put the music back on and told us she'd be right back, then she disappeared into the bathroom and I thought I could hear the shower going, but I really wasn't sure. Little Pauli was still very alert and wanted to go in and join her in the shower.

"Do you think she really has a sister next door, bro?" I said to Jens as we did another fat line and washed it down with some Veuve.

We both looked up as the bathroom door opened and out came Linda, completely undressed. Her long hair hung in damp tendrils and her fair skin was glowing with water droplets. She hadn't even toweled off. . She looked like a blonde version of the girls on the Lords of Acid's *Voodoo U* CD cover with a strange, faraway gaze in her eyes. I didn't stare at her eyes for very long; too much else to take in. I strained to be free, like a racehorse at the starting gate. *Fuck, she is hot*, I thought, *crazy or not.*

I turned the lights down and... Here I encourage you to delve into your wildest teenage *Penthouse* magazine fantasies.

The next morning, in regular Jens fashion, we had room service bring up pancakes, French toast, a Monte Cristo sandwich, scrambled eggs, sausage, bacon, orange juice, apple juice, five cappuccinos. Jens and I hid in the bathroom giggling like schoolboys while the attendant was setting it up – he must've thought Linda was on a food binge or something.

After a huge breakfast, Linda took another bath and holed up in there for an awfully long time as Jens and I occupied separate beds watching a rerun of *The Dark Knight*. I ordered three more cappuccinos from room service and dusted them with blow– fuck cinnamon, I'm in Vegas, baby. What better way to start the day? Wired and fired up just for the fuck of it.

I thought Linda would come out fully clothed and ready for us to get the hell out, but I was wrong about that. To my surprise, she emerged half-naked in a deep purple teddy with black garters. I quickly shut off the TV and cranked the music as Linda became our new and only religious leader.

Eventually Jens and I made it back to our room at the Palm around two in the afternoon to shit, shower and shave. I called Linda and we made plans to meet her at the VIP Stoli party at ten that evening in the Ghost Lounge at our hotel. I kept wondering, but we never brought up the question of whether she had a sister or not. She did, however, have her inner demons to deal with, and I for one was just glad to help her exorcise them.

I took a nap. I'm not sure what Jens did, but when I woke at eight he was sitting on the sofa counting pills out onto the glass-topped coffee table. I think he was channeling Hunter Thompson in *Fear and Loathing*...

"Hey, Pauli? You think Linda likes X?" He laughed his devilish laugh.

I replied, "I sure hope so!"

We met Linda outside the club and we were glad to see she was punctual. Sometimes you meet people in Vegas and they just disappear on you. She was five minutes early, and not alone, which was a good sign to me.

She introduced us to her sister Ashley, who was a few years older, with dark brown hair and a very attractive smile. Jens, who now couldn't contain himself, shouted, "I've got X!" The girls squealed with delight. I had my eyes on Linda who looked hip and ready to party, wearing dark blue, skin-tight jeans with some kind of cool sparkly motif on the back pockets and seams; a cropped, low-cut, black lace, spaghetti-strap top; a Manhattan-style, dark grey, sur la tete beret; and her hair was in schoolgirl pigtails. She topped it all off with a short, fitted jean jacket on top and a Burberry cashmere scarf wrapped around her bare neck. This chick was not only hot looking and adventurous as hell with sex, drugs, and rock 'n roll, she knew fashion. I wondered briefly if she'd marry me. Little Pauli was up for it, as usual.

We popped some X, did a few lines, and drank free Stoli lemon drop shots by the dozens, dusted by yours truly. We all danced together, and I was secretly thrilled that Jens and Ashley really seemed to be hitting it off so I could be alone with Linda and her demons.

We all went back to our suite at the Palm around 12:30 am, so high that we didn't know what to do with ourselves. I say that facetiously, because we knew exactly what to do. Apparently the Sunday school teacher bit was abandoned because Linda only carried a small clutch purse this time with no room for a Bible of her own.

The suite was wired for sound, and Jens hooked up his best playlist. He escorted Ashley to his bedroom and as he softly closed the door, I spied Ashley giggling in the background. My complete focus turned to Linda. Now it was time for me to exorcise my own demons. I aggressively undressed her before she even had a chance to find the Bible in the bed stand. I proceeded to tie her up (gently), blindfold her, and kiss her all over her body. She loved every minute of it, and when she couldn't take it anymore, it became like sexual combat; we wrestled and fought for access to various body parts, like crazed maniacs, and I think we both sustained some minor injuries. Not-so-little Pauli still has a small scar; I'm not sure how that happened but it was totally worth it. It was the most erotic sex I'd had since I was nineteen and moved in with my first girlfriend in Copenhagen.

In the morning, calorie-starved and drained, we ordered everything possible from the breakfast menu again and had a lot of laughs. We found out that Linda and Ashley were from a wealthy Maryland family, that they now lived in Philly, and Linda did indeed teach Sunday School, which we pretended sounded perfectly normal. Linda was also a fitness instructor and part owner in a gym out there, so it was no wonder she was in such good shape. She didn't mention her age but we guessed she was in her early thirties. The more I got to know her the more I liked her. Hey, she might never cure cancer or win a Nobel Peace Prize, but she sure saved an over-stressed, hard-working man in one wicked awesome weekend.

Linda and I exchanged phone numbers but Jens didn't offer and Ashley didn't ask for his number. I think she had caught on that he was taken, since he kept getting texts and stepping away to make calls.

In the end, it was all good. We never made it back to the convention center but I think we achieved more than we ever hoped to, with everlasting memories (and some football level injuries) that we won't be able to talk much about but will always remember.

Jens' girlfriend, Christie, picked us up at the airport and asked where our bags were.

"Right here," said Jens, pointing to our luggage. She looked pissed beyond belief. It didn't click right away but I figured it out later. Usually when I come home from that event, I've got several swag bags loaded up with free booze and paraphernalia – she was probably expecting that. But if she really knew Jens as she should have after living with him for two years, she would have known that he was up to no good. Although if you asked him, he'd have said it was all *very* good. I think I agree with that.

I was ready to head home, nurse my sore, tired body, and jump back into the Cricket Room chaos. Maybe I could figure some things out after a massive Vegas blowout and release of tension, like what to do about my limp career prospects. It was time to face the music.

CHAPTER 13
SUNSET BOULEVARD

A year later, my life was changing dramatically. I had locked my music into several CBS and MTV shows, which was great, but the financial payoff was nowhere near enough for me to quit my job at the Cricket Room. I took it as a positive sign that my music career had just been hibernating and was now ready to come out of its cave, ravenous and growling.

Linda had visited me a few times in LA on her own dime. I guess Jens and I had been unforgettable. We pretty much repeated the Vegas performance until it was obviously getting old and we finally just stopped calling each other. What happens in Vegas just isn't the same somewhere else. The thrill of forbidden fruit becomes bland and tasteless when it's readily available in your backyard. I felt sure she'd be back at Sodom and Gomorrah in the dessert, desperately seeking strange stuff but I no longer cared.

Jens was still always up to no good, full of mischief, and I knew I could count on him for keeping things interesting and exciting. Every now and then I'd get a call from a hysterically crying Christie asking if I'd seen Jens.

Sniff, sniff, "He hasn't been home for two nights," she'd complain.

"No, sorry, Christie, if he calls I'll tell him to phone home right away."

The truth was, I knew exactly where he was: holed up on the top floor of the Viceroy with a couple of hot sex maniacs. For me, it was an occasional phase; for him it was his lifestyle.

I was actually beginning to feel like it was time to meet a real woman, someone of substance who was worth settling down with. Someone I could love and show who I really was. After so many quickie, shallow, meaningless encounters, which were incredibly hot and physically satisfying but ultimately unfulfilling, I wanted someone to laugh with me, sing with me, travel with me, grow old with me. Turns out that everyone has the same body parts and when you smash them together it's great, but not everyone is compatible on a deeper level.

I knew I just hadn't met the right woman yet but if I were going to, I'd better stop spending too much time with Jens because every time we saw each other we'd get so roiled up, it's automatic trouble. It's as though I'm dry kindling wood and he's a match. We get together and a fire starts, like Stephen King's *Carrie*. I knew enough to realize that my dream girl wasn't slumming amongst the kind of company we kept. So I needed to grow up and start attracting what I wanted in my life. It's that simple. But could I do it? That remained to be seen. Maybe I'd just burn up and burn out before I could find the future Mrs. Hartford. I might need a muzzle for Mini Me.

It was a typical Wednesday night in the Cricket Room and I grabbed Jens in the service hallway as I motioned toward the dining room and whispered, "She's kissing me right now!"

"What the hell are you talking about?" Jens asked.

I told him to peek through the peephole at Pamela Anderson – every man's dream – who was vigorously sucking on her cocktail straw.

"So?" I think he thought I'd lost my fucking mind. But stick with me.

"So, I kissed the straw before I gave her the drink. She's kissing me!"

Jens laughed, "Dat's funny, Pauli! Maybe next time I stir her drink with my dick!"

Ariella had been listening. "Oh, you're both sick!" She shook her head and giggled as she walked away, bouncing and jiggling like an anime sex toy.

Goddamn she's hot, but I know she's just trouble too. Remember you're looking for a good woman. Hey, maybe Pam Anderson is my soul mate! Wouldn't that be awesome?

I'd just been informed by Mr. P that Johnny Depp would be dining in my section again. He either requested me or simply a certain table in my section, but it was nice to hear anyway. Although I have to focus on my ridiculously long list of duties, this news lifted my mood and the atmosphere crackled with excitement and expectation. Every guest at the Cricket Room is to be treated with the utmost respect and gentility, and while I've done it all before I really pulled out all the stops when it came to guests I admired. Mr. Depp adds a welcome earthiness to the elegance and refinement of the Cricket Room, and he's a bright spot on the long horizon of another busy evening ahead.

My immediate concern, however, is Gore Vidal, the illustrious and mighty author of some of the most important literature of the twentieth century. He was there as usual, cocked half off his ass on Grey Goose martinis and singing along with the piano player who knew all of his favorite oldies. I'd served him his usual meal of warm, buttery croissants followed by an order of our luxurious Washington State Kumamoto raw oysters. Gore liked them served old-school style, with our homemade cocktail sauce and a side of horseradish. His male nurse looked on, eating a NY steak with our made-to-order red wine sauce, and a side of fresh, steamed broccoli and glazed baby carrots. I loved Gore – he was one of the few who just said it as he saw it. Plus, he carried a certain refinement, reminiscent of old Hollywood, which is so fitting here. He was wearing a white collared shirt, ascot, navy blue blazer with gold buttons, khaki slacks, and chocolate brown loafers. He was like a throwback to the heyday of the Cricket Room when people of substance and class gathered there, clinking glasses, laughing elegantly, and holding brilliant conversations. There was no one like him. We didn't see his type much anymore, not because they were dining elsewhere, but because they didn't exist.

Since his partner Howard Austen had died quite some time previously, Gore had been rather melancholy and sometimes he'd just burst out crying in the middle of dinner for no apparent reason. That just broke my heart. I'm not sure why he got so sad. It could have been because the piano player was tapping out an oldie that reminded him of Howard. I'd also overheard him expressing his deep lament for the current state of the U.S. as he perceived it. He felt that the news and entertainment media, controlled by the "elite one percent," were spreading their brainwashing campaigns to a mostly illiterate and uneducated public. A lot of his anger seemed to stem from his belief that the U.S. government was spending its tax dollars on wars instead of educating its own people. He seemed to have quite a beef with most governmental policies and I also didn't think he'd ever get over his hatred for George W. Bush. Serving Mr. Vidal was always a treat – I never knew if I would get a world history lesson on the Persian or Roman Empire, or another fascinating sound bite from his spectacular life.

Mr. Depp sauntered in with his family, exuding his usual casual, friendly air. He carried little Jack in his arms, and Vanessa Paradis, the beautiful mother of his children, held their daughter's hand. They were followed by their regular contingent of bodyguards and assistants. Since it was still early in the evening, they walked in fairly unnoticed. I greeted Johnny as he entered the room dressed in a T-shirt, leather vest, navy scarf, jeans, and a Basque-type cap on top of his Depply-cool hairdo. He looked like he'd just stepped out of an upscale vintage clothing store in Berlin; like Stephen Tyler, Depp could pull off the quirky look. He approached his table with a confident yet down-to-earth smile on his face and said to me, "Hey, man, how you doin'?"

"Welcome, Mr. Depp, it's a pleasure to see you again." I greeted his daughter who will without a doubt grow up to be a looker for sure, and she smiled and said "Hi." Their kids, who look like cherubs in a Michelangelo painting, are extremely allergic to certain foods and must be protected against a careless kitchen staff at all costs. This I knew from prior visits, which was something not fully appreciated by management, cheap fuckers that they were. A new waiter from the never-ending conveyor belt would not have known that, had Depp dropped in as he does sometimes, and might not only have put the children in danger, but put the restaurant in legal jeopardy. Did people sitting in cubicles in another country ever consider such a thing? I doubt it.

I pulled out the table so they could all be seated in their half-moon booth comfortably. Johnny could sometimes seem a bit uneasy with the formalities we use in the Cricket Room but it can't be helped. No matter what kind of weird get-up you're wearing, you will be treated with gracious formality. Even before his good friend, the writer Hunter S. Thompson, used to frequent the Cricket Room, we had a long, proud history of proper service. I liked to think of my role as something close to Alfred the Butler from *Batman*, always at the ready with a towel hanging off my left arm, although without the British accent. Johnny's assistants and bodyguards sat in the booth next to him, keeping to themselves, but vigilant for knife-wielding whackos and overly exuberant fans. I can't remember their names but they were definitely European.

Vanessa, his then long-time girlfriend, was very adamant about describing the children's allergies. I nodded politely as if it were my first time hearing it all, listening with genuine interest. Something might have changed since last time. Although she was a French model, singer, and actress, she was hardly wearing any makeup and looked only like the concerned mother I knew her to be. I could tell that she was a sincere and grounded person just by listening to her talk and looking into her eyes.

"Jack," she said, "will end up in the 'ospital if any of this slips into his food." I assured Ms. Paradis that I had written down all her requests and would relay them to our chef.

Even though we had openly discussed the Depps' allergy issues at the pre-shift meeting, the busboy, Juan, mindlessly set down our regular bread basket on their table. I quickly pulled it away and gave him a look that said, "I'm gonna kill you, you fucking loser. What part of the briefing didn't you understand?"

Under Ms. Paradis' watchful eye, I told him not to bring any bread 'til we could be sure that it was safe for the kids. Two bottles of Fiji water rested in silver sleeves on the table, and I poured the water to one-third full in our signature stemmed water glasses. In an instant, Vino appeared at the table bowing and greeting Mr. Depp and his family. Vino, who was not about to make the same mistake as he had in the past by selling Depp wine he didn't really care for, mentioned that we had his favorite, Chateau Haut-Brion La Mission. Mr. Depp perked up with that news and asked us to open the '82 and '89, and "let's decant them both," he said with the devilish smile for which he's famous.

Chateau Haut-Brion produces one of the finest French wines that money can buy, and at about $3,800 a bottle it takes a lot of it. The man knows his wines and it was impressive that he was familiar with such an exclusive winery. It was obvious that Depp was not being a wine snob at all; had he been he could have ordered other more widely known labels often purchased not for their taste but for their snob appeal. Some celebs order ridiculously expensive wines just to show off; I know because I've served them when they were alone and they ordered Diet Coke. Depp simply knew good wine, could afford to indulge his palate, and seriously appreciated it.

Château Haut-Brion is rated a Premier Cru Classé (first growth), a title held by only three other Bordeaux wineries, and is produced in Talence just outside the city of Bordeaux. It is thought that the vineyard first took root in Roman times, and that cultivation of the land dates from 1423; the estate itself dates back to 1525. What sets this winery apart and makes it unusual is the fact that it is located outside of Haut-Medoc, which is the region that holds the appellation for Bordeaux, but its wines are still considered Bordeaux. Leave it to Johnny to choose the most unique and distinctive Bordeaux wines.

I left the Depps to read their menus and Vino ran off to fetch those exquisite wines. A-list celebrities have the effect of a magic wand on the entire staff, sparking everyone to life.

I decided to take care of the breadbasket issue myself by talking to the chef. On my way toward the kitchen, I caught sight of Roderick and Penny Stewart being seated in my other corner booth. "Okay, think quick," I muttered, trying to stay calm in the face of a celebrity shit storm. I hoped I was up to a Depp-Rod Stewart clash of the demanding titans. *Breathe.*

I flew into the kitchen just as the sous-chef was entering her office. *Oh shit, it's Lola – she's a total fucking idiot.* My shit storm had just gotten cloudier. Everything was a problem with her and even though it was the guests' allergies, she usually tried to act as if it were my allergies that were inconveniencing her. At the same time, I *had* to get my ass over to Rod's table, as the rules of service say we only have forty seconds to greet the guest and those forty seconds had passed. I really didn't want to keep them waiting any longer.

So I asked Lola with my sweetest voice possible, trying to pour on the Pauli charm, to put together a nice safe breadbasket for Johnny and his family. As I reminded her of the allergies at the Depp table, instead of just saying "of course," she answered with, "Why can't your busser do that? Doesn't he know what's in the bread?" Always looking for a way to shuffle things onto someone else's shoulders. No concern for the guest or for service. Or the most important thing: my job.

I said, gritting my teeth, "Look at him, Lola." We both turned and looked at Juan, who had followed me into the kitchen. He was standing there listlessly, staring blankly. I tell her: "Okay, you know what? You'll get your fifteen minutes of fame tomorrow when the headlines scream, 'Cricket Room sous-chef kills Johnny Depp's kids!'"

She yelled, "Fuck you, Pauli! Fuck you!" *Come on, Lola,* my eyes were begging. Finally, she hesitantly complied. "Okay, fine."

Why should I have had to beg for this kind of thing? I turned to Juan, who was looking on with his usual clueless stare. "Lola will make you a special bread basket. Bring it to Mr. Depp's table with olive oil. Please." *Dip shit.*

I dashed out but relaxed my pace before I hit the floor. I took a breath and remembered reading that Rod's third wife, Penny, had recently become pregnant. *Good for Rod,* I thought. *He's still as virile as ever.* They sat in peaceful oblivion, intent upon each other, unaware of the Depps and engrossed in their own world of conversation. As I approached their table, I bid them a warm welcome. Penny, a glamorous blonde English model, smiled and Rod said jokingly, "Hello, old chap!" I noticed how Rod always looks great – it's unbelievable. No visible plastic surgery either. He just looked tanned and fit, wild hair, like the rocker he is, but nowhere nearly as flamboyant as Steven Tyler. Rod usually wore a flashy outfit but this time it was just a nice white collared shirt with a black and white polka-dot ascot and medium length black cashmere coat. I couldn't really see the rest of his outfit but what I could see was very Rod-like. Classy but with an edge. That night he seemed to be focused on romance but he always gave off an impression of unpredictability; you never knew what to expect from him. No wonder audiences love him. He made the ascot look cool, which is something that even Gore Vidal couldn't do.

Penny asked for a bottle of Fiji water and Rod ordered a glass of chardonnay, no specific label, but then changed it to Pouilly Fuisse, probably figuring it would be cheaper. He does tend to be a bit penurious. But as they all do when they come here, he'll find out he's in the wrong place to save a buck. Actually, he should have known. It had been only a few months before when I was serving them and he almost choked on his tea when he saw the bill.

He had growled in his signature raspy voice, "A hundred and fifty dollars for a steak?" I explained that it was Wagyu from Japan, widely considered the world's finest beef. (This was just before the ban.) I told him that Wagyu refers to specific breeds of Japanese cattle which are known for intense marbling and may be raised with a regimen of massage and beer or sake added to their feed. He spat out, "Bloody hell, if I had known that I would have chewed it slower!" At that point, Penny calmed him down and paid the check with his card, leaving me a nice tip, then gave me a conspiratorial wink. They keep coming back despite the cost because Rod fancies the place and enjoys our fine musicians who entertain the guests. I think he also enjoys the pampering.

I hurried out with their drinks, pouring the wine from the bottle after displaying the label for Rod's approval. I always handle my single-glass orders to take the burden off Vino, who was busy up-selling great bottles of wine elsewhere. Rod tasted it and gave me the go-ahead. When I described the specials, I mischievously recommended the Wagyu beef, then told them I'd be back in a few minutes to take their order. I giggled to myself as I walked away. I loved pushing the envelope a bit in that stuffy place, but I always made sure to do it with a straight face, like the professional I'm supposed to be. I mean, we are supposed to recommend the ridiculously expensive beef, right?

Later, as the darkness of the evening descended on the Cricket Room, the main dining room glowed with a soothing golden ambiance. The warm light from the silver table lamps and the glittering lights from the trees on the patio added a gentle radiance. I looked through the elegant glass partition that separated the main dining room from the hustle and bustle of the front dining area near the bar, and I felt as if I were watching an old silent movie. The glass sparkled with the reflections of faces and tiny lights, but it cut out the sound and framed the scene like a tableau frozen in time. You could imagine a tall lanky dame in a shimmering white satin gown, elegant in a booth with a gentleman in a sharp wide-lapelled suit, both smoking cigarettes in long ivory holders. In my mind's eye it looked very much like the surprise hit *The Artist*.

As I looked a little deeper into the scene, I focused on the face of the brilliant new movie producer and clothing designer, Tom Ford, seated with his partner, Mr. Richard Buckley. I noticed that no one had approached his table yet, so I hurried onto the set of my silent movie and it burst to life, snapping me unpleasantly back to the noisy present. The reality was jarring when the sound returned; I much preferred my silent version and could sympathize with those film stars who hated the transition to talkies. Sound really did spoil the show.

Mr. Ford, who often modeled his own creations, always wore his crisp white shirt unbuttoned to the middle of his chest with a stylish dark blazer. Mr. Buckley dressed similarly, but more conservatively, often adding a classic ascot to his get-up. We probably saw more ascots in the Cricket Room than almost anywhere else on earth. In the "real world" you hardly ever see anyone wearing an ascot. Can't imagine one going over well at a football game, the mall, or a PTA meeting.

I approached their table quickly, welcomed them back, and introduced myself as we always did. Tom ordered a Belvedere and soda, and Richard wanted the same but with tonic, both with some limes and lemons on a side plate. Since this was not my first time serving Mr. Ford, I told him how much I had enjoyed his very stylish film, *A Single Man*. He thanked me humbly. I thought, *wow, he wrote, directed, and produced his first film and it's absolutely great. I'm impressed but not as impressed as all the gay men who are staring at his hairy chest right now.* Daniel, at whose table they'd been seated, was about to faint; he always got flushed cheeks and a sweaty forehead when he was turned on, and he was sweating like a fry cook right then.

I told Daniel, "Sorry to get in there before you but I just saw them sitting there, waiting for service. I'll transfer the check to you now."

"Oh, thank you, how will I ever repay you?" he said in his mezzo-soprano queen voice, with a bit of a suggestive look in his eye.

I replied playfully with absolute faux conviction and a sly wink. "I'll think of something, Danny boy. Just take good care of our sexy, hairy-chested genius."

"Oh, don't worry, I will," he assured me, licking his lips and patting his sweaty forehead with a small cloth napkin. *Oh boy, if Tom could see this he'd probably beg me to stay on as his waiter*, I thought. *Or maybe not?*

I briskly walked back over to Mr. Depp's table, where the artful staging of their dinner service was just beginning. Vino had been pouring the wine, Juan has replaced the cheese and nut bread with French-style white and wheat rolls, and a dish of olive oil for dipping had been placed in the center. I smiled at Johnny who always had a warm look in his brown doe-eyes, and he made perfect and sincere eye contact as he always did. Yes, even with his waiter.

Now I really do have to comment here, since I've waited on almost every superstar male actor in the world. Johnny Depp is without a doubt my favorite, with George Clooney and Brad Pitt sharing a close second place. They're all humble and seem to know how lucky they are, and they consistently display genuine compassion and respect for the help. And for me, as the waiter to the rich and shameless, that is all I need to go to the moon and back for you.

I whipped out my captain's pad and got ready to write down their order, all while hoping Rod Stewart and his pregnant wife were okay. Top-level service is a constant juggling act.

Ms. Paradis orders for the kids: "For Rose, the linguine pomodoro, with no cheese – please don't even bring it to the table. And for Jack, the linguine with olive oil, with an order of chicken fingers and fries to share between them. Can you make sure they're fried in fresh, unused canola oil?"

"Yes, ma'am, I certainly will." *Fuck. Lola is going to scream like a stuck Japanese cow.*

"And also for the three of us," she pointed to the kids and herself, "a side of steamed mixed vegetables, please." Ms. Paradis also ordered tomato soup for herself, which we – and by we, I mean someone else – would have to make from scratch since it was not on the menu. Then, she instructed, she would have the halibut, plain, grilled with spinach sautéed in virgin olive oil and garlic.

Johnny Cool took his turn after patiently waiting for his wife: "I'll have the tortilla soup with avocado garnish and a six-ounce portion of the Wagyu beef, please, sir."

"Just like that, sir?"

"Just like that," he said, smiling easily.

Wow, he's easygoing, and he actually ordered right off the fucking menu, I think to myself, as I inform him that the chef recommends the Wagyu beef be cooked to medium.

"Then that's how I'll have it, thank you," he replied. No typical tantrum or request to have it burnt to the point of resembling a lump of coal, or so bloody it looked like road kill.

I proceeded to repeat their orders back including every little detail. Once I had their nod of approval I poured water and more wine for Johnny. They were halfway through the '82 Chateau Haut-Brion and Depp was bemusedly eyeing the '89 like he wanted to kiss the bottle.

Quickly I skirted over to the computer to input my order. I asked Jose, "Where's Juan? I haven't seen him for a while."

"He's on break."

"Who's covering my station then?"

"I am," Jose said.

"Did he tell you about the allergies on table 43?"

"No, he didn't say nothin'."

"Not even in Spanish, nothin'?" I asked, getting madder by the minute.

"No."

Fuckin' loser Juan. He was *muerta* to me. Dead as the silent movie stars I'd dreamt of earlier.

I took a deep breath, gritted my teeth, and said, "Okay, table 43 is allergic to idiots, nuts and dairy, so no bread with nuts or cheese, or the kids die, comprende, amigo?"

"Fuck you, asshole," says Jose.

"Okay, sounds like you got it. Hey, seriously though, pay attention to them, their bill is already eight thousand and I haven't even rung in the food yet. They're gonna make our night." *If you and Juan don't fucking kill them. Murdering your client's kids tends to lower the tip substantially.*

Jose nodded and headed toward the dining room at his regular lazy-ass pace. I can't help thinking, *when are they gonna train these guys right?* Management exerts no pressure on them to grow or improve. I bet they'd even feel better about their jobs if they were held to a higher standard. But in the Cricket Room, all the pressure falls on the waiters, and it is only we from whom perfection is demanded.

I carefully input the Depps' order, then entered the kitchen to begin the dreaded review and specifications with Lola. As I was walking away, these words slipped out uncontrollably: "Now don't fuck it up, Lola. Please." I didn't dare turn around to look at her but Paco, the food runner, heard me and was chuckling to himself. The truth is, she always fucks it up. She didn't ever pay close enough attention to the tickets we wrote and in such a highly rated and exclusive restaurant, that is an unforgivable sin. But we couldn't argue with anyone in the kitchen. They had some special immunity from prosecution, like federal star witnesses in a mob movie. It was probably because the food and beverage director used to be the executive chef and all the wormheads with a chef title attached to them were his buddies from some other previous life before their Cricket Room gig.

All of a sudden, all those thoughts were washed away and replaced by the sound of someone screaming.

Then I realized it was Lola, screaming at me. "Get the fuck out of the kitchen, Pauli, and don't come back, you stupid asshole! Get the fuck out of the kitchen now, Pauli!"

I could just imagine her — I didn't dare turn around to look — her face beet-red with anger and that fast neurotic walk she took on when she got mad. *I better speed up my pace and get out of here before management hears all the commotion.* My back was still turned when I exited the kitchen. I could see Paco laughing to himself 'cause he knows what I said was true. She was always sending the food runners out to the tables with incomplete orders or a wrong item on the tray. Now I know you're thinking that the runners should have started checking the orders themselves before taking them out, but it's hard when she's already stacked the plates with tin covers on top of one another and is yelling, "Take this out to table number forty-nine NOW!" They are much too intimidated by her to stop, remove the covers, check the order, then proceed. They'd rather take their chances than face her wrath. And anyway, it's her responsibility, not theirs.

I scurried back over to Rod's table to take his order. He and Penny looked cozy, leaning in toward each other, shoulder to shoulder, bathed in warm candlelight, and still deep in quiet conversation.

Tonight Rod wanted our house-cured Balik salmon as an appetizer. We serve it with a nice side of poached white asparagus garnished with crème fraiche and black American caviar as well as fresh-griddled potato blinis. Penny ordered (shock!) a salad of mixed market greens with thinly-sliced fennel and carrots, garnished with shaved Asiago cheese. The dressing was white balsamic vinegar and organic Sicilian first cold-pressed extra virgin olive oil. For his main course, Rod asked for our juicy rotisserie chicken lightly herbed with rosemary, fresh tarragon, and Himalayan salt, but instead of potatoes Rod asked me to bring steamed asparagus with a side of Hollandaise sauce. I don't know what Rod's fascination is with asparagus, but one time I served him that small, skinny, wild asparagus and he picked one up with his fork.

As it hung flaccidly (probably overcooked), he said to me, "You call this asparagus? Go get me some proper asparagus."

So I did, I got him the regular asparagus stems that were cooked just right and could stand erect off the top of his fork. He liked that much better. Penny asked me for the caramelized sweet Nantucket bay scallops served over a fluffy butternut squash risotto and garnished with drizzles of truffle parsnip purée. I repeated their order back, and then, knowing that Rod never orders dessert – apparently out of vain concern for his weight – I decided to yank his chain a little more. I offered them a chocolate soufflé for dessert, which we have to prepare in advance. I mean, what pregnant woman doesn't want chocolate? Rod kinda looked at me like, *you asshole*, then turned to Penny who considered it but decided against it. I'll bet that little critter inside her stomach would've loved some, but I guess he'll just have to wait until he's old enough to order for himself. *Hello Brat Pack, here comes another Rod Junior.*

As I hurried to the computer to input the Stewarts' order, it struck me that I was a pretty lucky bastard to be waiting on people like Rod and Johnny. Well, I'm damn good at my job, so they're lucky to have me too. But they definitely made this thankless job a little easier to take. After all, there are only a handful of waiters in the world who have shared my experience, and if serving was how I was going to make my living, then this was definitely THE place to do it.

I then set up both the Depp and Stewart tables with the proper polished cutlery for both courses. I was hoping they'd figure out what was what and not use the wrong cutlery for the wrong course as most of our guests do, especially the Brat Packers who always make snide comments about so many forks and spoons. They usually deciphered what to do with the soupspoons, though. Bravo!

The clock struck nine and Mr. P informed me that Lola was furious with me. He told me I couldn't go back into the kitchen and all communication must go through him. That prompted an impassioned internal monologue:

Okay, great, is he gonna learn to speak English in the next few minutes? 'Cause if he's not I'm gonna call in a fucking translator. Dammit, all because I said, "Don't fuck it up." Why did I have to open my damned pie-hole? I have to just learn to keep my mouth shut like the rest of these one-dimensional gutless empty-headed cardboard figures that work here. It doesn't matter that Lola told me to fuck off and get the fuck out of the kitchen. Actually, I would have told me that too if I were she. No one likes it when you expose their weaknesses, but for me there's just too much at stake. I'm responsible for the well-being of every guest who sits at my tables even if I'm not the one screwing it up. I'm the face of the restaurant, the guest's representative, their go-to guy. To the guest, if a runner brings the wrong dish straight from the kitchen, it's my fault, not the kitchen's or the runner's. If it's cold, I must have been late somehow. Overcooked? My fault too.

So naturally, there is a lot of pressure on me, and whether I want to or not, I have to delegate certain responsibilities to my colleagues. Without their help, I can't get the job done. And if they screw up, it's my ass. Let's not forget that I serve the most affluent people in the world here with all of their quirks, demands, eccentricities, and allergies. They are paying for the privilege of getting what they want. And even if their expectations regarding the food we serve are not sky high, they do expect great service and to not wait more than a reasonable amount of time for their food. They don't expect to be poisoned or have their deadly allergies triggered and be carried out on a stretcher because the staff didn't listen or made a mistake on their order. This has happened more than once. There are so many things that can go wrong in the process, and I am responsible for all of it.

And besides that, I need my guests to have an exceptionally magnificent time. I want them to feel catered to and relaxed. That's how I make a living; guests show their appreciation by tipping us, thanking us, and coming back. I can honestly say that I really do care how they're doing when I ask, and I really do care if they're enjoying their meal. I really am looking out for them, period, and I can't stand it when some jackass drops the ball just because they don't have integrity or they know that the hammer will fall on me. That's why everyone I work with knows that you don't screw up on Pauli's tables. You just won't get away with it. I hold my team to a higher standard. You've got to pay attention, be strategic, and respond quickly. That's what I do, and I expect nothing less from my colleagues.

I don't know why I get so fired up about this stuff but Mr. P's warning got my blood boiling over and I felt like punching my fist straight through a wall. Preferably a wall with Lola standing in front of it. Luckily, while I was furious, I'm still smart enough to know that I would just hurt my fist and probably break some restaurant property. Not a good idea. I wasn't going to let Lola or anyone else push me to the brink. If you are ever so fortunate to have a fine server, whether it's a diner or a five-star restaurant like the Cricket Room, be sure to recognize it and appreciate the experience. It's not easy to pull off and therefore it's rare.

To blow off some steam, I decided to mess with Juan as he rounded a corner, about to enter the dining room with a basket of bread and butter. I stealthily put my foot out without looking him in the eye, and as his foot makes contact with mine, he stumbles and tosses the breadbasket in the air. In one smooth motion, I caught Juan with one hand and the basket in the other before either one hits the ground. My anger turned into a circus act! I slapped him on the back – "Gotcha!" – and continued out toward the dining room with the breadbasket in hand. Under his breath, I hear him grumble, "Pinche puto maricón." He always falls for that one. In the fast-paced restaurant business, we have such limited time to interact with each other that short jokes and pranks with instant gratification are often the only choice. I knew he would laugh about it with me later anyway. I would say that there are very few intellectual discussions going on amongst restaurant staff – it's more often sexual shenanigans and mischief that rule in this foxhole work environment.

The young comic writer Seth MacFarlane, creator of *Family Guy*, and the infamous Paris Hilton had just been seated in a cozy booth in my station, out of sight of the madding crowd. Before I approached them, I took a moment to gather myself and put on my best Cricket Room persona. Little did Seth know that he was seated in the same booth that one of the greatest authors in the world had just vacated. Only thirty minutes prior, Gore Vidal had left that booth to return to his beautiful house in the Hollywood Hills that he'd owned since 1977. His 4,800 square foot home, full of wall-to-wall bookshelves, sits just off Mulholland Drive. He was still singing and clutching his martini glass as his nurse wheeled him off to the car to be chauffeured home. What a legend.

I greeted Mr. McFarlane and Ms. Hilton by name, and I welcomed them back. I set the breadbasket down and explained the different breads, and as I made eye contact with Seth I could tell that he was excited to be there – he had a humble look and demeanor despite his tremendous success. Paris, on the other hand, was not eager to make eye contact with her lowly waiter and displayed a jaded, "over it all" arrogant attitude, as she often seems to feel about everything that isn't HOT. I guess that's telling me something; maybe I should go back to the gym and work on my abs. She's hard to read and impossible to impress. It's sad to me that someone so young can be so hardened to the joys of life. Imagine how bitter and nasty she will be in her old age. If she makes it.

The aloof princess ordered a bottle of Fiji water. Seth had a Jack Daniels on the rocks and talked Paris into having a Jack, but she ordered it with Diet Coke. I followed up by announcing the chef's specials. Paris couldn't have cared less and Seth was moderately interested, but much more interested in Paris. I let them know that I'd be right back with their drinks. They both said, "Thank you," but I actually couldn't believe Paris said it. Of course, she pronounced it with that Beverly Hills mall rat accent, "Th'nk yowwwwww," but she actually smiled a little bit and looked at me. Yeah, she made eye contact, wow! Maybe I am hot after all.

As I walked away, I couldn't help but wonder, *what's the comic genius doing with shit for brains?* I returned with their drinks and I was trying to eavesdrop 'cause I couldn't think of any reason they would be sitting together, other than her looks. Maybe he was about to humiliate her on the show and he just wanted to give her a heads up. My silent speculation continued: *That's probably it. Or maybe he's actually gonna try for it. I mean, I know he likes blondes. Maybe that's all it takes. Hell, if nothing else it's a nice notch in his belt – what's he got to lose, right? Respect? With a show like* Family Guy *you can't really rely on traditional respect anyway.*

I'd already cleared Rod and Penny's appetizer plates and confirmed that they had plenty of water and wine, proper cutlery, etc. I had also assured them that their main course would be arriving any minute. I always do try to be present at the table when the guests' orders arrive, to help the runners place the dishes in front of the appropriate person. All that information is already on the ticket, but sometimes people change seats after they order. I also like to make sure that each dish is prepared the way the guest requested it, often averting disaster.

I rushed over to my money table to check on the Depp family. Paco was just starting to serve their main courses, and I assisted him. Mr. Depp's steaming, perfectly sliced Japanese beef is broiled dark on the outside and juicy on the inside. Also on the plate: potatoes boulangère, truffled crimini mushroom croquettes, Brussels sprout leaves, and a side of homemade red wine sauce in a silver gravy boat. Vanessa's halibut with sautéed spinach looked scrumptious. The kitchen had sautéed some wild ramps (leeks) with chanterelle mushrooms to fill out the plate and made an American caviar sauce on the side if she should want it. I asked if everything was the way they liked it. Johnny was looking a bit fuzzy after four grand worth of wine and was already chewing a piece of the steak, said, and I quote: "Deeeelicious, mate!" I wondered if he was suddenly turning into Captain Jack Sparrow. All the weird characters he's played have got to be locked up inside his head, trying to get out at inappropriate moments.

I noticed that his glass needed more wine – he still had another $3,200 worth to consume. Vanessa seemed fine with the wine but asked for some balsamic vinegar reduction for her vegetables.

"Right away, ma'am," I replied, and went immediately to fetch her reduction. When I returned I was happy to see that little Jack was still well and hadn't started convulsing from allergic shock. Instead, he was eating up his pasta and French fries. I made sure to make eye contact with Ms. Paradis and her placid expression assured me that everything was as it should be. She smiled, I smiled back, and that was my cue to move on. One of Depp's assistants gestured for my attention at the next booth, and ordered a chocolate soufflé.

"Shall I have our pastry chef put that in the oven now for you, sir *(Mr. Idon'tcarewhatyournameis)?*"

"Yes please *(Mr. Waiterslavewhomakesalotlessmoneythanwedo.)*"

"Very well then, I'll do that now, sir." *The fake polite banter of servants engaged in subtle psychological warfare.*

Rod and Penny's dinners arrived at that moment and as I

assisted Paco in placing their plates, I noticed that their entrees looked perfect, just the way they'd ordered them. *Seems Lola straightened up tonight.* I asked the couple if they needed anything else with their dinner.

"I think we're fine for now, mate" Rod said.

I wanted to enter the kitchen to let Lola know that she hadn't killed anyone yet but it was probably not a good idea. Very tempting, though. Perhaps it was because she was dealing directly with Mr. P, but for some reason she had not fucked up even one order. It was a banner night and I knew I should just roll with it, but that's not my nature. I wanted her to know that I knew she was not being her usual fuck-up self. I managed to control my urges, however, for the sake of peace. And my continued employment.

I headed over to Seth and Paris to see if they were ready to order. Paris said, "Ah, yeah, I'll have the steak tartare, no onions and not too spicy, then I'll take your chopped salad with no cheese, and no egg yolk just egg white instead and turkey bacon." *If she eats like that all the time, it's obviously not brain food.*

"All right, very well, and Mr. MacFarlane?"

"I'll have the Siberian Ossetra caviar, just one ounce, and then the New York steak cooked medium rare."

I read back the order, they nodded, I thanked them, then offered another round of drinks. Paris asked for a fruit smoothie and Seth asked for a Jack Daniels single barrel on the rocks. *Normal, meet Not Normal. What is she, twelve?*

Paris excused herself to go to the restroom, but instead I saw her frantically texting for about ten minutes outside the front door. Their first course arrived at that moment but I was not going to send it back for someone who was just texting. Besides, she's a terrible actress and they both ordered uncooked items anyway. I placed the caviar down in front of Seth. It sat in the middle of a silver caviar server surrounded by finely chopped egg yolk, egg white, red onion and crème fraiche, all in individual, attached silver cups. It made a nice presentation. Paris' steak tartare was made with capers, raw egg yolk, Dijon mustard, finely chopped red onions, Worcestershire sauce, and a dab of Tabasco. It was sprinkled with parsley and served with some micro greens and tiny cornichons on the plate. I also set down a basket of warm, fresh toast points snuggled into a folded white linen napkin for them to share, and some warm potato blinis for Seth. Paris finally came back and as she sat down, I cordially placed her napkin gently in her lap. I noticed her soft smooth legs. There definitely is something very sexy and enticing about her. She had a few bites of the steak tartare then lost interest. What a surprise. Seth offered her some caviar but she declined. Seth ate every bite of his caviar; I could tell he enjoyed it immensely. Good thing, because it was obvious that this date – if it was a date – was not going to lead to bed.

In passing, I could see that Rod and Penny were fine. I gestured to Juan and gave him the silent signal to clear the Depp table. Of course, I assisted him with that so we could do it in one clean sweep. José came by and "crumbed" the table as Juan and I walked away with the dirty dishes. I returned quickly, poured the rest of their water and offered more wine. Johnny put his hand up, indicating that he doesn't want any more wine. Only someone shamelessly rich would just slough off a grand worth of wine left sitting in the decanter. Someone was about to have a nice after-shift drink.

I offered dessert menus and purposely suggested our most healthful desserts – our fresh fruit plate, sorbet, or cheese plate. I didn't bother describing our other desserts since I already knew their tastes. Ms. Paradis was not about to feed her kids chocolate mousse. They ended up just having some coffee and herbal tea. The kids were fine and half asleep but well-behaved. The soufflé arrived at the assistants' table and they shared it amongst the three of them.

Mr. Idon'tcarewhatyournameis asked me to combine the checks for both tables. I don't recall the final total but I do remember the tip because it was a new record-breaker for me. Johnny Depp left me a twenty-five hundred dollar tip. Yes – you read that right. Twenty-five hundred bucks. Man, do I love that guy! Of course, I didn't keep everything I made – I shared 35% with the rest of the staff including Vino. We all bowed graciously and thanked Mr. Depp and his family as they got up to leave. Johnny carried his sleepy son out the door, as every woman in the room swooned.

"Please visit us again soon," I said. Depp is a man of intelligence and substance, nothing like the crazy characters he plays. Guess that's the definition of acting, but don't we all, to one extent or another, expect stars to be just like we've come to know them on the screen? My job had taught me that was anything but true. At the time he seemed happy and comfortable in his family role as a caring father. If I hadn't known who he was, I would've admired him for that alone.

But fandom faded fast. He was barely out the door before Vino and I practically wrestled at his table for the crystal decanter with the remaining '89 Haut-Brion. We decided to share the remnants, just had to make sure we stayed clear of the house cameras and were not seen by anyone who might rat us out, like Lola, who now despised me with a fierce, hot hate. I was just glad that she'd turned her anger toward me into perfection for my guests. I made the big tip; she didn't. So fuck her and her broom.

We ended up settling into a hallway in between the small banquet room and the service area. This is where I often went to eat my steaks and faux Kobe hamburgers. There's a small table there pushed up against a wall that is used to pile up plates and supplies during a banquet. It's kind of cool 'cause you can't be seen there and it's just light enough without turning on the hallway light. We each filled a coffee cup with the remaining 1/3 of the bottle and sat on the table leaning our backs against the wall. Wow! That wine was heavenly. Vino told me that it's rated 100 points by Robert Parker. With each sip, we compared tasting notes.

Vino: "I taste cassis, earth."

Me: "Yes! Cuban cigar, slight black truffle."

Vino: "Ripe plums, tobacco smoke."

Me: "Hint of tar and mocha nose."

Vino: "Fruit, powerful, refined and elegant."

Me: "Oh yeah, a seamless finish, pure as silk and velvety."

Suddenly we were starring in a remake of the movie *Sideways*.

The sensuous flavors sent me into a reverie and my imagination took off on a flight to a sunny Bordeaux vista. I'm strolling down an unpaved country road lined with lush, mature oak trees, tall grass and tiny colorful flowers. I count the little puffy clouds that slowly change shape against the crisp blue sky. I hear the leaves whisper as the wind tickles them in fluttering waves. As I come to a crossing at a small wooden bridge that spans a babbling creek, I see, just up ahead in the distance, an immaculately well-kept large French farmhouse. I take a deep breath and my spirit inflates, my heart fills with the sweet sound of birdsong and the scent of wildflowers and vine-ripened grapes. Oh! What a joy...

"Hey, man, are you all right?" A waiter's voice rudely inserted itself into my reverie. It was Matt. How had he found me? *Shit!*

"Huh?" I mumbled brilliantly, still trying to recapture my French visions.

"Rod Stewart wants his check! He looks kinda pissed."

"Oh shit, yeah, fuck, okay, wow! I'm coming." Articulate,

right? Wakie wakie!

"Are you okay, dude?" Matt asked, looking at me askance and chuckling.

"Yeah, yeah I'm fine, thanks."

Vino was gone; his cup sat empty next to mine. I printed up Rod's check and brought it out with some unimpressive petite fours that Patzo the Clown, our pastry chef, had prepared for us two days prior. They were about as fresh as Paris Hilton's repartee.

"Mr. and Mrs. Stewart, it's been a pleasure serving you again this evening, thank you so very much for coming in to visit us." Rod handed me his black American Express card without looking at the check. He was probably not impressed that he'd had to ask another waiter for his check, or maybe it was just me imagining that because his table looked crumbed and clean. *He's probably just ready to go, that's all,* I told myself. *He never eats dessert anyway and he doesn't seem to like hanging around for too long after he finishes his meal.* I processed his card and brought back the folder. I stayed close by for a few seconds to make sure he didn't choke on the price again. He seemed fine this time, and no surprises. I hoped Matt was just jerking my chain, telling me he looked pissed.

I glanced toward Seth and Paris as the busboy was walking away with their dirty appetizer plates. I quickly set Mr. MacFarlane with a steak knife and made sure they were equipped for their main courses. I asked if they needed anything else to drink, and Seth ordered his third Jack rocks, regular Jack this time. As I was ringing in the drink, their main course arrived. I watched Paco set down the plates in the proper order, in front of Paris then Seth, and everything looked good. I picked up Seth's Jack rocks at the bar and by the time I delivered it, they'd both already started eating.

"Ms. Hilton, Mr. MacFarlane, how is your dinner tonight? Is everything as you like it?"

They both nodded and grunted. I'm not sure if I consciously time this inquiry for the exact moment that the guests' mouths are full, but the truth is, they're much less likely to complain. I looked at Seth's NY steak and noticed that it was cooked to perfection, a nice juicy medium rare, served with sautéed beech mushrooms, glazed Nantes carrots, and Madeira onion soubise.

"Good," I said, "I'll check back with you in a short while." Seth's eyes said, "Okay, no problem." Paris couldn't be bothered to express a notion of contentment or anything else. Her world apparently doesn't extend much beyond her nose.

Rod stood up from his table and approached our musician, saying, "I was watching you play the harmonica and I was wondering about something. Back in the early days I used to play the harp but now I can't seem to find the right tuning for the song."

The musician asked jokingly, "When was that, back when you were a one-man band?"

Rod laughed and said, "Yeah, I guess you could say that."

I secretly wished he had asked me since I knew the answer and would have loved the opportunity to get to know Rod on a more personal and musical level. The musician told him that when you play the blues harp you have to draw in the air quite forcefully to get that classic bend in the notes like on all the old blues songs. He also said that the harp has to be a 5th up in order to be in tune with the song. "For example," he said, "if the song is in the key of E you would have to have an A-tuned harp because A is five half-steps up the scale from E, you know what I mean?" The musician then demonstrated this for Rod on his guitar.

"Ah yeah," said Rod, "I remember it being something like that. That's right, thanks, mate. You sounded great tonight, by the way. I always like coming here and listening to you and the other fellow. Cheers then, good night."

Wow – the guy who was playing that night is an awesome musician, and now he could brag that he just gave Rod Stewart a music lesson.

Rod left me just over a 20% tip but what's more than that, he once again left me with the pleasure of having served a musical icon. It had been an honor. The Cricket Room was such a unique place to work; there really is no other place quite like it in the world. I swear, if it weren't for all the corporate bullshit and idiots who think they know how to run that room, I would work fourteen shifts a week. Hell, I'd even sleep here on a booth or something. I love this place – the dining room is my home away from home and I know that many of our guests feel that way too, though probably much more so in the past than under recent management.

Rod and Penny exited right past Mr. Ron Tutor who was walking on air that night. Ron "Miramax" Tutor, the seven hundred million-dollar man, was escorted to his table by the one and only Ariella, LA's most glamorous hostess. Her curvy body wiggled and bounced ahead, directing Mr. Tutor to his table. Ariella had probably already dated him despite his age – I wouldn't put it past her. He is in his late 60's, balding, and short but you wouldn't notice that at first since he always projects a very confident, winning aura. Ariella seated Mr. Tutor at a large table and shortly thereafter, ten other guests joined him. They all crammed together, making it nearly impossible to serve them properly. Tutor ordered five bottles of Cristal champagne at nearly $400 each. He was hosting a special celebration because he'd been named "Disney's Man of the Year." His date was a 10, a statuesque blonde bombshell about thirty years his junior, probably one of the best looking dates he'd ever brought along. Mr. Tutor always entertained a different girl; I really don't know how he kept track of them all. Rarely did I see any repeat performances. Mr. Tutor always seemed to get some. How do I know? Because he displayed it to the entire dining room – by the end of dinner he's always engaged in some immodest, deep French kissing at his table. We always wondered why he's not more discreet about it. Given his age, I suppose it's impressive that he's still got game. But then again considering his wealth, his immodesty isn't surprising, especially in this town. If money can't buy happiness in this town, nothing can. Hollywood is the ultimate power palace and power is built on money.

Mr. Tutor made his money in the construction and property development business, and had recently become the proud new owner of the Miramax films library, which Disney had to sell on account of Miramax going out of business. The deal was whisked away from the Weinstein Brothers who founded the company in '77 but were not bidding high enough for Disney. Tutor and his investors snagged it for $673 million. I have a funny feeling the Weinsteins are still part owners but it's a complicated deal. I remember a specific meeting they had soon after the deal was announced.

Harvey Weinstein and his lawyer arrived first and took a private table outside. It was about six in the evening and there was no one else sitting on the patio. Mr. Weinstein was looking very uptight and pissed off and said to his lawyer, "So should I just say…"

The lawyer replied, "No, don't say it that way, be a bit more prudent."

HW: "Well then, let's tell him…"

Seconds after that, Mr. Tutor walked into the meeting as if it were nothing special and handled it with superior poise and ease. I can't tell you what they all said, because I couldn't hear them clearly and I hadn't known about the deal at the time. But the important thing is that now Mr. Tutor was in the entertainment business, a much more glamorous business than his usual real estate deals, and especially great for attracting young actresses who want their chance at the silver screen. It was a given that his sex life had just gotten even better. I'd been watching older guys like Tutor for a while and was amazed at what Viagra and Cialis have done for them. They can spend more time on business and the infamous casting couch, and less time worrying about erectile dysfunction. Frickin' cheaters!

I cleared Seth and Paris's table because she no doubt had a Mensa meeting to attend. I also crumbed it since the busboy was nowhere to be seen, not an unusual thing around this time. It was ten o'clock and they were probably having a Mexican taco feast in the kitchen with the cooks. I hoped they would save some for me.

I brought back dessert menus and offered coffee and tea. Seth ordered another drink and Paris was too busy texting her Mensa buddies to even acknowledge my existence. She seemed over it – ready to go. Seth asked for the bill, so I delivered it with his drink and some petits fours which neither one of them even sampled. Seth signed and left me a $100 tip on a $418 tab, more than enough to get a couple of stars in my book. I bowed and bid them farewell and invited them to come back soon. I wanted to advise Seth to bring a better date, but of course resisted the temptation. Paris probably wouldn't go out with him again anyway, so he'd have to go back on the internet.

At ten thirty, Harrison Ford and Calista Flockhart were seated at a large table with seven other guests in my section. In another waiter's section near them is Bill Maher, whose bitingly outspoken political humor has made him the spokesperson for the self-titled intellectual liberal Democrats of our time. The permanent bachelor Maher was joined by his somewhat steady girlfriend, Cara Santa Maria and five of his pseudo-beatnik friends. They were engrossed in a discussion regarding ex-presidents Ford and Nixon.

I approached Harrison Ford who had a very urgent look on his face – that same urgency he displayed in *Air Force One* and *Indiana Jones* and, well, actually in all of his movies. Anyway, he handed me his platinum American Express card as if he were giving me a top-secret microchip stolen from the Iranians. I asked if he wanted to keep the tab open.

"Yes," he whispered into my ear. He continued to whisper in a conspiratorial manner, as if telling me a high-level secret that was going to change the world as we know it. "Make an imprint and hand it back to me. I'll sign it before we leave." What century was he living in? No one takes "imprints" anymore. This is the digital age, Indiana!

He seemed terrified someone else would try to pay the bill. In my experience, most of the Hollywood types were anything but aggressive about grabbing the check.

"Yes, sir," I said, and with that hot little card in my hand, I hurried to the service area to quickly start a tab, but I didn't get very far before I realized that I should've taken their order first. I returned to the table immediately. Ford was eyeing me suspiciously. I think he's read too many Tom Clancy novels and they have warped his mind.

"Ms. Flockhart," I said, "What can I bring you to drink this evening?"

She smiled and said, "I'll have a glass of the 2007 J.P. Napa cabernet." I smiled, thinking that if we held her up to the light we could probably watch the red wine enter her gossamer body. Even in maturity, she has not gained weight but remains very beautiful, with flawless skin. Actually, she looks like a fifty year-old teenager.

"Very well. Mr. Ford?"

"I'll have a double Grey Goose on the rocks, no fruit."

I gave him a knowing wink as if his secret were safe with me, regarding the microchip that is. At their table, there were also orders for a Ketel One martini and a Sapphire martini both up with olives, a Beck's beer, two more 2007 J.P. Napa cabernets, a mojito, and a fruity tequila margarita served up. As I passed a few Colombian spies on the way to the kitchen, I polished my decoder ring and said, "Okay, I need nine waters on table fifty please, no bread, just some bar snacks, thank you. Pronto, amigo!" Silently: ...*before a bomb explodes somewhere or the evil narco traffickers attack!*

I served their drinks and returned Mr. Ford's credit card, stealthily. *Ssshhhhhh... we're being watched.*

I was struck by his resemblance to my late father. Same nose, the same lines near his mouth and on his forehead, the hair, just his facial features in general, although my dad didn't have the scars Ford has on his chin and mouth that give him the rugged look women love. It makes me nostalgic. My father had passed only a year prior, due to heart failure. He'd had a close call back in the late nineties after I had taken him to Roscoe's Chicken and Waffles for a late-night munch out. That time he was saved by a triple bypass. We were estranged many times during my life, but I missed him and it was a tough loss for our family. I thought about how I used to look up to my father as a child and how he always looked so strong and seemed so brave, just like Ford's characters. My father had a five-speed Fiat 128 back then and was quite a good driver. He would always chauffeur me and my little brother Judas around when we came to visit him from across the Atlantic. He would wear his black leather driving gloves, you know, the ones with the five small holes down the length of the fingers and big holes for the knuckles? We'd weave in and out of traffic going through all the gears up and down, all the way down Route 9 in Framingham, Massachusetts. He used to play this cute game in which he was a racecar driver and he would do his own commentary: "Here comes Dolph in the navy blue Fiat, racing around the corner, moving up on the Chevy Malibu and nearing the finish line! He passes the Malibu and wins, he wins! The race is over and Dolph in his 128 does it again, it's incredible, it's amazing, ladies and gentlemen!" The funny thing is, I was never scared. I always felt safe, 'cause he was my hero. I couldn't help but feel a little of that playfulness with Mr. Ford, although he had no idea why I was winking at him. Maybe he thought I was flirting with him; I'm sure that happened a lot.

I picked up a flyer off the floor near their table; I'd seen the same flyer on Maher's table. Apparently, their late dinner was because they were all coming from a fundraiser for the Peace Over Violence organization, for which Flockhart is a national spokesperson. POV is a non-profit headquartered in Los Angeles focused on the prevention of sexual and domestic violence, stalking, youth violence, and child abuse. *So this is where they come afterwards to have their political and intellectual after-parties.* I heard them say that POV was established in 1971 by pioneering feminists. I don't know if Ford is a feminist or just going along with his wife for matrimonial harmony, but it's always nice to see celebrities using their fame to support important causes.

Speaking of child abuse, I better check to see what Tutor is up to with his young date. She should be home by now; I'm sure she has homework to do and it's past her curfew.

As I returned to Tutor's table, a toast was being made in his honor, "Blah blah blah blah, Disney's Man of the Year!" Everybody clapped, even some of the staff. Tutor turned to me and asked me to bring some assorted appetizers. I recommended two margarita pizzas with melted fresh mozzarella, thin slices of tomato and fresh basil garnish, three of our house-cured Balik salmon plates, two jumbo white shrimp cocktails served with fresh avocado and homemade cocktail sauce, and two orders of Kobe beef sliders with aged cheddar cheese and skinny fries.

"Sounds great," he said. "Whatever," is more like what he was thinking. Luckily, Vino was keeping everyone's champagne glasses full, but half of them were drinking mixed drinks as well so I was constantly running drinks out to their table. I passed by Juan to ask for appetizer set-ups on Tutor's table. He replied, " 'Ow many?"

"Eleven," I replied. He gave me a look like, *you asshole*, which was his general attitude anyway, but in this case he was pissed because he had to place eleven settings at a table made to accommodate seven. "It's a party, for God's sake," I told Juan. "This isn't fine dining anymore, we're past that hour of the night. This is party time for the rich, so just slap down the settings the best you can and don't worry about it too much, 'cause they couldn't care less anyway."

At that particular table, the goal was just to make yourself invisible and get the job done without being noticed too much, because it ain't about you, it's about Ronnie-boy and he's having his moment. I mean who wouldn't be, with that gorgeous blonde next to him and being honored and all? Even Daniel would be getting wood.

I returned to Ford's and Flockhart's table, and Harrison sort of flagged me down, as if I weren't going there anyway. *Get a clue, Indiana Jones. I'm coming right at you.* He waved his finger around the table to see who wanted what and then gave me his order last. Basically, most of the guests including himself and Flockhart, wanted another round. As I looked at him again, my father's face flashed before me and I thought, *Okay, Dad, right away.*

A few minutes after I brought the drinks, some of their guests were getting up to leave already. Ford gave me the secret look to bring the secret documents over to his side of the table so he could sign them in urgent secrecy. Ford left me a $100 tip on a $300 tab. I told him thank you and that it was a pleasure serving him and Miss Flockhart, and that I wished they would visit more often.

"We will," he assured me. He thanked me and then instantly forgot me. *Good night, Dad. Drive carefully.*

Tutor didn't actually pay the bill. I really can't remember who did, but they sure got socked with a hefty check. We added the tip in since it was a large party, and in these events if the payee is faceless to us, we just don't take the chance. The manager okayed the gratuity charge, and the final total neared twenty-eight-hundred bucks. The table was shared by a few of us so we split up the tip. Mr. Tutor rose to leave with his Amazon Barbie and I bowed slowly, which allowed me to furtively soak up the luscious curves of his girl. Then I said, "Congratulations, Mr. Tutor, we look forward to seeing you again soon." But I really meant *congratulations on that fine date of yours.*

Ariella snarled with jealousy over his beyond-hot date. "Goodnight, Mr. Tutor, thank you (creep)," she whispered under her breath.

"Thank you," Mr. Tutor said as he walked out with a big smile on his face and his girl under his arm. *That is one happy dude, and probably about to get even happier.* Money might or might not be able to buy happiness, but apparently it sure can buy awesome sex.

And so the night drew to an end. It was eleven thirty, and we reset the dining room for the next day's lunch. We also attended to our nightly sidework duties of polishing glasses and folding hundreds of napkins, wiping down coffee stations and refilling and cleaning salt-and peppershakers. It's at this time of the night when most of us, with the exception of the two closers in the front of the house, get a chance to talk about more personal stuff. Talking is a way of making the time and drudgery of the sidework speed past and also helps us bond as a team.

I felt that some of the other wait staff was envious of me for the good night I'd had. They kept asking how my night was, as they knew it had been good but not how good. I was not about to tell them. I never kiss and tell. In this case, it was better to fib, so I told them, "I only wish Depp had tipped on the total, then I could've bought myself that Taylor custom electric guitar I've had my eye on!" We all laughed, and everyone felt better, believing I'd made a regular tip from Depp. Now we all felt somewhat equal. Only I was more equal, they just didn't know it. Never any point to creating a jealous work environment.

When I said goodnight to Mr. P, who knew my little secret, I handed him two crisp hundred-dollar bills. "I even ironed them for you in the back room."

He laughed, and said, "Thanks, Polli!"

I asked if Depp had made another reservation.

"No, but I make chure you serve him when dey come back — they were very hoppy. I talk to dem on de way out."

I gave him a friendly pat on the back and as I bid him a good night, he said, "Polli, be careful wit Lola, jew know che's got protection." He pointed up, as in upstairs.

"Yeah, I know, Mr. P. Sorry to put you in that situation. Are we cool?"

"Yeah, we're fine. Jous be careful, okay? Watch jewr mouth."

"I will, thanks. Goodnight, Mr. P."

"Goodnight, Polli, good yob tonight, eh!"

As usual, I rode my scooter home in the pitch, past-midnight dark, down Sunset Boulevard toward the Palisades. At that hour, I was alone on the road, slicing through the night past quiet estates and mansions. The air was refreshingly cold and wet as the night breeze blew in from the Pacific in foggy patches. You could smell the trees, the grass, and there seemed to be a faint, sweet scent of jasmine or plumeria in the air. I wondered if it was the wrong season for that. *Who cares, it smells wonderful and I'm feeling content and happy.* Those moments alone after a long fruitful night put my mind at ease, and set my thoughts adrift. I had served some of my heroes and earned my biggest tip so far. It's funny, these stars I serve. It's so obvious when you get up close, they're just regular people just like you and I, some with tremendous insecurities and some very confident and comfortable with themselves. Some are assholes just like some of us regular people but the really big celebrities are usually not assholes. I'll go out on a limb here and say that in general most are sweet, respectful people who know how lucky they are. When they come to the Cricket Room, they are not on stage. They just want to relax and be themselves, and have a nice meal with family or friends.

As I laid in bed that night, my final thoughts revolved around how my latest song was coming together; another one was playing on a couple of television shows, and I'd started writing a love song for my sweetheart, a draft pick yet to be named. And despite tonight's thrills and adventures, for the first time in a long time, I felt lonely.

CHAPTER 14
IT'S A WONDERFUL LIFE

The holidays are spectacular at the Cricket Room and it all begins around Thanksgiving. The reservations generally numbered in the six hundred range for lunch and dinner. Preparations required several days because we needed to set up extra tables throughout the restaurant and garden area. No more well-spaced tables for privacy; fuck privacy – we packed them in. Extra cloth napkins, tablecloths, and table skirts had to be brought up from our banquet supply storeroom along with all of our banquet silverware, logo plates, and fine glassware. For the three days ahead of an event like this one, the waiters spent countless hours polishing glasses and silver, and folding hundreds upon hundreds of logo napkins in our signature style.

The menus are always multiple courses for a set price and multiple choices for each course. I hate to admit it but these menus were normally far from spectacular and aimed at pure profit by numbers. Seventy percent of the orders are for turkey and stuffing on Thanksgiving and ham or turkey on Christmas. Could the pilgrims have designed a better for-profit meal than cheap turkey, bread stuffing, pumpkin pie, and all the traditional fixins'? It's what people want, even in Beverly Hills, and it's all comprised of very low food-cost items. They just don't want to prepare such peasant food at home, so they come to the most expensive restaurant in town for cheap food, say grace over it, leave a big tip, and feel good about themselves. Win-win.

For Christmas Day and Eve we spent more time transforming the room than the kitchen did on preparing the meal. First, four well-lit colorful Christmas trees flanked both sides of the red carpet as guests approached the lobby from the outside. Once inside the lobby, our guests were greeted by a glowing fireplace and holiday-themed décor in hues of traditional red, gold, and green. Four more Christmas trees with ornaments and colorful lights stood in each corner, with luxuriously wrapped faux presents set underneath. The Christmas trees were always decorated in different themes each year. Some years they were sprayed snow-white and in other years left traditionally natural with colored lights and ornaments, and many variations thereof. This cozy decor completed the Hollywood tableau guests have come to expect and love throughout the decades. Santa Claus dropped in several times over the holidays for lunch and dinner to give candy and presents to our younger patrons. Santa came straight from central casting; the real deal – no fake beard or coloring in his hair. If I had been a kid I would have bought it hook, line, and candy cane.

All the planters around the booths and walls were densely filled with lush red poinsettias, and in the garden area the planted flowers were replaced with a thick carpet of poinsettias. Since the garden was so cozily lit on a regular basis, no real change was needed with the lighting.

Guests passed underneath a bouquet of mistletoe to enter the now-open private dining room, and immediately on the left in front of a huge mirror, were two very large gingerbread houses, complete with miniature cars, blinking lights in every window, and an "icing" of snow. It seemed to me that LA people love the surf and turf lifestyle, but when the holidays rolled around, they hungered for conventional, middle-America traditions like everyone else. And they were willing to pay to get them.

Christmas Day lunch and dinner went off without a hitch. We served over seven hundred guests and the room grossed well over $100K to set a new record for our highest-grossing day ever. So, approximately $20K in tips was distributed amongst twenty waiters that day. A more normal menu would not have produced nearly the profit that serving the cheaper holiday fare did. The corporate monkeys should have been ecstatic but I felt sure they were gleefully chortling and trying to figure out if they could serve some fancy version of turkey every day. ToFurkey and caviar, anyone?

At this particular time in my life, things had changed for the better. I had finally met a nice girl, someone I could take home to Mama and feel proud. This beautiful and amazing woman, Juliana, a writer, professional businesswoman, very intelligent, warm, funny, sweet, and caring, not a typical LA girl at all – would have her hands full, taming this wild bartender/waiter/rock musician. She claimed she was up for it. She's a very classy woman and doesn't care much for the glamour and glitz, latest fashions, or gossip. I felt so good with her, we moved in together after just a few months of dating. It felt right from the very start. I knew it was time for me to change and rise to the challenge of a mature relationship. I also knew I would need to change many things about myself if I wanted to keep this fine girl of mine.

Unfortunately for Jens, he'd had to find a new bosom buddy 'cause this woman wasn't gonna stand for the kind of trouble I always got myself into with him. Although it had been fun, deep down I knew I had just been passing time and blowing off steam. It was time to focus on love and music, which suited me just perfectly.

Holidays are supposed to be a time for families to be together and rejoice, but year after year I kept getting gypped out of that precious benefit, always working on important holidays. Even though I'd gotten used to the restaurant lifestyle, deep down I was longing for a more normal life. At first, all I had ever thought about were the great tips I'd make on New Year's Eve or Christmas Day. But as the years passed, I became disheartened watching families gathering at beautifully adorned tables, holding hands, saying grace, smiling, exchanging small gifts. I thought about how nice it would be to switch places with them; screw the tips. Then a bill would arrive in the mail and slap me back to reality. I was making some money on my music, but still not enough to quit my high-paying night job.

I'd noticed a substantial change in myself over the past two years though. Instead of getting excited about all the money I made, I felt depressed. In this restaurant setting I could see how the wealthy lived and it became obvious that we were merely fancy vending machines in their self-centered lives. On the holidays, I imagined these rich fucks had given their own live-in help the day off and probably didn't know how to cook and clean themselves. The pride in what I did began to taste bitter.

The residents from the nearby estates of Brentwood, Bel Air, Pacific Palisades, Beverly Hills, and even more humble Pasadena arrived with their little darlings decked out in beautiful dresses and/or cute little suits and ties, and even grandma and grandpa usually attended. I often felt like I was looking in on a Norman Rockwell painting: happy families with adorable pink-cheeked kids enjoying their best moments. I could appreciate the fact that their family was together for a nice dinner and they all looked so sweet together. I almost got excited for them until I remembered my girlfriend sitting at home alone waiting for me. Then I started wishing it were us sitting together in a cozy restaurant somewhere. It's such a humbling experience. It reminded me of my place in this tableau – nothing more than a servant. Waiter to the rich and shameless was turning into an uglier Scrooge version of a Dickens tale: jaded servant to the spoiled and shameful. I felt about as appreciated as a cold sore on a hot first date.

I had not spent a single holiday at home or with family since leaving my bartending position many years past. Back then, somehow I had managed to get Thanksgiving off a couple of years in a row. But as a waiter, I was required to work every major holiday, no exceptions. Everyone wanted the holidays off, so no one got them. Juliana was already starting to get a bit frustrated. Naturally, she wanted to spend our first holidays together and both of us also had birthdays in December that had gone uncelebrated because of my schedule. We barely had enough time to celebrate a late Christmas and both of our birthdays before I had to get back to work for New Year's.

New Year's Eve was just like any other holiday at the Cricket Room: we were open for business and packed with reservations. Every year we started preparations for the festivities the night before. It was traditionally very slow on the night of December 30th so we actually had time to perform the prep work necessary for our big night ahead. First we opened up our private party room to accommodate additional regular seating. We managed to squeeze in an extra twenty tables, some of them quite large, so all in all we gained seventy settings. A small parquet dance floor was brought in to cover the middle of the now-opened private room, and a three-piece band would be squeezed into the room's back foyer, with that entrance closed off. The band was necessary but not revenue-producing, so they got no extra space. If management could have figured out a way to stack them on top of each other, they'd have done it. Next year it'll probably be Grumpy, Dopey and Sneezy stuck in that corner.

Then, early on the 31st, we decorated all the tables with beautiful New Year's floral arrangements in a very chic but classy design using white roses, green leaves and silver-sprayed baby's breath in heavy square glass vases; wide silver bows tied around the vases were the finishing flourishes. This arrangement included a sterling silver candleholder with a silver shade as well. We inflated hundreds of black, white, and silver balloons with helium, then tied them with curly, festive, black and white ribbons. These balloon bouquets were then positioned decoratively throughout the restaurant, and a couple hundred more were stowed in a net over the dance floor to be dropped at the stroke of midnight.

There was only one seating on New Year's Eve, with 250 people arriving between eight and ten o'clock and staying until well past midnight. All guests would enter through the main door so a strict count could be kept, and those who were to be seated in the private room were walked through to the back of the restaurant. At the edge of the main dining room, our regular piano player performed with a stand-up bassist. Again, if they could have forced the bassist to stand on top of the piano, they would have.

I decided to drive and not ride my scooter to work just in case some drunken holiday reveler couldn't see me in the dark of the night on Sunset Boulevard. Celebrities get extra points for killing waiters and other lowly servants on holidays. It's a little-known Hollywood tradition.

I arrived at work at 5:30 pm with the sunroof open. It was a decent day – a little cloudy but still about 65 balmy SoCal degrees, one reason real estate is so expensive. Who wouldn't love that?

After the usual rituals of getting into my uniform, saying hello to everybody and wishing the day staff a happy New Year, all the waiters gathered in the kitchen for the pre-shift meeting and the Chef's tasting with course descriptions. The restaurant was dead, like Sleeping Beauty waiting for her Prince to arrive. No guests were allowed in without a reservation and no one would be arriving for their reservation until nine o'clock. So for once – and this is the only day of the year when this happens – we all had enough time to do last-minute side work, take our dinner breaks, attend the entire pre-shift meeting and actually hear the Chef's full course descriptions. It was important to make things sound as wonderful as possible, in order to justify the ridiculous prices being charged. "Here's your check, sir. Would you like to provide the title to your car or a credit card?"

Our new executive chef – the latest in a string of overpaid prima donnas – and the ever-lovely Lola stood before us but they weren't quite ready to present the scrumptious dishes of the evening just yet. Mr. P stepped in and began assigning our stations. No one was given more than four tables because, for once, they recognized we would all get swamped at the same time. They showed some compassion and actually staffed up enough to do the job right, which they could well afford. The only upside of everyone working every major holiday.

Mr. P explained how he wanted us to ring up and fire all the different courses and then pointed out that, "Ees a seeks kors deener, wit multipel choice korses." Some of the newer staff had a quizzical look on their faces but we would translate later. He went on to say, in a nutshell: "It's $250 per person, no exceptions, only one glass of

French champagne (which is technically the only kind of champagne there is) included and it will be served around eleven-thirty along with party hats and favors. I don't want any screw-ups tonight! No freelancing, no customizing, no substitutions or special requests. Everybody focus and double check your orders before you send them to the kitchen."

At that point, I glanced up at the usual fuck-ups who for sure would have some kind of problem. Their eyes were fixated on Mr. P as if they were actually listening. As for me, this was my tenth year with the company and fifth year doing the waiter thing. I'd never had much trouble with the mechanics of serving our distinguished guests, as I knew this job like the inside of my head. I took great pleasure in the opportunity to – for once – stay with my tables and guests for the whole night and actually get a chance to serve them without having to rush around covering other servers' tables while they were on break. As I explained, we only had four tables each and even the weak straight-from-Denny's waiters should be able to handle that. I made up my mind early on not to move out of my station to help any clown who couldn't handle that much – they could fucking choke for all I care. *Damn! There's that grumpy burnt-out waiter voice again. Shit, maybe it's time to move on, but what will I do? Music? Become a day-trader? Do porn movies? I'm sure my girlfriend will love that. Anyway I'll have to figure that out later 'cause here comes the new executive chef, Alex, an Asian man in his thirties, with his team and all the dishes, and boy does it all look great for once.* He and Lola outlined the menu for us:

Amuse Bouche (French for "amusement for the mouth.") – Served on a small, white, square plate with rounded raised lines around the edges:

An open eggshell perches delicately on a cushion of black rock salt and is filled with fluffy scrambled organic egg, flavored with a hint of wild truffle and topped with a dab of black caviar. The plate is sprinkled with shavings of fresh black truffle, a dab of crème fraiché on the side garnished with fresh wild chives, and a tiny silver spoon to scoop out the egg. An amuse bouche is usually one bite, maybe two. If it doesn't amuse the hell out of you to pay a butt load of money for one bite, you're not alone.

First Course (Two Options) – Elegantly served on a

medium-sized, oval, black glass plate with specks of gold leaf:

1. A terrine of farm-raised duck, organic brown lentils and chopped leafy winter greens. The terrine is accompanied by a fresh fig, halved and spread apart into a delicate design with squares of port and black pepper gelée.

2. Chilled Maine lobster tail served in the shell, topped with sweet, tender Dungeness crab meat. On the side is a trio of white and purple, lightly buttered, roasted baby potatoes, as well as a string of braised wild leeks and a small scoop of Hackleback sturgeon caviar.

Second Course (Two Options) – Served in a medium-sized, white china pasta bowl with gracefully rounded, swirled ridges:

1. A sunchoke-stuffed homemade ravioli served with a light Compté cheese sauce, salted pork belly and tiny Brussels sprouts. (Sunchoke is the tuber of a type of sunflower, with a flavor somewhere between an artichoke and a potato.)

2. A brothy saffron and Prince Edward Island mussel soup drizzled with a garlic and spinach puree and topped with a dusting of olive oil-roasted breadcrumbs.

Sorbet/Palate Cleanser Course – Served in a fluted crystal cup atop a matching crystal saucer with a cloth doily:

Yuzu citrus and lemongrass sorbet, meant to cleanse the palate of strong flavors and prepare for the main course, which follows.

Entrée Course (Three Options) – On an exquisite white china plate with a modern angular rim:

1. An aged prime beef ribeye cap, the most tender cut available, accompanied by a caramelized onion mousse and a mound of sautéed black trumpet mushrooms garnished with a touch of roasted hazelnuts.

2. A European turbot fish cooked on the bone, served with a green baby spinach and herb risotto, crispy frog legs and lemon Marcona almonds.

3. A beautiful oven-braised veal osso buco with flageolet bean cassoulet. Prepared with prosciutto and a slight trace of roasted fennel. ("No, sir, you may not substitute a Kobe burger with fries. No.")

Dessert Course (Two Options) – On a luminous jade square plate with speckled gold inner rim and an inch-thick toasted dark brown rim:

1. A lemon pain de genes, which is a lemon almond cake layered with vanilla *panna cotta* (Italian for "cooked cream") and a thin layer of lemon curd, topped with baked meringue and candied lemon zest.

2. A 40% Valrhona chocolate cake with a layer of coffee cream and a scoop of caramel ice cream on the side, garnished with a vanilla/dark chocolate wafer stick. ("No, ma'am, we do not have pumpkin pie with Cool-Whip topping.")

After this mouth-watering presentation, I had to admit maybe for the first time ever, I was really impressed with the menu and the presentation of the courses. I mean, people were paying a pretty penny for this dinner but they were mostly shelling out for the privilege of celebrating in the Cricket Room. That's how I usually felt about the food there – that it was not the star performer you would expect for the prices. But on this special night our new chef had really stepped it up more so than on any other holiday I'd worked in the past ten years. Maybe we wouldn't be bombarded with stupid requests for substitutions. It has always driven me crazy when some spoiled brat celebrity or just plain ignorant tourist is not willing to try something they don't eat at home.

Timing a six-course meal was always tricky as hell, especially because most of the tables were larger parties of six or more and people just couldn't sit still on New Year's Eve. They were always moving around, switching seats, talking with guests at other tables, stepping outside to do whatever. We also got incomplete parties with people starting their six-course dinners at different times, which really sucked. Once a table's order had been sent into the kitchen machine, it created a lot of confusion if you added to it or changed it. Plus, when you went into the kitchen to explain, you quickly realized that all the chefs were stressed out and didn't want to even hear your voice or look you in the eyes, because you might just have a guest request that's gonna stress them out even more. A waiter has to take control of their table and keep changes to a minimum or chaos in the kitchen will ensue. Unfortunately, taking control didn't mean we could just bitch-slap guests and tell them to sit the fuck down. Wanted to, though.

Each person's course also had to be served with the correct cutlery. I'm sure you've been to restaurants where you had to ask for a soupspoon or a steak knife because the server didn't bring it, but that was out of the question at the Cricket Room, where five-star service was our raison d'etre.

I pitied the sorry bastard who messed up his order that night when things were so tightly choreographed, but there was bound to be someone, that was for sure. You had to be on top of your game with your eyes on your tables at all times, even when the guests were playing musical chairs and making cocaine runs to the bathroom every thirty minutes.

Miraculously, my night went off without any problems. All my guests were served on time, every course was served correctly, and there were no complaints at all. As a matter of fact, I did have a couple of joiners who were two courses behind their hosts but I let them catch up by stalling the other people's courses just a little bit at a time. I have always taken pride in being able to maneuver, manipulate, and strategize like a battlefield general. Most guests have no idea of the timing, planning and logistics that my job requires. Great service is a thing of beauty and one of the few relics from a gentler past that we should try to save for the sake of civilization.

Poor Shakil – a sweet guy but he always had trouble. He managed to screw up the table of Mr. Ealy Ortiz, the owner of Mexico's biggest newspaper, and his nine guests. Mr. Ortiz had brought his whole family in for the evening, no doubt to show off his ability to pay for such an elite dining experience. They had ordered special meals in advance and something had gone wrong because half of their table was done eating when the other half got their food. Not very impressive. Shakil got stiffed, no tip on a $20,000 ticket. The manager wouldn't let him add the tip in even though it was a large party, because the service got screwed up so badly. That's heartbreaking to a waiter. Fuckups like Shakil have feelings too.

By the time dessert rolled around at my tables, we were just starting to hand out party favors and glasses of Piper Heidsieck. The absolute best thing about New Year's Eve is that on this one night at around midnight the managers let us have one glass of champagne each. But to me and Jens, of course, that meant we had free license to drink as much as we could possibly get our hands on. Just like the guests, we dressed up in party hats, with horns in our mouths and noisemakers in our hands, and we joined in the fun. I did keep my eye on the prize long enough to set down the checks on all of my tables first; this was the critical time when you had to keep an eye on people. They might think they have already paid and decide to go dance in another room or simply just not return. You usually don't have scammers at this level, but I don't trust anyone with that much money at stake. I actually ended up with an extra table: I took one of Germaine's 'cause as usual, he was busy talking to someone – running his mouth – and neglected the table. I didn't transfer it back to him either; I kept it, and therefore kept the tip. Maybe that would teach the fat ass blowhard a lesson.

After I'd collected all my checks and closed them out at around 1:00 am, Jens, Ariella and her boobs and I hit the champagne. Hard. We'd secretly stashed several glasses in a side cupboard that we were actually supposed to give to the guests. It was easy to do since management over-poured by about twenty glasses. We entered the kitchen to hug the cooks and chefs – everyone was getting drunk so there were no inhibitions or grudges in sight. Jens had secretly dusted our glasses of champagne, God love him. Everybody loved everybody on New Year's Eve. Shakil the Muslim didn't drink, though he really should have. His face was as long as a fiddle 'cause he missed out on a $3,000 tip. What can I say, only the strong will thrive, baby!

For these few minutes of freedom, we all just hugged and danced. The chefs broke out all the amazing leftovers we had barely tasted at the beginning of the night. We feasted on duck terrine, chilled Maine lobster, turbot, and plenty of veal osso buco. Our gay waiters were all chatting, hugging, and kissing in their own corner, tossing sparkly shit in the air. I went over and gave them all a big hug, getting sparkles all over my uniform. Macho Matt had grown a big boy mustache and looked like Freddy Mercury, and Daniel belted out "Happy Days Are Here Again," a Barbra Streisand tune, as I squeezed him. Stereotype much?

I bumped into Álvaro, the old wiry fucker with the dyed hair who had made it back from the dead, so I hugged him very carefully since I didn't want to crack him in half. His casket was probably parked in the lot somewhere. Amy came in and I gave her a hug praying that she would keep her breath to herself. The truth was I loved them all – they were like my family. For the past ten years, I'd been spending almost forty hours a week with them. Working teams become close in spite of differences that would not normally be overcome, simply because we shared our life events, good and bad; gay, straight, male, female, Muslims, Christians, we all had ups and downs that bonded us together. We also shared the pride of working in a beautiful hellhole that was the most iconic and historic restaurant, maybe in the whole world. We were all proud of that, whether we admitted it or not.

Mr. P walked in and we hugged. I could tell he's straight as an arrow. "Good yob tonight, Polli. I was watching jew, jew had control, Güey."

"Hey, in another ten years I'll be as good as you – watch out," I said, and we laughed.

I gave Shakil a big hug – he seemed to be feeling okay by then even though he'd only made about six hundred bucks. He was undoubtedly disappointed but you have to roll with the punches. That, as they say, is show biz.

I ended up grossing thirteen hundred bucks. Not the best I'd ever done by any means, but nothing to flinch at, that's for sure. Hookers, drug dealers, pole dancers, strippers, and waiters like me could make that much cash money in one night, but not many white-collar, college-educated, Volvo-driving, loafer-wearing, cappuccino-drinking, organic food-eating dandies could. But unfortunately for me, every night isn't New Year's Eve.

Vino walked in and presented me with a small glass of MX Beckstoffer To-Kalon Cabernet. It was leftover from my eight-top of Brazilian millionaires. It paired wonderfully with the veal and even the duck terrine. But wait a minute – where was Jens? I had lost track of him and started to wonder if he was doing bumps in the walk-in fridge, or maybe he was on the phone planning an after-party. I searched the dry storage room where the chef kept bags of onions, rice, oats, pasta, and the like. And there was my friend and mentor.

I couldn't fucking believe it! Jessica Rabbit was on her knees with her pouty mouth wrapped around his lollipop, giving him the Holy New Year's Eve, Batman, blowjob of the century. Jens's skinny, blindingly white butt was as naked as the day he was born. He turned around smiling uncomfortably; more of a grimace than a grin, like "Great timing, buddy." I laughed awkwardly and shut the door quickly.

Ahhh, the bad old days. Little Pauli had no sense of loyalty; I looked down and thought, *is that a banana in my pocket or am I just happy to see that?* Even though I had a steady girlfriend, a small part of me kind of felt left out. I silently toasted him: *Here's to a new year, guy. Will we be standing here this time next year?* I was beginning to hope not.

CHAPTER 15
ORDINARY PEOPLE

Every waiter sees things he'd rather forget, but almost any night at the Cricket Room could qualify for the Olympic Hall of Shame. The great Shakespearean-level human tragedy plays itself out daily on a grand scale. Whenever and wherever you gather the top tier of affluent society in one place – and it's a place in which they can have just about anything they want – you have to expect some kind of circus to ensue. Of course, awful things happen to regular people all the time, but when they afflict the cultured, coiffed, and catered-to celebrities and Jon-Lovitz-"Master Thespian" moguls we serve, somehow it becomes more dramatic. Or maybe just funnier to an acerbic witness such as yours truly. In any case, they certainly do fall from spectacular heights and it's amusing to watch, not because the tragedy isn't real – it often is – it's just that most of our rich and shameless guests take themselves so seriously it's hard not to mock them. Many of their best bloopers could be categorized as one or more of the Seven Deadly Sins (Lust, Gluttony, Greed, Sloth, Wrath, Envy, and Pride). I'd have to say that lust topped the charts.

Amber Lynn, the legendary porn actress, came in one evening accompanied by a couple of guys dressed in business suits. It all started innocently enough, but after a few drinks things were getting rowdy on table 44 and they were yelling across the dining room like they thought they were on the set of *Amber Fucks the Third Fleet*. Mr. P decided to move them into the private dining room where guests like Prince, Al Pacino, and others have preferred to dine in dignified seclusion. They made perfect use of the long, beautiful oval oak table with mahogany and ebony inlays. Amber got butt-naked and the men who'd come in with her were doing vodka shots out of her belly button and snorting lines off her Mega-breasts by Monsanto®. Even though the doors were closed and you could not see in from the dining room, several members of the staff were peeking through the window from a hidden corner of the garden area and it was fantastically sleazy. Of course, we only watched to make sure they were getting good service; we were concerned, as always, for the well-being of our guests. I mean, she could put an eye out with one of those things. You can't be too careful. I don't think Amy, our only female server, joined the peeping Toms, though she was more or less shaking her head in disgust through most of it. She just told us to make sure we disinfected the table. "Waiter! Alcohol swabs, stat!" By lunchtime the next day, our old sommelier was fired, one of our hosts was let go, and two waiters were suspended – their prize for committing two Deadly Sins at once: lust AND envy.

Speaking of fantastic (we were, weren't we?), Jenna Jameson, another famous porn star, was in with her boyfriend-of-the-month one night. Before dessert, they made a detour through the hallway by the lobby and had steamy sex behind a too-small-to-hide-anything fire extinguisher case. One of the cooks was smoking a cigarette near a back passageway into the restaurant when he got to see the action first hand. He said it was better than on film. She has even mentioned the event in an interview so I know he wasn't just projecting, so to speak. Why he didn't alert anyone else, or share his view, I couldn't tell you. Maybe he couldn't walk. Jens was pissed.

Amber and Jenna can make a man hungry for more, but a nicely dressed Bel Air woman in her late 50s made everyone nauseous. She was sitting at Don's bar (which used to also be mine) drinking her second Grey Goose martini, sucking on the olives, when a strange look came over her face. We all knew this cougar because she's the same plastic surgery face that used to try to court me many years earlier when I was behind the bar. A few more facelifts and she now looked like if you touched her face, it would pop like a balloon. Kiss her and you'd get a mouthful of collagen. Scary. She briskly paid her bill and got up to walk out, wobbling a bit on her spike heels. Just a minute or so later Mr. P noticed a trail of putrid brown stuff all the way from the bar through the lobby and out to the women's restroom. He was baffled and asked Don if there had been a service dog at his bar that had left recently. As he was asking, he noticed a nasty smell and a small pile of what appeared to be feces on the bar stool. The Hansel & Gretel crap trail was visible and plentiful all the way out to the lobby and into the bathroom. Mr. P called security to wait in the lobby to see if the poor woman was all right. I mean, don't you shit yourself when you die suddenly? When she came out, she was surprised to be greeted by security officers, said she was fine as if nothing had happened, and called the valet to get her car. She just wanted out of there as soon as possible. If this one isn't the sin of pride, it's the opposite and it's still funny. Later it was a sorry sight – our poor cleaning crew on their hands and knees with surgical masks scrubbing that long strip of carpet. The barstool was immediately removed and carefully de-stooled. We never saw her again after that, so at least she had the good sense to be embarrassed. Who knows, maybe her plastic surgeon pulled her face up so tight her asshole broke loose.

Since we're on the subject of talking shit, Kiefer Sutherland – a "Lost Boy" who used to be a favorite of mine – came in with some friends, expressing his dismay with the Hollywood executives who were contemplating the conversion of some of his favorite old films to 3D. Kiefer was in a feisty but playful mood that night, and asked our busboy, who went by the nickname of Anglo, if he liked Communism. Anglo said he thought it was good for some countries but not for America. Kiefer came back with, "How do we know if we don't try it first?"

Anglo replied, "I just don't think it would work here, that's all."

By the way, Anglo was the only Caucasian busboy I had ever worked with, which explains his nickname. He was only about twenty-three at the time and he really didn't know who he was talking to. Kiefer playfully taunted him: "Oh yeah, you want to fight about it?"

Anglo, trying to keep it light, jokingly replied, "Yeah, sure, I get off work in about three hours, I'll see you outside!"

As Anglo proceeded to pour water for the other guests, Keifer suddenly reached over and inexplicably swatted him in the balls. Anglo cringed, spilling water on the table, and gave Sutherland a dirty look. Seemingly playfully, Kiefer stood up and said, "Let's go, now, come on, let's go."

Anglo walked away, angry and bewildered at why a rich guy would be picking a fight with a busboy in a five-star restaurant. Once he got back to his station, and Germaine told him that the person he was about to fight was movie star Kiefer Sutherland, he decided to let it go. Was Mr. Sutherland just buzzed and really didn't mean to swat the guy as hard as he did, or was he being a jackass and picking a fight for no reason? Whatever it was, Anglo was almost ready to lose his job over it. I kinda would have liked to see how it would have gone down. Lots of movie stars who play tough guy parts think they're actually tough. They quickly forget that it's usually stuntmen who do the hard stuff, while the stars sit in makeup chairs drinking imported water like the pussies they are. Some movie stars have huge, prideful egos; in other breaking news, the sun rose in the east today.

Although Hollywood is the most egocentric place on earth, its headlines are usually ruled by celebrities' Freudian ids running wild. Britney Spears was in one night with her two assistants at the time. Where do you take your boss when she's the hottest news topic around but accidentally decided to shave her head bald? To the safe haven of the Cricket Room in a hurry! I served the three of them – including Britney in her Marilyn Monroe wig – some sodas at a table in the garden where they were trying to hide her on a chilly night whilst trying to figure out what to do with her. Before I knew it she was up roaming around, glassy-eyed with a strange, blank stare. I watched her as she slinked out of the restaurant and meandered around the lobby, gazing absently into the distance. I went back to the table with the check and her assistants asked me if I knew who they were with. I said yes but with a questioning look like: *Why the hell is she wearing that wig? Halloween was four fucking months ago.* They both looked exhausted and one of them said to me, "You've got to help us keep an eye on her."

I had no idea at that time what was going on but I replied, "I'm your waiter. I bring you drinks and food. You can chase her around; I can't help you with that." She got up, shot me a dirty look and walked in Britney's direction while the other one paid the check. The next night Britney was in the lobby, wearing her wig and had some shady looking dude by her side. They were both smiling and she shouted out a "Hey!" to Mr. P and me. I replied, "Hey!" but I could see that her eyes were still looking totally crazy. I thought she was going to come back in but she never did. Never saw her again, though I read plenty about that incident later. Perhaps she wasn't being gluttonous, exactly, but she definitely appeared to have overindulged in something.

At the other end of the spectrum are those lucky souls who not only hit the genetic lottery but have the talent and savviness to back it up. One early evening on table two I served Don *Miami Vice* Johnson and Michael Krupin (an eccentric regular who drank Belvedere over crushed ice, served in a large red wine goblet with Perrier), who was Don's good friend and insurance advisor. After Krupin convinced Don to order one of his bizarre concoctions, Don started bragging about buying a residence on Broadway in New York City for $6M and before he could even fully move in, some geek with a Band-Aid on his glasses knocked on his door and offered him $12M. Don greedily sold it just like that. Wouldn't you? I know what you're thinking: "Wow! That happens to me all the time!" Sure, me too. But he's always been a lucky dude; he's the son of a farmer, starred in not one but two popular TV shows, one of which he wrote. Plus he sued the studios and won a $15 million copyright settlement. He must be one of very few to beat the studios.

One of the few in that same fortunate category, George "Aren't I Great Looking" Clooney came in with his Italian girlfriend of the moment, Elizabetta Canalis, whom I had the pleasure of escorting to the ladies room. Her low-slung jeans revealed a fancy tattoo at the top of her butt. *Nice tramp stamp, honey!* When she got back she nearly choked on her water because Clooney had switched it out for vodka. Vanity isn't a Deadly Sin and neither is tomfoolery, but Clooney scores high on both. Known for being a practical joker, he and his guests were laughing pretty hard at his little prank. Apparently Elizabetta doesn't drink and he was trying to liven her up a bit. She was not all that amused and she also seemed annoyed at all the people who kept coming up to their table all night trying to talk to Clooney. He was very gracious about it so the staff didn't interfere.

Unlike Clooney's ex, some people appreciate the many blessings of Bacchus. Later that evening out in the garden I had the pleasure of serving Mr. Khaledi, the owner of Darioush wines. He is an older Persian gentleman, very refined. There were three Persian couples all together and they were loud and lively and even though I couldn't understand much of their conversation, I could tell that these were good people with good family values and certainly a decent taste in wine. I wouldn't say outstanding wine taste though, since they had brought four bottles from their own home cellar which, surprise, were all coincidentally by Darioush. At the time, we carried his wines and served the merlot for $25 per glass. Some might accuse him of the sin of greed, but who can blame the man for not wanting to pay top dollar for his own wine.

With the wine, they enjoyed several fruit and cheese assortments and a couple of soufflés for dessert. Corkage fee was $35 a bottle unless we had your wine on our list, then we charged the same price as on the wine list, but it had to be the same vintage exactly. We didn't have the vintages they were drinking so I charged $140 to open the four bottles. In case you are thinking this is a ridiculous practice, let me assure you that all good restaurants use this method to discourage guests from bringing in their own wine, even if they own a winery.

In the midst of their casual enjoyment, little did they know that sitting in a booth just thirty feet away was one of Mr. Khaledi's good

Persian friends and fellow winemaker, one of the creators of Mithra wines. There he was, adulterously smooching with a girl who looked nothing like Mrs. Mithra, when he was suddenly struck with the fear of God in his eyes. I believe he almost crapped his pants when he heard the Khaledis speaking Farsi nearby and laughing. I'm sure they all knew his wife. He could not exit the garden without passing them so he sat there for hours longer than he had intended to, just praying to God they did not get up to walk around or stretch their legs. Finally, he couldn't stand it any longer and made his date walk out ahead of him. As he passed the Khaledis' table he amicably greeted his friends and hurried out. Busted! Karma will get you, as many philanderers will attest. Whether he suffered wrath at home, I'll never know.

Another top contender for the Olympics of Shame is August Busch IV, descendent of the founder of Anheuser-Busch and known as a marketing genius. He and his entourage used to come in often, always seated at table 12. We would set it up with cheese and crackers, two wine buckets full of Bud Light and Bud, and all kinds of special perks. He is a great looking guy who partied often with friends and beautiful loose women whom he'd bring back to his hotel suite. One time he requested one of the waiters bring him three bottles of spray whipped cream and a roll of cellophane plastic wrap. Wow! That must've been a kinky night. I'd hate to be the maid assigned to that room, but Jens was taking notes. Busch had three of the seven sins all wrapped up in cellophane to go with a cherry on top.

But sometimes it's not the guests, it's the help who screw up and make terribly funny mistakes. Like the time I messed up royally. As I remember it, our waiter Daniel had been serving a table of four well-to-do Texans, all quite happy to be in Beverly Hills and especially in the famous Cricket Room. There was one woman, her husband, and a gay couple in the party.

The woman was a very beautiful, quite classy lady with a gigantic bust hidden beneath a thick turtleneck. I believe this is what Howard Stern calls "Sweater Meat." Mr. P and I would often bring sexy women to each other's attention by enticing one another to either pour water or check in with the table to see if things were as they should be. Quite a childish game actually and perfectly suited for the limited and often juvenile attention span of front-of-house restaurant staff. Well, after this well-to-do family finished their dinner, I spied Mr. P with his back turned to me, having a conversation with Daniel while they were facing the Texans' table. I saw my chance and slipped up behind Mr. P, casually resting my hands on his shoulders and whispered ever so softly into his ear so that Daniel couldn't hear me. "That woman has lovely biiiiiiig breasts!" I said in an exaggerated, lustful tone. Daniel had a straight face, seriously listening to Mr. P. Mr. P did not answer me and the two of them went on with their conversation. I was surprised that Mr. P would ignore me, so I waited a moment for a better opportunity to point out the wonderful sight facing Mr. P. As I waited with my hands still resting comfortably on Mr. P's shoulders, I looked over to my right and there, by the host podium, was none other than the real Mr. P with a questioning look on his face.

Fuck! I instantly withdrew my hands from the imposter's shoulders in horror and quickly scampered away into the back office area. As it turned out, it was the woman's husband himself to whom I had been whispering so lustfully, which explained why there was no real reaction at first. He had been wearing the exact type of suit as Mr. P and looked just like him from behind! I was mortified! In the back office, I tried to catch my breath, waiting on the man to hunt me down and beat the snot out of me. But as I thought about what I had done, I started giggling madly. I tried to hold it in, but after a few moments I fell to the floor, laughing harder than I can remember ever laughing before. My entire chest cramped up from the convulsions. I couldn't even breathe or speak. When I finally got myself together and crept stealthily back to the dining room, my pride firmly back in place, I discovered that the Texans had left and Daniel and Mr. P were waiting to ask me what I had whispered in that stranger's ear. Once I explained, Daniel and Mr. P burst out laughing too. It only took a minute for the story to spread throughout the dining room and kitchen, and for me to become legendary – the entire staff was having a good laugh at my expense. Even some of our regular guests heard the story and I became quite well known for it, which was very embarrassing. Luckily the Texans left the restaurant without mentioning a word about it or ever calling to express insult.

We cherished that tale for at least six months afterwards. My girlfriend and I had a good laugh about it too and that's probably because I told her that Anglo had done it, not me. I have always wondered what went through the Texan's mind. Was he flattered that a waiter admired his wife's breasts? Or did he go home and show his appreciation for them himself? I'll never know, but I hope it was the latter.

Ariella, who was usually under immense pressure, as was her brassiere, forgot to tell the chef that James "Actors Studio" Lipton had called ahead to let us know that he'd be in with Anthony Hopkins and his wife for a late dinner. By the time they arrived, the chef had gone home for the night and only one late-night cook was working. Mr. Lipton had brought a party of eight, planning on having a full meal. Mr. P tried to save face by telling them that everything would be fine. An unsuspecting Lipton, Hopkins, and entourage were told they could order from the dinner menu. I heard the music from *Jaws* in my head; disaster was approaching. There was no way the late-night cook on duty could manage the complicated dishes all by himself. He was used to making burgers, salads and fancy quesadillas, which is the usual late night fare. Eventually, it took so long to get them some food that they walked out, furious. It was truly embarrassing, although we the staff enjoyed eating their forsaken dinners approximately fifteen minutes after they left. The late night chef really didn't do a bad job at all. It was all quite tasty. Impatient wrath had not served them well. Should we have called them to come back? Nah. Greed and gluttony, you say?

We're good at that. Late one evening service had ended and the kitchen had a leftover leg of lamb. After we all finished cutting off pieces and gorging ourselves, Ariella grabbed it like a primeval weapon and started chasing me around the back of the restaurant as if she wanted to club me. Greasy fat and meat were hanging off it; it looked like something prehistoric from *The Flintstones* or maybe *Jurassic Park*. I ran from her, not from fear of being hit, but fear of getting lamb grease all over my uniform. There's that evil vanity again, chasing my ass around the room right along with Ariella.

Just as she rounded the corner into the empty dining room, with her hand high in the air holding this nasty looking meat club, Michael Bolton walked in looking for Mr. P. I remembered him eyeing her and, with a big grin, saying, "Well, that's interesting."

Ariella burst out laughing and dropped the lamb limb into a bus pan, grabbing a cloth napkin to wipe her greasy hands. Her face was flushed from chasing me and her enormous boobs were threatening to make an escape of their own. It was embarrassing as hell, even though we all knew him very well since he liked to close the place down at least once a week. He seated himself in his usual booth and never made any further mention of the "games people play." I think he just got a kick out of it, catching us off-guard and more than a bit informal in the stiff and stuffy dining room. Cool guy.

Another guy who's so cool that he's almost cold, Roger Waters (co-founder of Pink Floyd) had been coming in every night along with some of his band members and their management following their week-long, sold-out performances of *The Wall* that they'd been staging at Staples Center. I had read it was a spectacular show and the kind of intelligent rock that I really like. Unfortunately, my work schedule prevented my attending, although I would have loved to. Waters, who in my opinion looks like a case of "separated at birth" from Richard Gere, is without a doubt, a true musical and lyrical genius filled with the ability to project insightful imagery through his words and music. He invokes the deepest questions in all of us. I would have asked him or his nervous manager, Mr. Twitchy Face, for a ticket but truthfully they were not approachable and quite arrogant. It's the kind of conceited cold shoulder I could never get used to.

Two nights in a row, they managed to convince Mr. P to stay open and feed them after we were closed. Waters' stupid girlfriend sent back her omelet three times and he was pissed that he couldn't get fresh black truffles on his omelet (the chef had locked them up before he'd left that night and the night cook only had canned black truffles). Each night Waters downed multiple glasses of Pinot Grigio as if it were water. Twitchy Face, whom Roger playfully called his father, always ended up footing the bill.

One night over dinner with Twitchy Face and several others, Waters was having an argument with his lead singer Robbie Wyckoff, or Wackoff as Waters called him. They were getting really loud in their heated argument and out came that distinct voice of Waters' that we've heard on so many songs like at the end of "Don't Leave Me Now" – Roger at the top of his lungs. "You don't know what you're talking about you fucking nimwit, you don't know the fucking difference between an M16 and an AK-47 because you're stew-pid!"

That edge in his voice was so recognizable from those desperate wails on *The Wall* album – I half-expected Floyd's huge orchestral sound to crescendo and back him up. While they were busy arguing, I asked the Cricket Room guitar player (the same guy who Rod Stewart had consulted with earlier regarding harmonica playing) if he would play "Wish You Were Here" since he does such a nice job with that one. He was coincidentally facing the other way and had no idea Waters was in the room. A few minutes into the song and our guitarist is singing: "We're just two lost souls swimming in a fish bowl year after year… Running over the same old ground and have we found, the same old fears… Wish you were here." When the song reached its peak, Twitchy Face realized that he'd been hearing one of his client's songs and tapped Waters on his shoulder while he was in the midst of his wrathful yelling match with Robbie.

"They're playing your bloody song, Roger! Roger! They're playing your bloody song!" as if it were a crime punishable by death. Roger stopped for a minute, listened, and stiffened for a few seconds. He then said to Twitchy, "It's okay, it's okay!" *Oh, goodie, no public hanging tonight.*

Once the guitar player finished and found out who was in the room, he wasn't too happy with me for setting that up. Surprisingly, deceit isn't one of those Deadly Sins. No musician likes to sing or play someone else's song in front of them. It can go extremely well, or horribly wrong, and it's a gamble not many musicians want to take.

On their last night in town, Twitchy Face kept asking me if there were any hookers in the room. I replied, "Why don't you order some good bottles of wine so they'll come out of the woodwork?" I felt like saying, "Hey, dumbass, I'm a waiter not a pimp." So he ordered three bottles of crappy cabernet, but the girls still gathered like flies on fruit. Actually, most of them were forty-year-old groupies that they had invited to join them after the show. Later, when Twitchy revealed that the "fucking shows" were over and that he dreaded the next three performances which were to take place in Mexico City, one of the groupies yelled out, "Yay, Viva Mexico! Sangria! Margaritas!" A sinful combo pack of lust, wrath, and pride.

A genius of a different and more eccentric stripe, Quentin Tarantino, sat down at table three, then quickly ordered a Goose and OJ, and then a single barrel Jack rocks with a $130 per ounce serving of caviar. An hour later, the gorgeous Tia Carrere showed up to join him, and had a Hendricks martini up with olives. Quentin had a few more drinks, Tia had a few more drinks, and they talked about possible movie roles for her. Tia and Quentin then had a couple of glasses each of red Bordeaux, and they also shared an eight-ounce $200 Japanese Wagyu steak with fries. Quentin was his usual spastic self, eccentric and genius-like, talking expressively with no end or deadly sin in sight, his arms gesturing in all directions. Her beauty and his strange, rough looks made them a real odd couple. They don't call it Holly-weird for nothing.

Meanwhile, Woody Harrelson walked in with an entourage of

men who all smelled like "medical" marijuana – the whole table reeked of it. They ordered some light food, mostly appetizers, and a few drinks. Suddenly, Woody looked around, saw Tarantino, then got up and walked over to Quentin's table to talk to him. Perhaps he was smugly trying to get a part in anything Quentin might be currently writing or directing. Woody said he was really into playing a cop right then, referring to his role in the poorly rated movie *Rampart*.

The arrogant Tarantino, who was riding high on his horse that night, said, "You should study Michael Chiklis on *The Shield* if you want to know how a cop should act." Woody's face dropped, he looked down, disappointed, then thanked Tarantino for the conversation and went back to his weed-smoking friends. I thought the Tarantino play was rude and hurtful for no good reason. Speaking of conceited...

A few minutes later, a regular guest paid the piano player to play the theme music from *Love Story* for Quentin and Tia. The regular leaned over to Quentin and said, "I asked him to play this for you and your new friend." He probably didn't even recognize her. Quentin laughed and lustfully crammed his tongue down Tia Carrere's throat, like a snake devouring a mouse. She gladly accepted the assault on her tonsils and it really got messy for a while right there for everyone to see. After putting up with that, I hope she got a starring role in his next movie. She sure deserved a reward.

Now for tonight's faux reality news: The lovely Mrs. Lisa Vanderpump, who's about as real a Real Housewife as I am a billionaire, came in with her husband, two older guests, and NBC4 reporter Ron Kovacik. They were sitting in the bar area squeezed into the booth nearest the bar itself, on table twenty-five. Some male jackass who'd had too much to drink at the next table and was visibly intoxicated, started harassing Mrs. Vanderpump loudly enough for everyone to hear:

"I've seen the show! You're wearing a lot more makeup now and your eyes are even darker and sexier than they are on TV! What are you doing sitting with old people?"

He then proceeded to stand up and approach the table, still ranting, when Mr. Kovacik, the reporter, stood up and said, menacingly, "Stop harassing us."

He was answered with a swift and firm right-hand punch to the face thrown by the drunken idiot. Er, I mean valued guest. Vanderpump's husband Ken with the pretty hair then stood up and was quickly shoved to the floor by the man. Wow – Ms. Vanderpump can still drive a man into a lust-ridden frenzy. It was surreal to watch. Security was on the scene in no time, and Beverly Hills cops, without Eddie Murphy or Judge Reinhold unfortunately, were there in minutes. The man was arrested though no charges were pressed at that time. Later there were several lawsuits filed. Ron Kovacik was left with a split lip, and there was blood splattered on the mirror behind their booth. It looked like a crime scene from *Seven*. He was taken to the Vanderpump home where he got stitched up by Paul Nassif, the plastic surgeon who was married to Adrienne Maloof, another so-called Real Housewife. When you watch Kovacik reporting you can see a visible scar on his upper lip. Poor guy, he really didn't deserve that. Who knew keeping company with a housewife could be so dangerous.

Maybe Kovacik didn't quite say, "I Would Die 4 U" like the artist whose real name is Prince Rogers Nelson, but he certainly took one for the team. Around that time, Prince walked, or rather glided, into the dining room on his own very special day. Formerly known as about twenty different things, including Joey Coco, The Purple One, ♀, Alexander Nevermind, Christopher, Jamie Starr, Prince, Prince Nelson, and The Artist Formerly Known as Prince, he stood no more than a whopping five-six, even in his high-heeled boots. His size, walk, and appearance were distinctly feminine yet weirdly interesting. When he speaks, he's as soft-spoken as the late Michael Jackson. But don't let the voice fool you – his luscious girlfriends are a clear testimonial to his deadly straight sexual preference.

That particular night he was seated in our private dining room with a small entourage to celebrate his birthday. I tried to understand his delicate voice but he ended up having to repeat himself three times before I got his order of Far Niente Cabernet, a Seven-Up and a few fruit and cheese plates. We'd been specifically instructed ahead of time not to stare at him but it's really hard not to. I noticed that his head was very large and ill-fitting on his little body; he may sound like Michael Jackson but he looks like a neo Little Richard. That's not a compliment.

I boldly mentioned to him that I had heard a cut from his then-new album, *Lotus Flower* on the radio. He was startled and immediately asked me where I'd heard it. I said, "KCRW," (a local NPR station) and when I described the song as his cover version of "Crimson and Clover" he seemed relieved. I guess back then he had only allowed that album preview to be played on "Jonesy's Jukebox," hosted by the Sex Pistols' Steve Jones. It's all very complicated, I'm sure, and unless you're a real music fan you wouldn't give a shit. I love that stuff though.

I saw him perform several times at Glam Slam, a nightclub he owned in downtown Los Angeles. I would get a call from my friend who bartended there. "There's going to be an all-nighter here with Prince, do you want me to put you on the list?"

"Ahh, hell yeah!"

The show was awesome and you had to envy anyone who was part of it. First, Carmen Electra would come on stage and perform her Saturday night dance revue with several undulating dancers, and then Prince would start up around 1:00 am and go for however long he felt like it. He usually lasted at least two to three hours. He played his guitar with just his left hand, tapping the strings on the guitar neck, and simultaneously harmonizing on the keyboard with his right hand. I knew he was good but discovered he was truly a performing genius. One night, the crowd was so small and intimate that drummer Michael Bland handed me his drumsticks at the end of one of their rehearsal shows for the *Love Symbol* tour.

Back in the private dining room, Daniel proudly brought in a birthday cake with candles on it. We, the staff, gathered to sing Happy Birthday. The man formerly known as a sign looked angry and disturbed. In his ultra-soft voice he exclaimed, "In my religion, the candle represents the Eternal Flame, why would I want to blow out the Eternal Flame?" He seemed genuinely perplexed and I also worried whether, if he did bend over to blow out the candles, his large head would tip him over face-first into the cake.

Daniel's heart sank and we all felt terrible. Why didn't we know this? Who forgot to tell us? Maybe some exec who took the call from his assistant and hated Prince's music was, at that moment, sitting on his sofa snickering away. We removed the cake and candles, and Patzo fixed it up a bit, smoothing the icing. We returned the now non-offending cake, apologizing. I think the guy's a vegan and probably doesn't even eat cake, but he cut the first slice for his guests, which was a gracious gesture.

The celebrity sinning showdown continued as Johnny "Jackass" Knoxville sat at table twelve near the piano, accompanied by a loud and silly entourage, while our most awesome pianist was entertaining the room. Since it's Johnny's "brand," maybe he feels obligated to act stupid at all times. That must be a burden.

In contrast, Brad Pitt had just finished up a dinner meeting with a *Moneyball* producer and stood up to shake hands and say goodbye to him. Star-struck guests walking by were trying to get a photo of him by pretending to photograph themselves with him in the background, even though all they got is the back of his head because he was facing the window. Brad ignored them and sat down again, this time to join the rowdy Knoxville party. They all laughed and clowned around for a while; Pitt really seemed to relax and enjoy himself but he didn't stay long. A little jackass apparently goes a long way.

Knoxville, in true jackass form, decided he would pull a seriously inappropriate joke on one of his friends. He coyly and discreetly reached under the table while holding court. He flicked his lighter awake and held it to his friend's pant leg. Once it caught fire, he put the lighter back into his pocket. In less than ten seconds, the flame is crawling up his friend's pant leg. The friend started screaming out in pain and Knoxville handed him cocktail napkins to put out the fire but that only made it worse, giving the fire more fuel. Now there was smoke rising – this could have gotten seriously bad, especially if it spread to the table skirt or drapery.

Álvaro, the old waiter, reacted out of instinct, grabbing a chair cover from one of the banquet chairs and urgently diving under the table, wrapping and smothering the fire on the man's pant leg. The poor guy, panicking by now, screamed out in pain again. The entire Knoxville party was in tears of laughter as the restaurant filled with smoke and the smell of burned hair and skin. Hilarious. There should be an 8th deadly sin: stupidity.

The staff dressed the man's burns with ice and Neosporin. His injuries weren't terrible and I'm sure he got Johnny back at another time; that's what they do for a living – pranking. Lucky for Pitt he'd left right before this childish and potentially dangerous trick. In fact, we were all lucky the entire dining room didn't burst into flames, sprinklers coming on, and people being trampled. I'm always up for a good prank, but this was just dumb. I couldn't help but wonder what Frank Sinatra or other classy entertainers of old would have thought. Sinatra probably would have had one of his guys shoot Knoxville and then ordered another drink.

One quiet evening Daniel asked me if I would take over one of his tables, which was a party of three plus one child. Daniel forgot to mention who it was – he only said, "They've been sitting there forever and they won't acknowledge me."

So I approached the table with a certain assertive attitude

thinking *I 'm going to make these fucking people order right now.* I walked up, cleared my throat very loudly, and firmly announced, "Excuse me."

Tom Cruise turned around to face me and boy, did I soften right up. I couldn't tell it was him from behind. At his table were a male guest, his then-wife Katie, and their little daughter Suri. They had seemed to be a regular family out for dinner, maybe tourists. Oops.

"Good evening, sir, madam, my name is Pauli. We'd like to welcome you back to the Cricket Room. Is there anything I can get for you at the moment? Beverages, perhaps?"

Thanks, Daniel, I almost made a perfect fool of myself, not something my pride is fond of doing. They proceeded to order, however, and I have to say that there were signs of trouble in the relationship already back in those days. When Tom picked up baby Suri by one limb and handed her to Katie like a ragdoll, Katie exclaimed, "That's no way to handle a child, Tom!" Her face flushed with anger and maternal protectiveness.

"She's fine, don't worry!" he said with a smile. Suri didn't seem to mind but to an outsider it didn't look, shall we say, normal. He was manhandling the kid like a sack of potatoes for no obvious reason, as though it were important to show his manhood. That spells little-guy insecurity to me.

Simultaneously, two tables over, I was serving Bruce Willis with his new wife, Emma, and to my surprise Demi and Ashton had joined them for the evening. But they were all so quiet and reserved I found that Cruise was much more exciting to watch. Cruise was gesturing passionately in his trademark couch-jumping style, jerking his head and hands around with his hair bouncing in perfect rhythm. He said to his guests, "When I go see a movie I want to be entertained! Not depressed!" *Like a movie such as "Minority Report" isn't depressing? I beg to differ, Tom.* In spite of being handsome, he looks for all the world like the former seminary student he was, or maybe a prep school rich kid, with a "III" or "IV" after his name (which he has).

My thoughts at that very moment were: *Not everybody is entertained by the same things you are, Tom, that's why there are different kinds of films... As a matter of fact I hate half of all the films you make, for the very reason that all they do is entertain then leave me feeling empty afterwards.*

Later on, it was odd when he got up and walked over to Demi's and Bruce's table – I watched the clashing of the titans before me. Tom with his ultra-clear-look-you-in-the-eye stare and very intentional conversation, weighing up against Willis's smug, crooked, introverted smile. It was an odd moment for everyone, I believe. I didn't get the feeling that Willis liked Cruise or thought about him very much at all, while Cruise strove mightily to always leave a powerful impression. These two giants of the movie industry collided awkwardly: Willis' self-confident swagger vs. Cruise's insecure macho bravado.

After Cruise went back to his table, probably expecting applause, Willis asked me for the check. I handed it to him and he gave me back the folder asking for a pen. I said, "May I have your credit card first, sir?"

"I gave it to you earlier," he said.

"No, sir, I'm afraid I did not get it."

Demi and Ashton appeared to be getting a little uncomfortable and Demi started to open her purse like she was used to this. Bruce stopped her, dug out his wallet, rummaged through it, and came up empty handed. He looked at me as if to say *See? I told you I gave it to you.* As I stood there, watching this very awkward situation unfold, it was starting to measure up to the discomfort level of the time when Lisa Kudrow's platinum card was denied and I had to ask her for another one.

At that time I tried to be discreet by saying, "Ms. Kudrow, do you have another card?" But she didn't catch on, and asked in true Phoebe style,

"Why? What's wrong with that one?"

"It was declined," I said painfully.

At that point, she immediately gave me another card without another word. But here I was watching Willis squirm and finally he reached into his shirt pocket and pulled out his wayward Platinum card, then handed it to me like it was my fault. *Fuck me,* I thought, *why didn't I think to reach into his pocket and pull out the card? Was he waiting for someone else to toss down a card to pay the check?* I'll never know, but I did notice that Kutcher never made a move to pay, he just looked kind of confused and like, "Wow dude, where's my car?"

My attitude: "Sorry, man, I don't care if you're President of the United States, I have got to get fucking paid, that's the bottom line." I guess he'd put the card in his front pocket for easy access so that when the check arrived he wouldn't have to look through his wallet. He left me a good tip and I served him several more times after that, never with a problem. As a matter of fact he returned a month later with Emma for a prime NY steak and a bottle of Jonata Syrah for which we shamelessly charged $450 without flinching. Fuck it, it's the Cricket Room! We got license to charge.

When I came in to work the next night, I had no idea that somewhere in the cosmos it must have been declared vomit night at the Cricket Room. Just as things were going great, an eight-year-old girl got up from her table in the main dining room and projectile-vomited all over the carpet like Linda Blair in "The Exorcist." It was seriously smelly and disgusting, and there was a lot of it. Many guests had to be moved and some were comped because they lost their appetites. Poor Juan had to clean it up alone. Where the fuck was Anglo when this shit happened? He's never had to clean up any poop or vomit. With timing like that he should be a stock market investor.

Later that same evening, the young Princess Al Saud from the royal family of Saudi Arabia came in with her servants and they were all seated in the garden. She ordered hot tea and biscuits. By biscuits, she meant dry cookie-like pastries you'd find in Great Britain. Thirty minutes later she stood up to walk to the bathroom but she didn't make it. She walked right into the garden podium and puked her guts out on the immaculate patio tiles. She finally got herself together and wiped her mouth, then walked out fairly composed with her bodyguards at her side, trying mightily to maintain a princess like, haughty demeanor. They escorted her to the lobby bathroom.

Meanwhile on the patio floor she'd left huge pile of puke behind her – it looked like a heap of cow manure. Mr. P. gallantly helped poor Juan clean all that crap up again. Believe me, royal puke is no better than peasant puke. In fact, it may be worse. We were shocked when she returned an hour later gluttonously asking to order some dinner. I served her but kept a wide margin, wishing for an umbrella by my side just in case. Luckily, she kept it down as far as we knew. I was thinking heroin use, and Ariella was thinking pregnant with quintuplets. I knew from the tabloids that she wasn't married so some dude might be facing serious Saudi justice.

Whatever the cause, Juan told me he didn't eat for three solid days after that puke fest, which should've done him good, but all that happened was that his legs got even skinnier and his belly stayed the same.

Another great evening started with Leo DiCaprio and his then-girlfriend du jour, model Bar Rafaeli. They drank tap water and he had an Arnold Palmer, which is lemonade and iced tea. He had an ounce of Ossetra caviar and our Monday herbed pan-fried chicken special. Bar had a tortilla soup and our famous chopped salad. Geez, if her parents had been hard up to find a name for their baby girl, maybe they should have consulted Prince. He's good at coming up with them.

Anyway, Leo was yelling at her to shut the fuck up and she was crying through most of their dinner. They both decided to take their entrees to go. He was ignoring her for most of the time, just constantly texting on his phone. He'd been in before and generally does not seem to have a good time with his dates. I think it just takes a lot to interest him; maybe they bore him. If you are going to talk, it better be interesting or just shut the fuck up. For instance, when he was dining with Amanda Seyfried, she was telling him that she had just gotten back from NYC and how much she liked it there and how badly she wanted to go back. She was very excited about it. His reply was, "Oh, you're going through that phase, huh?" To be as brilliant an actor as he is — my favorite role was the mentally handicapped boy in *Gilbert Grape* — his mind must race and he's reluctant to slow down for dates to catch up. That's just my guess. He could just be an asshole.

All these stories aside, and in spite of a continuous parade of the seven deadly sins, plus all the laughs we've had, the bulk of the experience was slowly fading into a grey abyss of sameness and servitude. I was beginning to feel that I should be doing something more valuable with my life. I didn't want my picture to end up hanging in the Cricket Room Hall of Shame with the plaque reading:

Paul Hartford
He coulda been a contender.

Chapter 16
Under the Tuscan Sun

My personal life unexpectedly screeched into a one-eighty within a few months. Jens had moved in with a new girl crazy enough to take him in, and right around that same time I got engaged to Juliana. She and I realized pretty quickly that we belonged together, and I popped a rock on her finger on a rainy night in a quaint, romantic restaurant in Topanga Canyon. I had intended to do it on a hike in Malibu Creek State Park where we had enjoyed so many beautiful walks and long talks. Juliana would have loved that since she always talked about the time we found ourselves in the middle of a field of daisies and laid down on our backs to watch the sunset together. But, as the date approached, heavy rain was forecast and hiking in the rain is no fun . The cozy little restaurant I chose had a lot of meaning for us, as we often stopped in for candlelit dinners after our walks. It all worked out pretty well, though the damn ring box kept getting stuck in my inside blazer pocket and I nearly ripped the blazer apart trying to get it out. Luckily she said yes.

You can probably guess that Juliana wasn't too fond of Jens, especially after the night when she had to pick us up at two a.m. after a long day of partying that started on Venice Beach and ended up at the Geisha House in Hollywood. Neither Jens nor I could remember where we had parked our cars. I think I realized then (or the next morning) that Jens was not going to be very good for my relationship with Juliana and I had better make a choice. So I left her. Just kidding. Jens became part of my frivolous past and I had found my reason to focus on the future. Juliana "got" me, we had more fun together than I remembered ever having with anyone, and for the first time, I felt my partner was also my best friend. That became a fantastic basis for an awesome relationship. So in restaurant lingo, I had 86'd Jens and Juliana was the new house special.

Jump to the following spring: the featured cinematic event was set in Florence, Italy; the night air was still crisp after a beautiful 70-degree day. Juliana and I were there to bond our souls in matrimonial bliss, and where better to do that than the country of our ancestors' origins. As I gazed into the ancient Arno River, I suddenly felt grateful for my job in a way that I never had before.

We were living a dream come true for both of us and my heart was beating double-time every day. But in all honesty, sometimes I wasn't sure if my palpitations were from adrenaline or from anxiety about how much money we were spending. As we strolled along the medieval streets, Juliana calmed me down, speaking in reassuring tones and reminding me that it's our experiences in life and not possessions that matter. I knew she was right; she always is. And I'm grateful that my lucrative job at the Cricket Room has allowed us to afford this experience. *Thank you, big spenders!*

The next morning, we had to sign our Nulla Osta, a civil document that all foreigners must sign at least three days prior to marrying in Italy. The rainy morning traffic was thick, and our cab driver swerved onto side streets to try to save time, but pedestrians were dashing across the street in all directions, zigzagging between vehicles, trying to dodge the rain. From the back seat, it looked like a video game of Dodge the Taxi. Bicyclists and people on scooters were draped in plastic bags or raincoats; chaos reigned, but that's normal in Florence, rain or shine.

Nadia, our wedding coordinator from San Marino, showed up to meet us at the U.S. Consulate a little late, in genuine Italian style, but with enough time to keep our appointment. Thanks to Nadia, we were guided competently along every step that we needed to take in this adventure. No one can create quirky, tangled, complex, incomprehensible laws and regulations like the mercurial Italians. It's a national sport and you better have a good coach. Nadia got us in quickly, we got our papers signed and stamped, and we were back on the street in less than an hour. It should actually have taken five minutes, but anytime you can get something done in Italy in an hour, you are fortunate indeed.

Nadia struggled with her English but managed to ask if we wanted a ride home; she had instructed her driver to wait at the curb. The Tuscan sun had broken through the clouds and Juliana and I looked at each other, smiling, and told Nadia that we'd prefer to walk around the city a bit and get some lunch. She shook our hands and reminded us about our meeting the next day for our Atto Nottorio, which is a sworn statement that we are each free to marry. We all nodded our heads in understanding just like Chinese tourists do in the U.S., then went our own ways, hoping but not entirely sure that any of us really got it right.

Nadia jumped into the taxi and we walked away, along the Arno, the pulsing backbone of this city, ready at any time with our umbrellas. The road led us to Via Nazionale, a central thoroughfare, and we stopped in at *Rosso Pomodoro* (red tomato) for pizza and beer. We drank *Nastro Azzurro* (blue ribbon) beer and shared a mushroom pizza. The mushrooms were pale but had the rich, bright, nutty taste of chanterelles. They certainly didn't taste like the bland mushrooms from home. It was our first full day and first time in Florence so we reveled in watching the people, listening to but not quite understanding their animated conversations, and viewing the sights. It was like Fellini's *Roma*, a barely functioning but beautiful city; chaos was everywhere. It amazed me that anything got done, but somehow it does, and has for many hundreds of years longer than anything in America. To fully appreciate Italy, you have to really let go of the concept of time, and just "be."

It was two o'clock, long past American lunchtime, but hordes of Italians were on their lunch breaks, smoking cigarettes, conducting loud discussions, and gesturing wildly over their espressos. It amused us to watch, as everyone sounded so agitated and expressive when all they were really doing was having an everyday conversation. I loved it; we both got a kick out of their passion, and even though we had both studied Italian before this trip, they spoke so quickly that we usually had a hard time figuring out what they were discussing.

Right across the street outside the Central Market there were two very precise rows of tiny parked cars and a third long row of scooters, bicycles and motorcycles tightly stacked side by side. After lunch, as we got up to pay the bill, some guy on a scooter with a three-quarter helmet, sunglasses, and a cigarette hangin' out the side of his mouth was cut off by a miniature car the size of Shaq's sneaker. Make that Shaq's sneaker when he was twelve. We heard awful crunching sounds that could have been bones breaking as his helmet flew off and he rolled across the uneven cobblestones like a rag doll.

At that very moment a large city bus rounded the corner, and I feared that both of them – the car and the scooter rider – would be crushed. I instinctively jumped out into the street, waving frantically, until the bus driver saw me and came to a brake-grinding stop. When I turned around, the cool scooter dude was getting back up and began yelling at the driver of the sneaker car. One of the blue, mirrored lenses was missing from his sunglasses, and he limped toward his helmet in his fashionably-worn Diesel jeans, which were now authentically distressed. Everybody was now honking and screaming, gesticulating wildly. I ran over to help the Italian scooter dude, picked up his scooter, and in heartfelt gratitude for my saving his life, he yelled at me to back off. Amazingly, he yelled at me in English, when I'd been told all my life I look like an Italian Guido. Well, fuck, another myth shot to hell.

Meanwhile, Signore Millegrazie was also yelling at the driver who he thought had caused the accident. I threw my hands up in the air – what else would an Italian do? I backed off, grabbing Juliana by the arm. "Let's split."

We walked off quickly before things got any more melodramatic. The bus driver had also gotten into the melee, and was screaming at both of them and looking around for the *idioto* who had waved him down.

"I guess we come from a long line of hotheads, huh?" I asked. "Did you leave a tip?"

"No," she replied. "Why? I heard you only leave 3% if you're at a full service restaurant. This was a walk-up counter."

"That's right," I said, remembering what I had learned on previous trips. "No wonder Italian tourists are always stiffing me at work. Fuckers don't know how to tip for shit."

"Forget about work now, honey, we are here to enjoy and relax. If you can resist being Superman for five minutes, that is." She kissed me sweetly on the cheek.

"I was just trying to help that guy on the scooter for God's sake, it's not like I was trying to steal his bike or nothin'. Ungrateful little shit. I shoulda let the bus hit him."

Juliana just laughed, "Calm down! You did a good deed. He's just too mad to see it right now."

We carried on up the street toward the Accademia Museum where we stood in line for two hours before we were able to enter. Somehow staring at Michelangelo's amazing sixteen-foot statue of David made it all worthwhile. To be so close to such an incredible sculpture was thrilling – he almost seemed alive. I felt like I could see the twenty-six-year-old Michelangelo at work, coaxing this Adonis pulsing with life from cold, indifferent stone. We really felt we had entered another dimension at this point. The Accademia houses many famous masterpieces. One of my favorite sculptures at the Accademia was Michelangelo's unfinished "The Young Slave," in a contorted pose and still taking shape as he struggled to free himself from the raw stone. Michelangelo had intended it for the tomb of Pope Julius II.

Another of my favorites was "The Tree Of Life," painted by Pacino di Buonaguida. This complex composition features Jesus painted in the cross position as the trunk and foundation of the tree while each of the forty-seven circles on the tree limbs represents a leaf encapsulating its own related allegory. Upon close examination, some peculiar stories are revealed, like at the top where a pelican is piercing its own breast in order to feed its young with its own blood, or Judas' soul being pulled out of his body by a dark demon. Seeing these works of art awakened something within me – perhaps my Italian heritage – and a newfound passion and appreciation began to warm my soul. This became an added dimension to a trip that would change my life in ways I had not even envisioned.

For the next three days, we met up with Nadia numerous times, to get our Atto Notorio from the Italian consulate and then a sworn declaration from the Town Hall of Fiesole, the village in which we were to be married. Meanwhile, we managed to squeeze in tours of Uffizi Gallery (which houses works of art by great Italian artists like Botticelli, Leonardo da Vinci, Raffaello, and of course Michelangelo), and the Duomo de Santa Maria, the cathedral that dominates the skyline of Florence; it was designed by Arnolfo di Cambio at the end of the 13th century.

By the fourth day most of our fifty guests had arrived and we had a huge cocktail party hosted by my mother at a place called Negroni Bar on Via Dei Renai. The drinks were so strong everyone got plastered, and there were nothing but idiotic smiles everywhere. It was great seeing all my European friends who I had grown up with, as well as my many cousins and of course my brothers and sister and beautiful niece. We all wobbled home to our hotels laughing as we split up and said goodnight. Smiling, chattering, singing, and gesticulating, we blended right into the Florentine landscape.

The next day, the day of our wedding, I was so nervous I thought I would die. My heart was pounding so loud I thought everyone could hear it. My skin felt prickly, my palms were sweaty, and I probably looked like I was high. Nadia and her crew picked us up in separate cars after my fiancée had been primped and made up. We arrived in the small *paese* (town) of Fiesole around two o'clock and passed right through the center of town five seconds later. We wound our way up serpentine roads passing huge, medieval estates with rolling vineyards, finally reaching the top of the hill.

The car stopped and I couldn't believe my eyes. I was to be married in a twelve-hundred-year-old castle – a *castle* for God's sake – complete with parapets, towers and vines growing up the side of it. Surrounded by immaculately landscaped estates, the castle commanded a stunning view overlooking all the hills of Florence. In the distance I could see the curved red Duomo we had just visited. Once again, I had the feeling of being transported back in time as we approached this imposing ancient building. It had been raining off and on but the sun was finally shining, bathing the grounds in warm golden tones. In true medieval fashion, large torches dotted the gardens and musical fountains serenaded us. It was the perfect blending of old and new, as we prepared to make our vows, begin life anew together, and build upon the ancient foundations of our heritage.

Our guests were picked up at their hotels by two busses that we had leased, and dropped off at the castle at four-thirty for our five o'clock ceremony. Not unexpectedly, none of my co-workers were able to make it since they all had to WORK. Upon our guests' arrival, cocktails were served to loosen them up in the intriguing Armaments Room of the castle, lined with antique tools of battle. Not a foreshadowing of my impending marriage, I hoped. Ironically I was the one who really needed a drink but since my best man/older brother is a recovering alcoholic, he wasn't thinking of bringing me that double Grey Goose vodka on the rocks I so needed. Where was good old enabling Jens when I needed him? Probably engaging in some sort of debauchery in a hidden corner of the restaurant back home. A fleeting thought of – make that a longing for – my old life and its freedoms nearly caused me to run screaming for the hills of Florence, but good sense prevailed. This was my future and the past had no place in my thoughts.

A string quartet welcomed everyone into the Chapel Room and as soon as they were all seated, Nadia motioned for me to approach the altar. Later on, watching the video of the event, I could see I did so with a subtle Guido-ish gait. I greeted the priest and then turned around and glanced at all the smiling, expectant faces that I hold so dear, all whispering to each other and waiting in silent affirmation. Inwardly I knew they were all cheering for me – "There's hope for Pauli! Who knew?"

In the front row there was a framed picture of my late father and next to him was a photo of Juliana's late parents in a beautiful pewter frame. Pachelbel's Canon started playing and that was my cue that my lovely bride was about to enter the chapel. Instead of staying turned around to watch her approach, I nervously faced the priest until she was standing right next to me. I really had no idea how to behave – I felt like laughing, I felt like crying, I felt like eating, and I definitely felt like drinking. Can you tell? I was a mess.

She looked beautiful beside me and my heart swelled with love for her as we stood in front of the small bespectacled priest who was chattering through his scriptures in broken English. Through it all, I couldn't help but notice how the priest's breath reeked of cigarettes and espresso. Finally, it was my turn to say my vows and I was still a mess: laugh-crying through the whole thing. As we turned around to walk out of the chapel and face our friends and family as a couple, now legally wed in the eyes of the law and of God, the string quartet burst into a request I had secretly made earlier.

The cello led the way, pumping out two bars of steady eight notes then the rest of the violas broke into a string arrangement of "Starlight" by Muse. It couldn't have been more perfect if we had been married in Heaven, and as a matter of fact it felt like sheer Heaven up there on the mountain, my wife's hand in mine, the music filling the chapel and my heart, and I can still feel it all when I close my eyes today.

The Francia Corta bottles were popping at regular intervals at the bar and once again, the sun broke through the persistent clouds, lighting up the rolling hills in the distance as if they were Michelangelo's own magically painted backdrop. The golden lighting was perfect for our photo session, and we watched as the late-setting Tuscan sun gilded the entire city of Florence. No Hollywood producer could have created a more perfect setting. I once heard that God has a particular affinity for sinners, and that day I could totally buy it.

I finally did get my double Grey Goose vodka as our guests were offered some amazing appetizers by haughty white-gloved waiters. There were: salted almonds with parmesan flakes; hot truffled dumplings; brioche with warm veal paté and rosemary; polenta cake with red onion and gorgonzola; hot toasted bread with wild boar ragù and tiny Tuscan mushrooms; whole meal bread with bull salami and smoked scamorza cheese; tomato, avocado, shrimp or fresh basil mousse on toasted bread. Incredibly, we also served some fried delicacies that included parmigiano with sweet cinnamon; pecorino fritters; calamari fritti; and crispy battered squash blossoms. I could see the appreciation on our guests' faces as they bit into the appetizers with delight. Not for the first time, I was grateful for my intense training and experience in the legendary Cricket Room, where I had learned the fine art of food, beverages, and service. Along with my bride's innate good taste, it made for a great menu that all of our guests would remember for years to come.

While we mingled about the garden with our guests, it was great to hear how touched everyone had been by the ceremony and the magical setting. After about an hour and lots of photo-taking, Nadia summoned us to a sit-down meal with wine parings of white and red Tuscan IGT wines (a local high-quality designation) followed by many ooohs and aaahs as our guests savored the luscious foods. I have to say that it was a superb culinary showcase and certainly the most delicious meal I'd ever had in Italy – and that says a lot because the food in Italy is tremendous. In my opinion, it is more earthy, honest, and simplistic than in France, for example, and therefore better. Italians have a way of taking the simplest of ingredients and raising them to the level of art. The main menu included these four courses:

Fresh pasta gemelli w/guanciale, broccoletti & Tuscan pecorino (shocking that we had pasta, I know!)

Risotto with "morellini" artichokes

Gilt-head bream flambé with Armagnac, dusted with thyme and coriander, and vegetable ratatouille

Chianina beefsteak, flan of aubergines with truffle heart, and potato crisps

For dessert the chef prepared a traditional *Millefiori* (a thousand flowers) cake as we watched, layered with a pastry crème so good that Thomas Keller only wishes he could serve it at his famous Napa restaurant, French Laundry. As every great chef knows, the secret to the flavor of all food is largely in the origin of the produce and the quality of ingredients used. Italy takes great pride in utilizing mostly local dairy and produce and when you travel there, you can taste the vast difference in eating garden-fresh produce, handmade cheese, and so forth, as opposed to products designed for long shelf life.

While we all danced the night away, a chef stood by busily preparing fresh crepes filled with hazelnut cream, or fresh fruit with whipped cream or melted chocolate. The bartender stayed quite busy as well, as my childhood friends from Denmark really know how to enjoy a party. It was such a small gathering that everyone had the chance to feel part of the celebration, which was intentional on our part. Finally at around one-thirty, all the happy drunken and sated guests were rounded up and bussed back to their hotels. There was singing and joke-telling on the busses, and I have a feeling my wife and I were not the only ones with everlasting memories of that evening.

The next day we all met again as my new bride and I hosted a brunch at a Florentine restaurant, Hostaria Del Bricco. There were fifty of us, most of us a little hung over, and we indulged again in a superb multi-course brunch that was home-cooked by the owner's mother. Hostaria Del Bricco had a very warm, rustic medieval vibe and the dishes were especially good after a late night of revelry. Served with red table wine in a clay carafe were:

Crostini misti: warm bread with various toppings of onions, peppers, liver, eggplant, mushrooms

Panzanella: salad with home-baked Tuscan bread, tomato, cucumber, onion, basil

Ribollita: vegetable soup (they're famous for this fabulous rustic soup)

Farfalle al fattore: bowtie pasta with artichokes and ricotta

Maialino in porchetta: oven-roasted suckling pig with peas and fava beans

Cantucci col Vin Santo (dessert): special biscotti to dip in Tuscan dessert wine

After many hours of laughter, revelry and countless photographs, we bid our guests a sentimental farewell with plenty of Italian hugs and kisses.

The next day Juliana and I took the train to Venice, which felt like it was a scene straight out of a 1940's European film. No trip to Italy is complete without a visit to Venice; I fear the city will disappear one day beneath the water as it encroaches daily on the buildings' foundations.

We ordered lunch in the dining car (can you tell I'm kind of obsessed with Italian food?), and the spaghetti marinara was better than anything I've tasted in the finest American restaurants. As we watched the green rolling hills speed by, we enjoyed a bottle of Masi Corvina blend and freshly baked bread along with side dishes of sautéed string beans and mushrooms. Our Italian waiter was a pervert with his eyes fixated on my wife but I decided to take it as a compliment.

We stayed in a quaint hotel for three nights in Venice and joined a fascinating tour that outlined the history and geography of the city. We learned about the cisterns that each island keeps to catch rainwater and how St. Mark's piazza floods every year. The tour guide showed us how most buildings have metal ramps at their entrances that can be folded up to keep the water out. That relieved some of my anxiety, but I know I'm not alone in my concern for the longevity of Venice. It's incredible to me that those ancient buildings can stand in water for eons and not crumble.

I had long forgotten about the Cricket Room as Juliana and I toured the city, beaming with huge, silly smiles on our faces. I was happier than ever before, spending my honeymoon with the love of my life in my ancestors' homeland. Was it too good to be true? Was I perhaps in the midst of *Pauli's Magical Adventure* and at any moment I could wake up and find out I'd been tricked by a dream? Juliana's sweet kisses answered that question pretty quickly.

We took the train to Rome where we had rented a one-bedroom luxury apartment opposite the Vatican. We preferred an apartment to a hotel for our four-night stay as we could shop for groceries and cook our own breakfasts, and not be seen by any human eyes until we felt like it. This was also a great way to get a feel for the lifestyle in Rome and really immerse ourselves in the culture. Best of all was our tour guide who took us back in time as he led us through a most memorable exploration of the Coliseum, Palatine Hill, and the Forum. This man had a gift of historical storytelling that would make even Gore Vidal jealous. I swear I could see the ancient Romans milling about the marketplace or the age-old streets of Palatine Hill. He brought it all to life right before our eyes. The Romans built a tremendous amount of infrastructure, like roads and small footbridges that are still in use today. I can't imagine much of what's being built today lasting as long as the Roman Empire's creations.

Our fifth day in Rome came much too quickly, and we took another train to a small town in the legendary Cinque Terre (the Five Lands). These tiny, jewel-toned, terraced towns, snuggled along the cliffs of the Ligurian Coast since Roman times, are connected by spectacular walking paths that wind through thick forest and precarious rocky outcroppings. We didn't realize just how small these towns are until we got there and stepped off the train in Corniglia. Tiny and picturesque; everything seemed doll-sized to we Americans accustomed to wide streets and large buildings.

The road up the hill to Corniglia from the train station was very steep and the ancient stone stairs were impossible with our luggage as they went on for several hundred feet. Corniglia is the only town in the Cinque Terre that is not at sea level; instead it is perched on a cliff at 330 feet elevation and parts of it reach even higher as we would find out later.

We took a taxi up the hill, which was less than a five-minute ride but a necessary one nonetheless. We had been unable to connect with the person who had rented me the apartment in which we were to live for seven nights, and I was getting quite worried. In the taxi I finally received a mysterious text from someone whom I could only suspect was the apartment manager. It instructed me to go to Bar Matteo, so we got out of the cab at the tiny main piazza because the side streets were not wide enough for automobiles. Since we are typical American travelers, we totally over-packed compared to the hikers who voyage there to rough-it for a week at a time bringing just a backpack. Americans tend to make a competitive sport out of over-packing and conspicuous consumption: *Look at me! I have more shit than you and I brought it all with me!*

We looked like we'd just come off the red carpet at the Grammys and were dropped off in another era. My wife and I really had had no idea what to expect; to say we were over-dressed is an understatement. Our inappropriate shoes alone should have landed us in an Italian jail for dumbasses.

On two benches in the tiny square sat five grizzled elderly women of indeterminate ages, who stopped talking when they saw us and just stared. They all wore colorful scarves on their heads, and their gnarled fingers spoke of ages of hard work. Even a small child who peeked out from behind her mother's skirt stared at us in deafening and mocking silence. I swear, even the birds stopped chirping and dogs stopped barking. Aliens had just invaded their little town and scrutiny by man and beast was required.

Mortified and feeling like a serial killer whose face had been plastered all over town on posters, I left Juliana there in the main town square, which was about the size of two tennis courts, to try to find this Bar Matteo. For all I knew at this point my carefully-made reservation had been handled on the Internet by some random huckster in Nigeria, who was now living it up on my deposit money and laughing his ass off. Juliana sagged against an olive tree with our luggage stacked around her like a protective barrier.

It was my job to handle all the reservations and I could feel the tension building as my dear wife gave me that look that only a woman knows how to give – that "What in the hell is this?" kind of look with her hand on her hip. I knew I'd better fix things quickly or there would for sure be trouble in Paradise. I had no desire to suffer from a lack-of-nookie headache on my freaking honeymoon.

I walked on down the very narrow, hallway-sized Via Fieschi, feeling daggers from Juliana's eyes landing in my back, which was, it turned out, the only street that lead through this small town. Dressed like a rock star and getting WTF looks from mostly everyone, I walked past two restaurants and a very small grocery/convenience store. Then I came to a miniature piazza with some outdoor tables, shaded by an awning that read Caffé Matteo. Bingo! I'm thinking *this must be the place, right?* I mean, how many Bar or Caffé Matteos could there be in this town? So, genius that I am, I walked in and was greeted by a fellow named Riccardo. The place was empty; it was siesta time, and a Sunday too, which explained the quietude. In broken tourist Italian, I tell Riccardo my name and the reason I'm there, expecting him to instantly say: "*Si Paolo, va bene, aspettiamo arrivarti!*" ("Yes, we've been expecting you!") and then start calling the whole family in to say hello, who would all be awed by the well-dressed American. But such was not the case. Of course not. Things had been going way too smoothly.

He had never heard of the apartment I was supposed to stay in and I was really starting to get worried. Riccardo poured me a small glass of Amaro (an herbal digestive liqueur) and brought me an espresso. In Italy, it is a widely held belief that either alcohol or espresso can fix anything, from being robbed to divorce. He told me there were other places to stay in town, and I was guessing he owned one of them. We sat there trying to figure out what may have happened to create this dilemma. I showed him the text on my phone but he still acted clueless. I was trying to figure out how I would explain all this to my now most likely furious future ex-wife. That is, if she hadn't already taken a cab back to Rome, hired a Mafia hit man to kill me, or been kidnapped.

Just as I was about to get up and leave, in walked his wife, Manuela, who asked me something in Italian. I stumbled along trying to explain that we were supposed to pick up keys at their bar for Appartamento Alto which we would be renting for one week. She looked at me and said, "Wait a minuto," then walked over to the register and made a phone call. Five minutes later, one of the old crones from the main square tottered in. Manuela introduced her as Signora Marilena Galletti. Mrs. Galletti, who didn't speak a word of English, was in her sixties and was wearing a white and blue-checkered sleeveless dress with some incarnation of an apron wrapped around her waist. She had the build of a farmer; you could tell she was familiar with hard labor by the outlines of her body. She looked strong as an ox with a brick of an upper body and legs like a rugby player. Nothing Hugh Hefner would be interested in for a centerfold.

Apparently, our mystery had been solved, but another mystery took its place: Why had the woman not recognized us in the square as her renters? No other American tourists had gotten out of a taxi looking lost in the main square right in front of her. She ushered me to follow her, using now familiar Italian hand gestures, which I did, as I thanked Manuela and Riccardo, my two new best friends. We proceeded in the direction of where my poor wife had been waiting for forty minutes with our luggage. Do I need to tell you that she did not look happy? If she had rolled her eyes at me any harder, they would have disappeared into the back of her lovely head. I helped her up and kissed her cheek, hoping she had not called a divorce lawyer.

We pushed and pulled our heavy bags up the elongated cobblestone steps and steep walkways wondering where in the hell this apartment was. It was obvious where Mrs. Galletti had gotten her sturdy build. Once we got to the building, we discovered that the apartment was on the third floor (another minor detail left out of the brochure) and Mrs. Galletti instinctively grabbed one of the heavy bags and walked up the very narrow steep spiraling staircase, carrying it like it was an empty briefcase. We followed slowly behind her with the rest of the bags, grunting and groaning like the lazy-ass Americans I'm sure by now she thought we were.

We were still very skeptical but once she opened the door we couldn't believe our eyes. There were two bedrooms and a full bathroom downstairs, and the master had French doors (or were they Italian doors?) leading out to a small balcony with a tremendous, stupendous, spectacular view over the entire town and the ocean below. Another large window looked out over the sea and to the right of our picturesque view rose a green, terraced and irrigated hillside, an example of the ancient agricultural techniques utilized by the local farmers. It was all so beautiful that I almost forgot that Signora Galletti was standing behind me waiting for payment. I gave her the balance in cash to make up six hundred Euros for the week, and she told us that she'd be by the next day with more towels. She rewarded us with a gap-toothed smile, backed away, and left us alone. I could tell by the look on my bride's face that I was now redeemed. Hope she remembered to cancel the hit man and fire the lawyer.

Once Mrs. Galletti closed the door and we heard her clomping down the stairs, my wife and I pounced on the queen size bed and hugged, we were so happy our hearts just welled over at the spectacular setting we were to live in for the next week. Of course, I wanted my reward for a job well done immediately and Juliana was more than happy to deliver. After reveling in the afterglow, I realized we hadn't even been upstairs yet. I went up to inspect the kitchen and living room, and yelled out in excitement, "Come upstairs quick! You won't believe your eyes!"

The kitchen was nothing special – very tiny by American standards – and the living room was simple with a basic dining table and a window looking onto the ocean, but what blew us away was the rooftop patio. Again, French doors opened up to an outdoor space with a painted wooden table and chairs and, of course, a wrought iron railing to protect toddlers, drunks, and the odd clumsy American tourist. There was an outdoor shower with a proper drain so you could cool off on hot days I supposed. The view was completely unobstructed as we stood in complete awe and amazement. To the left of us on another hillside was the charming town church where the mourning doves were cooing gently. Just beyond that and below us was the small town square where a grocer's truck had pulled up and was selling meats, cheese, and other products hard to come by way up in Corniglia. A few laughing children chased each other around the café chairs set out for hungry passersby, while old men nodded on a bench, their afternoon nap interrupting what I imagined to be their daily visit. Across the piazza we could see the base of the town's narrow main street winding up to the top of the hillside beyond, dotted with ancient houses piled atop one another like pastel jewels. The captivating view spanned the entire town and as I looked more closely, I could see a meandering pathway that lead down to the beautiful Mediterranean Sea.

A few people were sunbathing, stretched out on huge rocks,

and kids were jumping into the water from the edge of the stone pier. It felt like I could possibly see all way the way to Nice in the south of France. As I finally turned slightly to my right, I could also see some of the hiking trails that lead to the other neighboring towns and with a hard right, I saw the impeccably maintained hillside farming terraces. It was almost too much to take in and since I'd never been exposed to anything like this before I felt overwhelmed as I stood at the top of one of the highest residential points in this cliffside town. Juliana had her arm around my waist and was resting her head on my shoulder. Neither of us spoke as we tried to capture the view and the moment in our internal Kodak albums. We wanted to remember it always.

We admired what the local people had done with their tiny cliffside town that was set in stone thousands of years ago, and our senses filled with gratitude at the simplicity and beauty of this brilliant use of terrain. The keepers of the land had done an amazing job of leveraging what they had. No wonder the apartment was called "Appartamento Alto," as it occupied the highest point in this tiny town.

Realizing that my Diesel shirt and tattooed blazer were a bit of overkill for this humble town, I dressed in a pair of cargo shorts, a simple polo shirt, and some thong sandals as we headed down to explore the town a little more closely and buy some basic groceries. I also figured the change of clothes might throw off the lone Mafia gunman who might be lurking nearby with his sights set on me. Juliana had put on a green flowery sundress and sandals and looked spectacular, but then she always does. In fact, I'm not sure why I even worried about what I wore, because when we're together all eyes are on her.

We dined every night within the stone walls of Osteria a Cantina de Mananan, a highly-rated eatery attracting people from all over the world to this tiny hamlet. Their front door was plastered with stickers and ratings from numerous international organizations. Once we finally got in for dinner, we realized quickly that we would need to make a dinner reservation for every night at eight or we didn't stand a chance of getting in. The owners, Livio and Augostino, and Augostino's wife Marianne in the kitchen, became not only our chefs and servers but quickly befriended us and guided us in their own way through our every meal.

Our dinners consisted of only the freshest local sea fare – caught, cooked, and served the same day – and vegetables from

Augostino's own terraced gardens. Livio's style of serving the customers made us feel we were in the home of a generous and caring host, albeit one with certain culinary rules. He would not allow us to order a wine until he knew what we would be eating – the pairing too important to leave to chance. (Slapping his forehead: "Pauli! You canno' order de wine befora you know what to eating!") We grew to love his commitment to the dining experience and enjoyed every bit of advice he dispensed. Most fine restaurants in America would rather sell you the most expensive wine, your choice of menu items be damned. He usually gave us a Vermentino from La Spezia (a larger, neighboring town) or sometimes we craved some red wine so we would order a Rossese di Dolceacqua, a light and refreshing Pinot Noir-like wine from the north of Liguria.

Some of the native dishes we enjoyed while dining with our new friends were: an antipasto of smoked tuna carpaccio with anchovies prepared in three different ways (vinegar & lemon, olive oil & garlic, and fried); a white bean salad with squid and pearl onion; grilled baby artichokes with olive oil and parsley garnish; local salt cod, pan-roasted and served in a light broth with black and green olives, capers, and fresh tomato. Whole grilled Branzino (local Mediterranean sea bass), which Livio filleted for me at the table, was superb. Linguine with their own version of pesto sauce, which is legendary all over the Cinque Terre, was also delicious. We ate cozze marinara (mussels in tomato sauce), and of course their spaghetti frutti di mare (fruits of the sea) with gamberoni (jumbo shrimp) could not be skipped.

Once we had communicated that we were there on our honeymoon, Augostino told us the story of how he had proposed to Marianne under the moonlight on the beautiful shoreline walkway that leads to Manarola, the closest town south of Corniglia. Livio piped in saying that we had to take that romantic walk, and a few minutes later presented us with a bottle of Pergole Basse, a local red wine, for us to take along, with the words scribbled across it: Alla Salute, Augostino, Livio, Mari, Grazie. They asked us if we needed an opener and then Livio broke out some local Grappa and shared it with us along with an espresso and some biscotti that Marianne had made that morning. I was beginning to worry that we'd have to buy a whole new wardrobe soon, if we kept eating like this.

I appreciated the authentic food and joy of serving that made this place so special and memorable. These people truly enjoyed growing, preparing, and serving these wonderful foods; they wanted to see joy on their guests' faces, and like a doting grandparent, they kept piling our plates and every groan or "oooh" and "aaah" enticed them to serve more. They take such simple foods as pasta or olives and elevate them to exquisite heights through love and caring. Instead of covering something with sauce, for example, they let the food speak for itself, let the natural taste shine, enhanced with seasonings and flavors just enough to achieve sublime perfection.

I couldn't help comparing it to the cold and rehearsed manner of service at the Cricket Room, and it made me shudder. There was no natural human interaction with guests, such as I had experienced throughout our Italian adventure. I realized then that I hated corporate restaurant chains. In fact, I hated the whole idea of corporate anything – it just seems like an excuse to buy out the competition and corner a market and then use cheaper products to maximize profits. It's an ugly disease that we should resist at all costs. I was becoming some modern new incarnation of The Forgotten Man; someone who values individuality and uniqueness over mass production and efficiency. This mom-and-pop shop with great, unforced personal service and local food works! In Italy and throughout Europe they truly manage to achieve this personal feel, even in the largest of cities like Paris and Rome. Remember to look for it – it's there.

We also became friendly with Manuela and Riccardo as we ventured into their Bar Matteo several times after dinner to enjoy their homemade gelato and cookies. Manuela told us they would be visiting Los Angeles soon, so I gave her my home phone number in the hope of showing them a good time in our big city.

One day I ventured down to the stone pier by myself, leaving the old ball and chain up there perched on top of the hill in that sweet apartment. Juliana wasn't feeling well; she was catching a cold and wanted to take a nap. I walked down the winding dirt path to the water where I had been taking my Mediterranean swim on an almost daily basis. The water by the pier is lively but has no California-style breaking waves. The churning water creates a confusing illusion: the water is so clear that when you look down it's very hard to judge where to jump in, as it actually looks so shallow you fear you'll hit your head on one of the huge submerged stones. And yet it's quite deep.

A young mother and her small daughter were floating in bathing rings and a couple of hikers who looked like they'd arrived from the north, which would be Vernazza, had the pier to themselves. I knew Vernazza was about a 10-mile hike up and down steep paths –

no wonder they were stripping down to cool off in the sea. A couple of kids in their early teens arrived and were soon running around and playing tag in the water. A thin, white-haired man who seemed to be talking to everybody was swimming and jumped off the pier a few times. I asked him in my less than perfect Italian, "Is it safe here?" as I pointed from the pier to a spot in the water. ·

He responded, "Si, va bene," then dove in to show me where. I dove in after him and when I came up for air he was swimming nearby.

"Grazie," I called out.

He asked, "Tedeschi?" *(Are you German?)*

"No, Americano, ma non parlo l'Italiano bene. Parli l'Inglese?" *(No, I'm American and I don't speak Italian well. Do you speak English?)*

"Yeze," he replied in his thick accent.

His name, I discovered, was Renaldo and we ended up spending the late afternoon fumbling along in my bad Italian and his worse English and striking up a friendly camaraderie.

Renaldo told me that he comes from Corniglia (by the way, the "g" is silent as in "lasagna") and is the only one left in his family who still lives here. He later took me on a tour of his garden, which was just up the hill from the shore. There were several different gardens, not all belonging to him, he explained. He picked some lemons off his tree to give to my wife for her cold and also grabbed a bunch of "timo" as he called it (thyme).

"Is very good put for da fish, with pomodori," he explained.

"Tomato?" I ask.

"Yeze." He also managed to explain that during the summer months, Corniglia has a population of about 3,000 and that's because of tourism, but in the winter there's actually less than 1,000 permanent occupants. When I got back to the apartment, Juliana was worried and a tad angry. What could I possibly have been doing on my own for almost five hours? Had old Pauli returned and gone philandering with some cute young Italian signorina? She laughed (and was relieved, I think) when I explained how Renaldo and I had been talking in our terrible versions of each other's languages for almost three hours. It was incredibly easy to lose track of the time since the summer days there can last well into the evening. I showed her the lemons from his garden: proof of my alibi.

I made Juliana some fresh-squeezed lemonade for her throat and she rallied enough for some great makeup sex. And lest you think that lecherous Pauli forced himself on his poor sick wife, I can assure you that she was living la bella vita (the good life).

We then freshened up and walked down through the piazza to see Augostino and Livio for our standing eight o'clock dinner appointment. It was to be our last night, so we had to bid farewell to all of our local friends: Livio, Augostino, Mari, Manuela, Riccardo and Renaldo. We left the next morning with heavy hearts and an ever-lasting impression of this beautiful seaside town and its welcoming, earthy residents. Though we have traveled a lot, nothing ever came close to the feeling of belonging that I experienced in this little town. And to think it had begun so roughly, feeling lost, worrying about our reservation, and fear of being killed by my angry bride's hit man. All of that melted away in the beautiful Italian hillside town and left only beautiful memories.

We boarded the train and left to spend a week in Nice where we had rented an apartment overlooking the sea and the Promenade des Anglais. During our stay there, we visited the beautiful 2000-year-old village of Èze which had been carved into a rocky mountainside. We took a day trip to Monaco where I had some delicious steak tartare, and Juliana was thrilled to see such a legendary place. We also visited Cannes where I enjoyed a new food combination for me called "Moulles Frites," a traditional dish of local mussels in a white wine broth served with French fries in the same dish.

We immediately noticed a huge difference once we had crossed the Italian border into France: trains ran on time, conductors were sharply dressed and checked your ticket frequently, traffic and pedestrians moved in much more organized patterns. It was obvious that we had entered into a far more socially-organized society, one in which rules were enforced and in return a certain pride of service existed. But I still prefer the Italian way of anything-goes mentality; you just feel like no one really cares and no one is watching you for mistakes. My wife found that a little disturbing at times. Italy is definitely a little closer to a rogue state than France and you have to wonder how it could have been ruled by such a strict fascist dictator as Mussolini.

We continued our honeymoon/culinary journey by taking a scenic train ride from Nice through Marseille and up to Paris. There were no more reservations questions, errors, or confusion; all went quite well. The French countryside was picturesque and every town we passed through was truly a painted canvas of earthy colors alive with everyday country life. After becoming used to the vast sprawling open spaces of the U.S., everything on the European continent seems condensed, almost miniaturized. Roads are narrow, vehicles are small, and landscapes invariably evoke historical significance. The variety of cuisines and food preparation methods was endlessly fascinating and enjoyable.

Soon after arriving at the infamous Gar De Lyon train station, we caught a taxi to Paris's district of Le Maraise where we rented a tiny but comfortable condo on Rue du Bourg Tibourg. We stayed there for another week, exploring all of Paris by foot. My favorite visit was that of an accidental Sunday service in the cathedral of Notre Dame where the choir was singing and the cardinals were waving incense burners. But our visit to Versailles at the royal castle built by Luis XIV in 1682 was unforgettable. We learned a great deal about the lives of the privileged rulers, how they kept psychological sway over their subjects, and how it all fell apart leading up to the French Revolution. Even the paintings of the palace in its heyday depicted it as alone on a hill, which wasn't accurate but set it apart from the mere mortals scrounging about below.

Just as the French and Italian ways of life are very different yet both offer tremendous gifts, so go their unique cuisines. At its best, French food is earthy and satisfying; at its worst it can be pretentious and insubstantial, relying on fancy presentation instead of inspired combinations. Some of our favorite meals, in addition to the Moulles Frites in Cannes, were a peasant-style coq au vin (chicken in red wine sauce) with a thick, dark brown sauce and big chunks of mushrooms, and an earthy ratatouille of fresh regional vegetables. While Juliana would have none of the escargot or patés that I loved, she reveled in the picturesque candy and dessert shops that made her wish she had grown up in France. The ubiquitous *croque monsieur* or *croque madame*, grilled ham and cheese, or grilled ham, egg and cheese sandwiches, respectively, became two of our favorites. Ultimately, we decided that we preferred the lighter, more brightly-flavored coastal Italian foods which made us revel in just being alive.

Once you visit Paris and see all the cultural and historical treasures so mindfully restored and maintained along with the royal grounds and Palace of Versailles, you will finally come to understand why the French are such snobs. Even the brilliant and artful design of Paris itself left us humbled. France's national pride is legendary and well-founded. We were both impressed and inspired by the French way of life. Well, Juliana more than I.

After our visit to Paris, we stopped in London for a two-night visit then flew back to our beloved Los Angeles. Once we arrived, we brought our bags into our apartment, then walked to our favorite little restaurant for a bite to eat. We sat outside and took in the deep blue sky, the fresh ocean air, and a bottle of crisp California Viognier. Though we had just experienced a dream vacation, being home was just great. I felt really refreshed and ready to start the rest of my life with Juliana in the role of my sweet, loving wife.

It was time to make some important decisions about the direction our lives would take.

CHAPTER 17
ONE FLEW OVER THE CUCKOO'S NEST

Juliana and I settled easily into our married life. She worked days, I worked nights and luckily we usually got to enjoy our weekends together. It was the rest of life that kept getting in the way of my "major chord." As De Niro put it in *New York, New York* while he was trying to seduce Liza Minnelli in a cab to Brooklyn, a major chord is when you have the woman you want, the music you want, and enough money to live comfortably. My music was still missing.

Hard to believe, but my ten-year anniversary at the Cricket Room was only six months away. Thinking about it made me reflect on what I had accomplished in that time. I had made great money, enjoyed serving amazing celebrities and other luminaries, and reveled in witnessing – especially in the beginning – some culinary feats of accomplishment. But it was beginning to lose its luster. No, wait. It *had* lost its luster. The sheen had been rubbed off over those ten years, revealing fool's gold. The truly golden days in Italy with my beautiful bride had shown me the value of what's real. And returning to the Cricket Room reminded me of what's not.

Sometimes you start focusing on the strings rather than the marionettes, and suddenly the entire illusion is lost for you. That had been happening for me a lot in recent days. There was an alarm bell clanging in my head that screamed, "Wake up, dumbass. Wake up!" It was getting harder and harder for me to fathom why I kept coming back to work day after day. Money, sure, and you can't minimize the importance of that for survival. But there has to be more, right?

At first, it had been easy to be seduced by the reflected brilliance of our guests. After all, I may have been serving fine food like waiters in any other exclusive restaurant, but I'd been serving it to the most admired and worshiped people on the planet. And I'd been doing it up close and personal, where most "regular" people would never be. Surely there was great value in that, right? Lately, however, that was no longer enough. I was starting to realize that maybe it never was.

Was there something wrong with me? Or is there something wrong with humans in general, because no matter how good we have it, we always want something else? Was my feeling of discontent just a case of "the grass is always greener," or was I just being ungrateful? Did I think I had some greater calling? Was I willing to give up my fantastic pay to take a chance on something else? I had way more questions than answers, and the only thing I was sure of was that I was not happy. I was sputtering, burning out like a flaming comet in its death throes. But my discontent didn't come from lack of appreciation for the customers, or the rigorous schedule that never let me off on holidays. Not even from the idiots they kept hiring because they were cheap. It was the glaring discrepancy between my reverence for the history and lore of the Cricket Room, and the reality of the way corporate management was running it. That gap in values was a serious pain in my psyche and I felt edgy and irritable all the time. I had even become snappish with Juliana, which she didn't deserve. I often felt like a pit bull on a short chain, ready to bite even the hand that fed me.

One day out of desperation, I called out to God for an answer – and by the way, just for the record, I have never followed any particular religion. I believe very deeply in the Lord almighty and I can feel Him (wherever He is and whatever form He takes) trying to reach out to me all the time; I just don't know how to interpret His messages.

I could never understand being associated with any one way of worship 'cause to me they all start to look crazy, controlling, or restricted with ridiculous rules you have to follow. The "do this on this day or you will burn in the fires of hell" is bullshit to me. But I can still feel this burning kind of warm mushy energy in my core and usually it gets stronger when I'm surrounded by the beauty and serenity of nature. Like when I was standing on the stepped terraces of Italy, looking out over the frothy sea. That's pure heaven and you can really feel the spirituality of the universe washing over you in an earthy, natural place like that.

But at this time in my career, it was me reaching out to God and asking Him, "Show me what I'm supposed to be doing, and give me some guidance, Lord!"

Well, as you can probably guess, there was no burning bush or lightning bolt from heaven and I went to work on that night of unrequited prayer basically feeling the same way I had been feeling:

burnt out and mentally exhausted. My ankles had been hurting like mad and that pain was sending another message to my nervous system, demanding that I figure out an alternative way of earning a living. Something I could feel proud of, enjoy, and not feel this constant sense of pressure and dissatisfaction.

Just as I was feeling kind of defeated, I overheard a guest in the dining room talking about Russell Brand and how he was meditating and all these stars were doing it; he mentioned Ellen DeGeneres, Russell Simmons, Sheryl Crow, Laura Dern, Clint Eastwood, Scorsese. The man went on and on about it, describing how the David Lynch Foundation had a gala planned at the Los Angeles County Museum of Art in December to raise money for veterans with post-traumatic stress disorder (PTSD) and for kids in tough, inner-city neighborhoods having trouble staying focused at school. I found it hard to believe that the guy who wrote and directed *Wild at Heart* and *Blue Velvet* was now trying to save the world. I had no idea what meditation could possibly do for celebrities, veterans, children or anyone, but somehow it perked up my ears. Wow, it was difficult to imagine frenetic Russell Brand meditating. I couldn't even envision that guy sitting down for dinner without getting up and dancing on the table. *How the hell do you get Russell Brand to sit still and meditate? Now you've really got me interested.* Could this be a message for me? Was I supposed to overhear this conversation? I made a mental note to look into it.

The night went on and I forgot all about that conversation as I found myself watching Kirk Douglas walk in past the piano player who was pounding out "Let it Be." Kirk sort of slowed down and started conducting the music as though he knew what he was doing and his timing was actually great. He is one of the few remaining silver-haired elder statesmen of Hollywood. When he walks in the room, it's like, "Daddy's home!" Everyone sits up a little straighter.

Kirk took a table in the dining room away from all the noise and joined the great Arthur Cohn who has won several Academy Awards for producing best foreign language films. Kirk, who became a bit hard to understand after his stroke, had really recovered quite remarkably and was in exceptionally high spirits that evening. Mr. Cohn always orders fresh pineapple juice and Kirk joined him in that. Mr. Cohn also talked Douglas into ordering what he was having, and it's always the same thing.

He said, "I'll have my usual steamed whitefish, and bring that for Mr. Douglas too, please." We always served him the same dish, steamed white sea bass with mashed potatoes. I guess after coming there for twenty years he still hadn't figured out that we never carried whitefish, which usually comes from Lake Superior, and always served him local sea bass. Oh well, it's certainly not the food, it's the company and the ambiance that matters at the Cricket Room. We probably could have served him Gorton's frozen grocery store fish and he would not have complained. Especially if we garnished it nicely and charged forty bucks for it.

Hollywood business mogul Kirk Kerkorian was sitting at table one in the bar area with one of his indistinguishable blonde assembly-line sweethearts. They all had conveyor belt lines on their asses, I'm sure. Lately he had stepped it up with Joan Dangerfield, Rodney's widow, but that night he was back with an old standby whose name I don't know. Kirk was a kind and extremely humble old-timer. The valet parking guys had told me that he drove an older model Jeep, very unpretentious, and often in need of a wash job. He can't hear much out of his left ear, though, so he always sits at a half moon booth with his right ear to his date. Mr. Kerkorian always drinks the same thing: a mini bottle of Evian and a neat Cutty Sark with a side of rocks. He likes to mix his own drink and he'll nurse that thing all night. We always try to sell his date on an few glasses of premium wine or champagne with the goal of getting that check average up there because Kirk will always round off at the nearest hundred since that's all he carries, and usually tips fifty percent. Of course, we have always loved him for that and many other reasons, such as the fact that he never tries to show off. Kerkorian likes his Caesar salad chopped up in smaller bits and always shares it with his date, and a petit filet cooked medium served with mashed potato and nothing else on the plate. Tonight his bill was $265 and he shoved $400 in my hand and said goodbye. He doesn't stick around too long these days, usually not past 9:00 pm. It's just incomprehensible to think that this guy lost over $10 billion during the latest financial crisis and he's still worth more than $3 billion. Maybe being careful with every dollar, like sharing a salad, is how he became a billionaire. Ha, I wish.

Across from them, I was serving some new Russian starlet, Sofya Skya (show of hands if you think that's her real name), who was on some trendy celebrity white food diet. That was something new to me. She had a piece of roasted halibut served with white rice and finished it all off with coconut sorbet. I'll never forget that diet though I never did get to ask her anything about it. I just can't imagine the benefit of limiting your diet to white foods. Her face was remarkably beautiful, and when she stood up the whole dining room took a breath. She was all legs – six feet tall and wearing short shorts. Apparently she's a former ballet dancer and now an up-and-coming actress in Hollywood. Well, at the very least she makes a great spokeswoman for that diet, if it can make you look like her...

Through the window, I saw Neil Diamond at one of the garden tables entertaining a much younger girl. Maybe he was helping her with her homework.

It was that time of the night when we often get seated too many tables at once and our manager fails to control the scheduling of employee breaks. So now once again I'm running all over this huge restaurant, my ankles screaming at me to slow the fuck down, trying to cover tables for employees who are on break – and this time two waiters went to break together. This wasn't allowed but they get away with it time and time again. No one seems to give a crap and I continued to wonder why I'm the only one who does.

Despite all of these delights and distractions, my mind kept circling around the two issues that have been tearing at my complacency for quite some time. It was getting difficult to keep signing up for the same set of management challenges year after year with no solutions in sight, and it was continually just getting worse. The more management got away with, the more it emboldened them to push harder. New waiters came in all shiny and new, and in about two years' time they'd quit, tired, haggard and jaded. Management in a place like this should be concerned with consistency, giving their customers a pleasant experience with familiar faces and warmth. Instead, they run the wait staff into the ground so that it's a never-ending revolving door of new and untested servers. The Hollywood factory has two sides: one that churns out buxom blondes and one that turns out ambitious wannabe actors portraying waiters. Both products have built in expiration dates.

And, thanks to our idiotic scheduling system, my colleagues and I walked at least ten miles a night to cover the tables in our stations which are scattered all over the restaurant. It amazed me that our leaders were either unable to fix these problems or unwilling to present the situation to the upper management executives. But as much as these thoughts nagged at me, I didn't have time to worry about them, I just had to get the job done. My conscientious nature would accept nothing less.

Arthur Cohn had his hand up and was looking annoyed. I got to his table and he said, "I want my cookies and we'll take some tea. You want tea, Kirk?" Kirk nodded. When Mr. Cohn says he wants his cookies he's actually serious, they are his cookies – he has them sent over from Europe. They're just regular Linzer cookies with a red fruit preserve in the middle; you could probably buy them at any decent store, but he imports them. After I served their cookies I asked the grouchy Mr. Cohn if he wanted anything else. "No," he said, so I moved on. We never bring him a check as he considers this place his home away from home, so we just put it on his house account with a 15% tip. He never leaves any extra tip and quite frankly I'm always glad when he's done. If he thinks he's at home and we're his family, I felt like telling him I wanted an increase in my fucking allowance.

Nicole Kidman and Keith Urban, whom I'd served many times before, were seated at a discreet booth. They are a very quiet couple, extremely reserved, and Kidman comes off as quite self-conscious. Maybe it's her height; she's almost six feet tall and stands out in a crowd, literally. As a couple, they are very lovey-dovey although not overly touchy-feely in public. You could see a lot of mutual admiration between them. Since I know their drinking habits, I brought bottled water with gas (sparkling) for Urban and some still water for his distinguished wife. Two minutes later, Nicole's parents sat down to join them for dinner. I recommended they try the Krupp Brothers merlot by the glass, and once they tasted it they were sold. What really amazed me was when you looked at Nicole Kidman up close, you could see that her skin is so youthful – she looked like she could be in her late twenties. She must have at least a two-hour regimen of creams, lotions, potions, and magic tricks to make her face appear so flawless. She really doesn't look like she's been worked on at all. She looked truly amazing and very beautiful to boot. But, after a few minutes, I realized she looked other-worldly in an odd way too. There wasn't a whole lot of facial expression going on – her features were frozen. Probably Botox, but what do I know? Actually I noticed how Urban looked really young too. What the hell are those two up to, smearing human placenta on their faces before bed and sleeping in an oxygen tank? But once I looked more closely, her ravishing beauty became darn near creepy, like a living wax museum figure. I pitied Urban if that's how she looked in bed: expressionless and static. I preferred less perfection and more honest expression. I'd rather know from her expression of anger that my wife is pissed, rather than get a book thrown at my head by someone I thought was placid.

Nicole ordered her usual: the chopped salad without cheese or bacon and egg white with no yolks. For all the food value in that she might as well have grazed on the lawn. At least she might get some protein from a bug or two. Urban at least had six ounces of Wagyu beef, and Mom and Dad each had the $38 burger. They were drinking their water quite fast so I kept bringing new bottles and they kept thanking me all along. At one point, I returned to their table to refill their water glasses, and when I picked up the water bottle, Nicole suddenly shoved her hand in my face and said, "We're fine!"

What the fuck is that shit? Speak to the hand? Wow, I couldn't believe it, so I just went ahead and asked her folks if they wanted another glass of wine, which her father did. When I brought it back I was still pissed off about the hand thing. I mean it's not like they were engrossed in any secret conversation – they were talking about a house and some fucking furniture. It sounded pretty boring to me. I guess she wanted to control the water-pouring. The thought crossed my mind that a good slap might bring some color and expression to her face, but I still needed my job. Plus a night in jail didn't appeal to me. Maybe Botox causes bitchiness, like steroids cause aggression.

Urban finally asked for the check and left me a better-than-usual tip and Nicole took her uptight ass out of there and that was the last time I ever served her. Speaking of an uptight ass, I wonder if she'd had that lifted too. I had actually dropped the check without clearing the table. I would normally never do that. I guess I let my emotions get the better of me on that one. Oh, ye gods of service, I pray for forgiveness, please have mercy on my soul of servitude. Amen. And fuck Nicole NoKiddingMan.

Even I could tell I was turning into a waiter burnout. My attitude was getting too negative; I just was not enjoying the job like I used to. I probably needed a change of scenery. A year ago I thought the honeymoon would change all that but it only made me realize how nice it was to be elsewhere. It also reminded me how pleasant and rewarding it could be in places where service was considered more than honorable. Where great waiters were admired.

But it wasn't just me, I knew that. It would have been impossible not to notice that there was also an odd ambiance in the air lately, a vague sense of foreboding. In a movie you'd be able to hear the music become dark and ominous. I heard rumors swirling around regarding a scandal involving our big GM. I'm not one to listen to gossip; most of it turns out to be bullshit, but when I kept noticing executives from our overseas office milling around the restaurant like G-men, it made me wonder what was in store for us. They all but spoke into their lapel pins and rubbed their secret decoder rings. The suits brought about a feeling of unease that trickled from top management straight down through the ranks, all the way to the bottom of our culinary food chain.

Mr. P was nervous all the time. He kept stressing that we needed to keep to the rules of service at every table no matter what. "Jus' treat everyone like a chopper!" Meaning keep to the script, play it by the book, no deviations, upsell at every opportunity and act like a robot. This was not what I wanted to hear. My thoughts were rampant: *Whatever happened to genuine two-way human interaction, simple courtesy, and respect? The sophisticated guests at the Cricket Room don't want to hear our prefabricated scripts and pathetic attempts at upselling. Why don't they just get iPads at every table programmed to force upselling with popup windows and make the guests place their own orders?*

And now, after all these years of running back and forth, covering what feels like miles a night, the physical stress started taking a toll on me, and my body began breaking down. Foot and ankle problems exacerbated by constant overuse plagued me and interfered with my time off as well. I could no longer go for leisurely walks with Juliana, take long bike rides, or go hiking. That alone was depressing as I've always loved being outdoors and these little adventures made up some of our most memorable times together. I was slowly being reduced to a park bench sitter, feeding the pigeons and watching others live actual lives. "No!" I screamed internally, "Not Pauli the rock star waiter to the rich and shameless!"

Painkillers could only keep me on my feet for so long until one day I knew I would require major surgery to fix the wear and tear. I'd already had to go to therapy to help with all the anxiety problems caused by this job. Now my body was caving to the pressure too. Anyone got Nicole NoKiddingMan's phone number? Bet she has just the thing to preserve me like an Egyptian mummy.

I started to brainstorm about my alternatives – I'd dabbled in the stock market but dabbling can't do it – you're up one trade and down the next; might as well play Lotto. My music was really starting to take root – perhaps I should pursue that full time? But my flagging music career was what had brought me to the restaurant in the first place. *Shit!* I felt like a caged dog that just wanted to get out but had no idea where to run. More importantly, I yearned for the peace I used to feel before I started working at the Cricket Room, before the nightmares, before the foot and ankle problems, before all the missed holidays and insults to my self-esteem. While I used to identify with my job, suddenly I didn't anymore. It was an odd sort of peace I felt. The illusion of feeling important and valued had been shattered, which was a relief of sorts, but it had been a really nice illusion and I'd cherished it. Now I needed to find a replacement. Finding it though, was like trying to nail smoke to the wall, or remembering a dream that is just beyond your grasp.

As luck would have it, a friend of Juliana's soon invited us to the star-studded David Lynch Foundation fundraising gala in support of Transcendental Meditation, which seemed like another hint from above. I hoped it would provide some answers.

In the meantime, the fact remained: I knew I was trapped in the asylum, yet I had never tried to fly away. Who was the real cuckoo here? Was it time for the caged bird to sing?

CHAPTER 18
TITANIC

Seems like these days I'm walking around here angry all the time, getting into fights about things that won't change anyway, and not giving a shit about who I'm serving. If you're not Johnny Depp or Russell Crowe, you're boring the holy crap out of me. It's tough to work at a job that is a paradoxical ragout of heaven and hell at all times. Every day at the Cricket Room, I have a strange, euphoric feeling of doom, if that makes any sense. I'm on a train, heading for a wall, and I'm terrified of the impending crash, yet I can't wait for the trip to be over. I want off at any cost.

Mine could have been a great job, and was for a while – it was very exciting to serve such interesting, iconic people, but the creeping fear that at any moment I could be thrown into an impossible situation with no backup caused my gut to twist up in knots constantly. Hell, those nightmares come from somewhere, and that somewhere is my everyday reality.

I've established the fact that our upper management couldn't run a Denny's efficiently if their lives depended on it. Why? For the simple reason that they are cold, calculating number crunchers who don't understand the needs of sophisticated restaurant guests and they don't understand how even small adjustments to our budget tremendously impact the guests' experience. Imagine if the Rockefellers were operating a day care center and slashed snacks from the budget to help pay for their annual trips to Aspen. That would make for ill-equipped workers and some seriously cranky kids.

Lately they'd been running the place like it was the McCarthy era all over again. Paranoia and suspicion reigned. The corporate goons manufactured excuses to fire more staff in eight months than they had in my entire ten-year career. Many employees with a permanent position and benefits (the same benefits I was so proud of when I began) were being let go, for reasons that hardly deserved a reprimand.

One of our most beloved bartenders, Don, who'd been there for over twenty years, was fired a week before he was to retire. Don was soft-spoken and a great listener who always had a smile for his guests. All the regulars loved him. He knew their drinks and always poured a perfect cocktail. The guy never had a guest complaint lodged against him. He was a throwback to the Cricket Room's heyday and wasn't particularly hip to all the fancy mixologist-concocted new wave drinks. Bogart would have loved him; he was our version of Sascha, the bartender in Rick's Cafe Americain. Unfortunately, he was also resistant to learning the trendy new "junk" as he called it. Our classless twenty-something bar manager apparently thought that the Cricket Room should comply with the latest cocktail trends like a slick downtown bar run by Adonis bartenders. He started testing Don on all the new drinks, some of which the bar manager had created *himself.* Don failed miserably time after time. But the truth was that none of his guests even ordered that crap – they all ordered old-school drinks like manhattans and martinis, and an occasional raspberry lemon-drop martini which he made quite nicely. And yet just a week before he was to announce his retirement, he was fired for not complying with company rules. At that point, they could have just let him ride out the extra week and proudly leave a place he had served so loyally for two decades. But no, they chose to contemptuously dismiss him as easily as you would swat a pesky fly. "Waiter, there's a fly in my soup" became a metaphor for getting rid of unwanted payroll bugs.

It was a despicable act, which was looked upon with tremendous scorn and resentment by all of us, not just me. Morale plummeted, now at subterranean levels. After that, three more full-time bartenders and servers plus one assistant manager were fired for untenable reasons. I thought I wanted to rub elbows with the rich and shameless, but now I see that this isn't the same thing at all. Like Hollywood itself, the Cricket Room chews up the little people and spits them out like sunflower seed hulls. I suspect our regular guests and celebrities, who make news on a daily basis by championing various minorities and causes, would not approve of how their dear servants at the Cricket Room were being treated. *The Player,* please meet *Amistad.*

During this Grand Inquisition, we found out that the top brass had given our general manager no choice but to leave. Apparently, he was the cause of a class-action lawsuit claiming racism, sexual discrimination, and unfair promotions to employees of lesser seniority in exchange for sexual favors. Mostly true, he was a scumbag for sure, but probably not much different than many other corporate executives. In my experience, anyway. One national channel carried the news on this but the money machine was successful in shutting the media out a day later and it never surfaced again. Later we found out that he had settled yet another sexual harassment case using in-house funds, without the approval of the London office.

So, the GM left, and all of his evil minions were fired along with several other comrades in the chain of command. There was initially some joy in this, some sense of retribution for the perceived wrongs inflicted on the staff. But it was short-lived. The new high-powered firing machine that replaced him was headed by a freshly unmolded glob of gelatin in the form of a grey-haired GM who handled both of our Los Angeles properties. But did that improve things? No, because the fish stinks from the head, and all of the same ills and idiocies crept up again like a stubborn infection. It was a crippled and inept corporate culture that was too deeply ingrained to change with one surgery. It just left the rest of us twitching as if laser sights were on the back of our heads too.

There was tremendous fear and insecurity among the ranks. Everyone was walking on eggshells, adding to the crushing pressure we were already dealing with. Now we were covering for missing colleagues, missing managers, longer hours, and the job was more intense than ever. Everyone was afraid to screw up, to speak up, or to be noticed for any reason whatsoever, even for doing a great job. Dare to complain, and in retaliation your schedule is changed to shit. Take a few days off and suddenly you have no money nights scheduled for the foreseeable future. You are suddenly an enemy. If you wanted to last there, it was best to be a mindless automaton and avoid the spotlight. I was having serious trouble keeping my famous temper at bay. But one thing I knew: the celebrities and regular folks who came in to celebrate or dine in peace and quiet did not deserve shitty service just because our jobs stunk to high heaven.

When we finally attended the David Lynch Foundation's "Change Begins Within" gala fundraiser at LACMA (Los Angeles County Museum of Art), I was desperate for a sea change. The event was fun and Ellen DeGeneres hosted along with Russell Brand, who was surprisingly well-spoken and impressively entertaining. I was curious and intrigued to see and hear all the stories of troubled school children and even veterans with PTSD who were praising Transcendental Meditation for helping them get through their struggles. Once again, meditation was pricking my consciousness.

Several entertainers performed, amongst them some up and

coming stars like Eli Lieb ("Young Love" singer) and James McCartney (singer and son of Paul). After meeting Bob Roth, the executive director of DLF, he mentioned to us that as a special gift for attending that night, all of the attendees were eligible to learn Transcendental Meditation at no cost. Well, I guess it can't hurt, right? It seemed this was somewhat inevitable. And free. My favorite four-letter word.

We called later to set up an appointment with an instructor who had a most peculiar name: Puki. The appointment was set for the following month. I'm so used to seeing these uptight Hollywood types take, take, take that it was refreshing to see a hugely successful director pay it forward in this way. Lynch is such a creative mind that I figured if it worked for him, hopefully it could help me too. It sure as hell couldn't hurt.

On the other side of my schizophrenic, disgruntled, waiter-slash-frustrated-rock-star life, I was seeing good residual checks from my BMI quarterly statements and was getting a bit more work creating different styles of songs for films and TV. I started putting out as many feelers as I could to get more musical work, trying to build my brand and create a platform. This was why I had taken the damn waiter job anyway: it was supposed to leave me time during the day to pursue my alternate reality. It hadn't actually worked out ideally, as the job was so physically draining and stressful that I had little energy left for music. But this positive reinforcement in the form of royalty checks finally helped me steel myself for a more concerted effort.

My dabbling in the stock market was going well too. I had gotten myself into day trading triple-leveraged ETFs (exchange traded funds). I took a course on how to set and read many complex special technical indicators, and it actually all made sense to me. Maybe it was all related somehow – my ability with musical notes, an anal focus on service perfection, and an affinity for math – and resulted in financial gibberish being clear to me. But that delusion was about to pop like an overinflated balloon. Learning and doing can be very different in practice.

The trading had started out as a lucrative venture, giving me a tremendous sense of confidence in my abilities, but it was extremely stressful trying to keep track of constantly changing indicators. I eventually lost my footing when the artistic, musical side of my brain finally clashed with the calculating, stock trading, stick-to-the-rules side of my brain. The rock star wanted to color outside the lines and be creative; the number cruncher said "stop it!" It wasn't long before I took my eye off the ball and made a terrible mistake that affected our finances deeply. The longer I waited for that leveraged ETF to come back, the further down it went, along with my flawed understanding of all the rules that the teacher had given me. The trading instrument I had chosen was a triple-leveraged ETF that followed the Russell 2000 index. Even though the Russell 2000 finally came back and actually surpassed my break-even point, the ETF was nowhere near breakeven for me. What I didn't understand then was that the leveraged ETF was compounded each day and once the market started moving sideways it didn't pick up as much steam. And another thing I didn't anticipate is that losses are compounded in a unique way as well. Here's an example:

$100 into triple-leveraged ETF on Day 0
$300 exposure on Day 1 ($100 x 3)
Index goes up 10% = Your $100 becomes $110 which is $330 exposure
The $30 is "credited" to your $100 initial investment = $130 which is $390 exposure
Day 2, index goes down 10% = Your $390 loses $39
Your $130 loses $39 = Becomes $91

So, in two days of "equal" swings, you've lost almost 10% of your initial investment.

Not actually "equal," because in this scenario, (A + 10%) does not simply become (A − 10%) when you lose. It actually equals (A + 10%) − 10%, which is a bigger number than just (A - 10%). Understand? Neither did I, at first.

Long story short, in my case I ended up erasing all my profits from the previous twelve months, plus I lost an added $65K, and that was *really hard* to accept, financially, emotionally, and egotistically. My dream of leaving the Cricket Room had just gotten even further away.

To top it all off my best buddy and pretty much only work companion, Jens, was fired for using a manager's code to correct something on a guest check. When they upgraded the POS (point of sale) system they had allowed him to use it because he was the only person who was familiar with it from a previous job. But with the dining room being short-staffed and Mr. P unable to work every single day and night, they would send stand-in managers to attend to the now-fired assistant managers' shifts. These guys were unfamiliar with the system and too fucking slow to act, so Jens took matters into his own hands in a non-hostile way and got the job done. But he was still fired for it. He tried to explain that he was only doing what a supervisor would have done in the past, but they showed no mercy. He was so heartbroken and unprepared for joblessness that he told me he was planning to move back to Denmark the following month. That was just about all I could handle. I had to get out of there. I just couldn't enjoy the environment anymore, but I had no exit plan and considering that I lost a huge chunk of my savings, I regretfully had to stay put. I felt alone and more trapped than ever. Jens had always been a role model for me at work, and an amusing fellow to be around. He savored life and made me want to savor it too. Now work would suck even more, and I hadn't thought that was possible. The light at the end of the tunnel dimmed.

At the restaurant, the staff began to tell each other, "If the boss calls, get his name." We never knew from one day to the next who the fuck was in charge. Management was as distant and anonymous as a colony on Mars.

A couple of weeks later I helped Jens pack up all his stuff. We got drunk that night and reminisced about all of our good times, like taking the ferry to Catalina and drinking all day at Descanso Beach Club, and how our friend Jonathan slept on the floor in the hallway of the hotel that night. We shared memories and laughed but deep inside we were both hurting, for perhaps some of the same reasons. But I also had many other private reasons.

I called Juliana and told her that I'd be spending the night at Jens's apartment. She wasn't too happy, for obvious reasons. She wasn't very fond of Jens since I always ended up coming home high or sloshed after hanging out with him. But that night it made sense especially since I had offered to take him to the airport early the next morning.

As soon as I had gotten off the phone with her, Jens convinced me to go to a club with him and really live it up this last night together. "Come on, Pauli, for old time's sake," he wheedled. "You can't deny me this final night of fun." And I couldn't.

We went to Avalon on Vine Street in Hollywood because it was Jens's favorite place to party. Everybody knew him there – the bouncers and lots of nightclub hipsters were shaking his hand and slapping him on the back. Everyone wanted to buy him a drink. I felt like grandpa amongst all the 20 year olds. I bought a bottle of

"Sampagne," as Jens pronounced it and hoped it would make us look, or at least feel, important. Jens was decked out in his club gear with his shirt wide open and some kind of a scarf tied in a trendy knot. Someone sent us a round of lemon-drop shots and then some flaming Russian roulette shots. Jens disappeared for a while, probably to find drugs; I spent some time dancing by myself drenched in the rain of the laser lights. When I saw him again he was back at our table with two smoldering hot blonde Scandinavian girls hanging on him. Mia and Lena were barely dressed with short shorts on and cute little hats; not much else. By the time we got back to his apartment, he was already making out with one of them and the other was feeling up her friend. It was crazy, as usual, and brought back some fond memories.

I fell asleep on his large IKEA shag rug that he had kept after he and Christie broke up. I sort of heard him and his Swedish Double-mint twins going at it off and on throughout the night but I never jumped in. That's my story and unless someone has a torture device handy, I'm sticking to it.

In the morning the girls left and Jens and I went to Hugo's for breakfast. Halfway through, Jens got a funny look on his face and rushed to the bathroom. He probably threw up because he came back looking 100% more alive and ate the rest of his breakfast like a champ. I asked him what he would do with his apartment and all the stuff he'd left behind. He said he had given the keys to his friend Ozcar (his drug dealer) and told him he could do whatever he wanted with it.

"I've got everything I really need in my suitcase, Pauli, and I don't care about the rest."

We laughed a lot when he told me what he had done with Mia and Lena. He was pretty proud of himself and I felt confident that once he got back to Copenhagen he would be the big fish in a smaller pond and that would work out just fine for him. It was strange saying goodbye – I was too hung over to get teary-eyed but as I walked back to my car I felt envious of Jens. He was getting out of here and onto a new and exciting adventure that I was sure he'd make the best of. I needed a big change in my life too but I wasn't sure how I would go about that yet.

A few weeks later my wife and I spent the weekend with the DLF people. They were somewhat weird but not half as bad as some of those pretentious yogi people who change their names to Moon and Sun and Hummingbird Breeze and all that absurd stuff. If you don't live in LA you may not know the type, but trust me, you don't want to.

My teacher's name was Danny, a normal name, I noticed, and he was an okay guy. It was odd that he was always smiling, but he seemed genuine otherwise and very dedicated to his work. The teachers spent thirty minutes describing what we as a group would be doing and then I met Danny privately and he showed me the Transcendental Meditation technique. For the next few days we did a lot of meditating and talking in groups about what we were experiencing. There were several people from Oprah's new LA staff since she had offered it to any employees who were curious.

By the time we went back ten days later for our follow-up, I had already been in touch with Danny. The cumulative effect of the meditations had left me so high and focused that I could not figure out what to do with all my energy. Everything seemed crystal clear to me and some of my meditations were "super cosmic" as they used to say in the seventies. I actually felt like I was traveling through the cosmos and the energy got me so revved that I could barely sleep at night. I needed to come down somehow because I was unbearable to others and also to myself. I had diarrhea of the mouth and couldn't stop talking about anything and everything. Luckily, Danny showed me a simple yoga and breathing technique that worked; it brought me back down. I was completely exhausted from my ten-day high. So exhausted, in fact, that I called in sick for two nights and sat on the couch for both days, just staring. It was beyond strange. Later, once I started meditating again, everything was a lot more balanced and it really never got crazy like that again. It transformed into a wonderful feeling inside whilst I was able to sort through my thoughts and find an inner calm. It led me to a clearer, more productive lifestyle and best of all, I felt a keen connection to nature, life, and people in general. I was able to listen and accept people at a different level, and it helped me deal with the stresses of life at the Cricket Room. All in all, I think it humbled me. Yes, your wild and crazy rock star waiter to the stars used meditation and yoga to become more focused and relaxed. It worked too.

Nothing has been the same since I started meditating and even though my temper has come more under control, I still feel that this job leaves me wanting more. No matter how peaceful I feel inside, the fact remains that the Cricket Room has become a bore to me, and I need some new challenges. Among the many projects I took up with my newfound, clear-headed energy, I wrote and finished a comedy screenplay — a buddy movie that epitomizes the Hollywood movie business. I also started writing and drafting ideas for this book.

In addition, I used some of my newfound focus to draft a plan for management with suggestions on how we could humanize their "Rules of Service" and make them more efficient. I felt we should train every server to better "read" their guests at the very first introduction, before just blurting out mindless up-sell suggestions. The way the stupid rules were structured, if you approached a table of Muslims or Mormons you would immediately offer them expensive wine. My plan included the type of language to use and defined the tell-tale signs to look for before up-selling, as well as what the signs were to not push a sale. I also explained that there was much gratification to be had in the art of serving and enhancing a guest's experience, and that allowing the server to adopt this approach would bring dignity to the entire situation. It was a detailed, four-page proposal and when I presented it I was laughed at. I could tell that the grunts in lower management found it threatening, and no one was courageous enough to get it to the executives. They were particularly afraid of it getting out since what I was recommending – staffing for powerful success – meant they would simply have to hire a few more people. Mr. P, for example, was too afraid of presenting that notion since it would make him look weak, as though he couldn't handle the job, or like he's been operating understaffed for years without bringing it up. It's obvious that his longevity was based on his willingness to bend over and take it prison-style. He had turned taking it in the shorts to an art form.

When I suggested that I would show it to the new GM or senior executives myself, I was shut down quickly and told that if I wanted to last in the Cricket Room the smartest thing I could do was to keep quiet and follow the rules, that's it.

"Leave the executives to do their jobs and you do yours, Pauli."

I believe in the end the folks in lower management were scared it would make them look like they were not doing a good enough job, which they weren't. And, quite frankly, how could they when they were not given the right tools. The strategy of management by fear won out again and our immediate supervisors elected not to rock the boat even though it would make their jobs easier, and would likely improve the bottom line. What was I thinking? It was time to stop trying. Time to stop rearranging the deck chairs on the sinking Good Ship Cricket Room. I had given it my best effort and they returned the gesture with a rude "Fuck you."

I hoped I could find a lifeboat and fuck them first. *Ohhhhmmm....*

Chapter 19
What Dreams May Come

The idea of life beyond the Cricket Room has become a constant, nagging motif in my thoughts. I often imagine myself joining a rock band and giving it one last shot, or developing some of my writing ideas, including this book. I feel the urge to challenge myself but the fear of going through life as a broke artist yet again chills me. Don't get me wrong – I'm grateful for my experiences at the Cricket Room, grateful for the friends and money I've made and for the insider's view of an iconic American bar/restaurant, but I have to accept the fact that it's time to move on. Some of our servers will be here until they retire or drop dead preparing a tableside steak tartar, but I'm not like them, at least not anymore. Thanks to a loving wife, meditation, a kaleidoscopic array of colorful interests that include cuisine, service, music, real estate, finance, wine, and writing, I now understand that I have options instead of just opinions. And that's the message I want to communicate: So do you! Everyone has options; you just need to gain the confidence to exercise them. I had to find the courage to follow my convictions.

I keep thinking about Jens and Don and all the others who were offed lately. Great careers just hacked off, chopped like my un-wanted ponytail. It seems so unfair. Did my dream job change, or did I? Or both? It's probably always been like this; it's just that I finally saw through the illusions of my own contentment and now I'm faced with only one direction: forward. But how does one leave a great job like this and how can I believe that it would be better anywhere else? Truth is, I can't but I have to have faith and it's better to grow in life than to be stuck doing something that is stagnating and uninteresting. At least that's the theory.

As I was mid-yawn, in walked Katie Perry, the recently divorced Brand-ex and then-number-one pop star in the U.S. That was a wakeup call to my fractured psyche. How apropos – she happened to be entering just as the piano player performed his up-tempo version of "California Girls" by the Beach Boys. Of course, she thinks he's play-ing it because she's walking in so she can't help herself but to mouth the lyrics and bounce up and down a little like the vivacious doll she is.

Her hair is dyed powder blue and her matching and very tight dress accentuates her voluptuous body. Ms. Perry looks like an animated, X-rated cartoon figure who just climbed out of a Baskin Robbins ice cream cake and I don't need to tell you what Jens would be doing in that scenario. She's a real hottie and to her credit gives off an honestly positive air.

She joined a couple of businessmen already seated, and an hour later she left, but not before she was cornered by a female guest in the lobby who wanted a photo with her. She gladly complied and our security guards allowed it since she was into it. The room seemed darker after her departure. She glows vibrancy and energy.

Valentine's Day arrived again and the only interesting person in the Cricket Room was Charlie Sheen. *Come on, Charlie, bring on the crazy.* I'd been waiting for this day to come – he's the bad boy of all bad boys, my wife hates him and the show he got fired from, so I can never really watch the show unless she's out. Charlie was with a hot-looking date, someone I didn't recognize. She must be at least a little special, else why bring her in on V-Day? She ordered a glass of Champagne… or something. I can't even remember, as all I can think about is, *finally I got a big spender here again, and on top of it all, it's Charlie Sheen who's known for his impulsive generosity – among other things.*

Charlie asked for our best scotch, and I brought the bottle of Macallan Lalique 57 to show him. I explained, "Mr. Sheen, the Macallan 57 is $2,800 per glass, because it's been matured for 57 years in Spanish sherry oak casks and only four-hundred bottles were produced."

He gave me an engaging look and said, "Go on."

I assumed he meant continue, so I did. "It's rich, dark, and complex with spicy notes of sun-dried raisins and orange zest."

"Aren't all raisins sun-dried, Pauli?" he said with a devilish smirk on his face. "Go on, Pauli."

I continued nervously as I hadn't had much time to memorize this from my iPhone research. "With lingering touches of citrus and peaty smoke."

He approved with a knowing nod, so I brought out the bottle on my silver tray and poured him a shot at his table. He drank it served neat; scotch is best served with no ice and only a splash of water. When I checked on him a few minutes later, he gave me a warm glance then said, "I'll have one more, please."

"Yes, sir, anything else for the lady?"

"No, she looks fine, doesn't she?" He said it with his usual leering grin.

"Yes, she certainly does, sir." I placed a fresh glass on the table from my silver tray and measured a two-ounce shot as my manager looked on from afar, probably to make sure I didn't over pour. *Asshole. That's the kind of stuff that just drives me crazy. By this time, I should have earned a high level of credibility and unquestioned trust.*

"Nicely done, Pauli, thank you."

"My pleasure, sir." He seemed to be eating up all the old-school formalities but he was definitely calm and collected, not the crazy Charlie we had seen all over the news. Damn, just when I needed him for some entertainment, he gets straight.

The carte du jour was a set menu as always for Valentine's Day and really not a great one. Charlie had a meat dish and his date had fish. During his dinner, he downgraded to a couple of double Macallan 30's at a mere $1,000 a pop. When everything was said and done, his check was $7,400 and he left me a $1,700 tip. Charlie Sheen walked out content, collected, and self-assured and I shall remember him just that way. Shit together, check. Straight, check. Sober, hmmm, not exactly. It was interesting how, on this romantic holiday, he spent thousands on himself and just a couple of hundred bucks on his date. In fact, he spent more on me than he did on her. Maybe she wasn't that special to him after all. Full blown ego, check. It was clear to see that Sheen may have been off the testosterone cream but he was still the ultimate rock star poster boy for self-indulgence. And isn't that why we love him so much?

When I got home that night, my wife was still awake. I had brought her a beautiful flower arrangement that someone had left at their table. I'd had to get a backdoor pass from the manager on duty so that I could show it to the prison guard at the security desk on the way out. Even with the huge tips, it always felt like freedom – the air even seemed fresher – when I left the place. I kept waiting on them to install the razor wire and guard towers, but Beverly Hills building codes probably frown on them.

I gave Juliana a long kiss and told her that I yearned for the days when we could spend all of our holidays together. She let out a longing purr and then whatever was supposed to happen did happen. When I woke up the next morning, Juliana had already gone to work as usual and I sat at my computer writing in my journal and checking e-mail. I looked at the stock market and it was going up as it had been for most of the beginning of this first quarter. Fortunately, I was partly exposed to the upside in my 401K – a sunny spot on the dark horizon since my recent huge losses.

Back at work, things were getting more and more boring. Johnny Depp came in twice and didn't drink anything but iced tea. What the hell was going on? Russell Crow hadn't been in to the Cricket Room for almost a year. I think they were catching on that it has lost a lot of its old Hollywood glamour and was turning into a chain restaurant with more tourists than in-crowd. I expected to see two-for-one drink special coupons and early bird dinner specials any day. Some moron in a cubicle was undoubtedly designing pre-packaged logo snacks like airline peanuts. "Hey, we could call them Cricket Chips! This is gonna be great!"

There had been one good surprise: I made a $1,000 tip from J. Williams, a huge player in the entertainment representation business. In normal speak, that means he's an agent. He was hosting a client on Vino's night off and ordered two bottles of wine: a Peter Michael Chardonnay at $200 and a bottle of Grace Family Cabernet, $700. Later, when I asked if they wanted another bottle, he smugly threw out a suggestion he thought I'd never be able to fulfill: "You don't have the Harlan Estate, do you?"

Busted, chump. "We do, Mr. Williams. May I decant that for you?"

"Well, I only want it if you have the 2001," he said, winking at his guest.

I returned within a few seconds with the wine list, pointing to the 2001 Harlan Estate cabernet, which was listed at $3,200.

Bluff called. "Oh, fantastic! Bring it out would you, Pauli?" *Cha-ching!* He looked a little ashen but braved it out.

He pretty much had to say that in order not to look like a jerk in front of his guest, a potential client whom he was wooing. I went on to sell them chocolate soufflés and just about anything else I could think of short of hookers. I hope cubicle coupon boy doesn't think of that. By the time Mr. Williams left, he was in great spirits. We shook hands but I never saw him again, unfortunately. He probably got the credit card bill and a huge case of buyer's remorse along with it.

Johnny Depp finally came in, returning for a third time with Vanessa. He bought her a bottle of Cristal Rosé to share with her girlfriend but he didn't drink at all. At the time I thought that perhaps all the rumors of their breakup were false or maybe they're just friends. I don't see him as being a monogamous person and I don't think she's dumb enough to believe he would be. After all, if you have all the girls in the world throwing themselves at you for long enough, you're bound to break sooner or later. That's the price of fame. It also explains the rarity of long-lasting Hollywood marriages. Human nature, at least the male version of it, is what it is. (Honey, if you're reading this, I'm the exception. No worries.)

As he was sitting there, I reminisced about the last time he had tipped me ever so generously. It was about one year ago to date, and he had come in that time with Vanessa, Keith Richards and Keith's wife, Patti Hansen. Keith had been looking all rock 'n rolled out – in black, tight skinny jeans and black Converse sneakers, a red headband, and some weird shit sewn into his hair. Basically, a very modest version of Captain Jack Sparrow. These two had become very good friends and they talked about the "Pirates" movies and Keith's autobiography that Johnny had narrated for the audio version. I remember noticing that Depp was sort of putting on a British accent or something. Gwyneth Paltrow and Madonna do that pretentious shit too. Granted, he never really speaks normal "American," but now it was really much more like Keith's accent. Maybe he's such a character actor that he just adopts the accent of whomever he's with.

Johnny went on to order his usual two bottles of Haute Brion and luckily we still had them. Keith ordered a vodka cranberry to start. I guess he was going for that anti-oxidant healthy rocker thing. When I brought Keith his drink, he tried to suck on the stir stick as if it were a straw. It's true that our stir sticks are thick and designed in clear plastic with a knob at the end so they do look different, but they don't really look like straws. I think he just got confused for a second, or maybe that's a permanent condition. I stopped to watch him and once he was done trying to get some liquid out of that solid stir stick, he burst out laughing at the whole thing. Johnny was chatting with Vanessa and pretended not to see it.

After a polite pause, I asked Keith, "Mr. Richards, would you like me to bring you a straw for your drink?" I maintained a straight face, which I've gotten good at. I think I could be a spy.

He looked at me and replied in his trademark slurred, cockney accent, "No, it's just funny that's all, I thought it was a straw and I started sucking!" Now he was laughing and Johnny was keeping a straight face and wishing I would just leave it be, but Keith kept on laughing and saying in his accent, "It's just funny, that's all!" and shaking his head. It was funny and I was tempted to laugh but I managed to remain professional about it.

During that dinner, Keith and Johnny kept sneaking out to the patio to smoke. The rest of the night went off without a hitch and Johnny thanked me with another $2,500 tip, which had helped pay for my wife's wedding ring. A white gold band with eternity princess cut diamonds totaling four carats. I always think of that ring when I see him now. Thanks, Mr. Depp. (I could say that when I look at my wife's ring I think of Johnny Depp, but that would be weird.)

Oscar season rolled around and things always start getting really stir crazy around that time of year. First of all, there are many, many awards parties and ceremonies and a slew of movie and music stars staying in town that normally live elsewhere. And then you have all the tourists in town trying to spot a celebrity at a famous hangout. It's hard to weed them out without being accused of discrimination. The corporate monkeys like their money. But there is also a whole mess of more or less not-yet successful or small-time players and industry wannabes who are looking to grow their brand and/or find or make that big contact that will take them to the next level. Oscar season is ripe for picking up contacts.

All of this happens in the Cricket Room on an inflated scale around that time of year, and it's almost unbearable. You have all the small-timers trying to hold meetings in the front of the restaurant so they can be easily noticed. They also like to keep an eye on who is walking in so they can approach them at their tables later. Well-known, "important" people don't work this way. It's annoying to the waiters (and the regulars) since these unnamed and faceless people have revolving meetings at the table as if it were an office, so a lot of the time we give them lousy service in return for treating our restaurant as their own personal workspace. They turn the Cricket Room into a speed dating bar, with a parade of losers who order almost nothing and tip like they think they're at the Waffle House.

Once time I even walked up to a guest who had been holding those kinds of meetings in our restaurant for months and asked, "Is there anything else I can get you, sir? Stapler, pencil, whiteout, paperclips?" I think he got the message 'cause he handed me a Benjamin, asked me for a cup of herbal tea and told me to keep the change. But I still didn't like him.

So in the midst of all the annual Hollywierd madness, all the executives from our international corporate office in Europe decide to have a party, celebrating themselves. "Hello, I'm Omar, your boss. Aren't I awesome? You may kiss my ass if you like."

They used the newly remodeled lobby as their excuse to celebrate. It is my opinion, and the opinion of many of the regulars, that the lobby lost its rich, warm, classic charm for a colder, more modern-looking theme, unsuitable to the property. They erased Hollywood glam and replaced it with faux chic Euro-style stone and glass. But some contractor convinced the top honchos that it was a good idea, and since they had so much money to waste, well, why not? Money, I might add, that was saved by cutting hours, short staffing, and firing good people with benefits.

Boy did they spread it on thick for this party! It was a 1920s theme put on by Tribute Productions. It all started with the executives arriving in automobiles from the 1920s, treating themselves like celebrities. Once they got out of the cars, they walked down a red carpet (obviously it had been their wet dream to do that) leading to the lobby where they were met by fake photographers with old-style cameras and flashes. The "paparazzi" actors were dressed in rumpled old suits like journalists from "The Daily Chronicle." Their photographs were taken surrounded by lookalike actors dressed as Laurel and Hardy, Greta Garbo, Clark Gable and many other old time "stars" who were roaming about to greet the corporate execs. Have you ever heard of anything so fucking cheesy?

Meanwhile, while we were running the Cricket Room short-staffed as usual, they all walked through the restaurant to get to their private room in which we had a special banquet staff to take care of them. The real Cricket Room staff was told (threatened) to be cordial, to greet them all and smile, so we were bowing and all that bullshit, but I was trying to pick out which one of them was the asshole who set our budgets. I knew it was some executive from our stuffy headquarters in London, but whether it was a man or a woman, I had no idea. I kept entertaining thoughts of poison, accidentally "dropping" a knife in their chests, and other creative ideas for mayhem.

As I looked at these individuals walking through, I could see that they were clueless as to the bigger picture. Most of them were just performing duties as described by the top execs – following orders like the Nazis. The CEO is a white man from the continent of Africa; the COO is from France, nicknamed by the previous GM as "Ding Dong," and then next in the food chain is a female VP of sales. Their names are not important but their word was the law. No, more than law – their word was Biblical scripture, to be followed on pain of death. It might as well have been carved on stone tablets, but of course that would have cost too much. They, along with thirteen other executives, run ten four- to five-star properties including several restaurants and bars. Each one of those properties has its own hierarchy of more junior executives as well. I can just imagine what kinds of salaries these people sauntering through this restaurant tonight are making. Kissing ass must be a line item on their paychecks.

As the night went on, I spied on them from our back area as they enjoyed 1920s-themed musical entertainment, amazing hors d'oeuvres, and finally a sit-down dinner with the finest meats and seafood. The kitchen was going crazy – all the executive kitchen staff was there, each of them screaming out orders to their underlings. It took forever to get a meal out to the regular diners in our main dining room because the kitchen staff was putting this party on the VIP list and forgetting about the rest of the routine dining room service. It was all smoke and mirrors, really, as it always is when any of the executives showed up to eat in our restaurant. If the executives enjoyed their service, they just assumed that all the guests in the Cricket Room were getting great service too, and this scenario repeated itself time and time again. And on this particular night, it was amplified twenty times over. Pathetic, really.

I walked back into the kitchen to show Lola an over-cooked $38 burger that was sent out to my table. She took the plate out of my hands, screamed at the cook again, then told me to get out, and that they would re-make the order. Ten minutes later, I was waved down by the same guest and he showed me that the burger was rare instead of medium rare and had the wrong cheese and no onions on it. I apologized once again to the guest, and he looked like he was not having any more of it. He asked for the check and as it turned out he had a house account. I didn't recognize him at first but he's a successful movie producer with the last name of Pressman. I had to get Mr. P to take something off the check and he was nervous too and hard to find since the executive committee was holding court. I guess he figured his job relied upon a massive amount of bending over. Drop those shorts, Mr. P.

I ran into the kitchen to show Lola the burger she'd sent out wrong again. Like the customer, I'd fucking had it!

"Look at this!" I screamed. "It's bloody rare and has the wrong fucking cheese and no fucking onions on it! For the sake of all that's fucking holy, Lola, why don't you look at the ticket before you send stuff out? How can I make a living when you guys don't pay any attention? The guest is a VIP and now he's leaving, still hungry, and mad as hell! He won't leave a fucking tip either, like it's my fault you can't do your job!"

Lola opened her mouth ready to scream back at me but right at that moment Paco was bringing another dish into the kitchen that was being sent back from one of my other tables – a no bacon chopped salad full of bacon. Behind Paco was Jose with a plate of rejected medium rare salmonella-laden chicken and limp vegetables. All of these orders just happened to be from my tables. As usual, the whole staff was so concerned with giving the corporate asses an unrealistic, manufactured, perfect evening that they were letting our regular clientele suffer. It's ridiculous how the staff is programmed to screw the ones who matter in order to pretend the Emperor has no clothes. And the Emperor remains blissfully unaware.

I felt the years of frustration and anger building up in my throat and suddenly I really lost it. I called Mr. P. into the kitchen with Paco and Jose standing there helplessly and I let him and Lola have it. I hardly remember what I said, but the incompetence and misplaced priorities finally broke the proverbial camel's back.

I think my tirade went something like this: "You weak bastards never stand up for what's right in this place! You're so afraid of asking for anything or making any improvements that you get stepped on and abused and that's what you think you deserve! Shit rolls downhill through you two and you don't do a thing about it! Look at these assholes in the other room! Spending tens of thousands on a party to celebrate the fact that they wasted a million dollars on ruining our lobby – when a few dollars invested in the kitchen and floor staff would improve EVERYONE'S experience! And you're too afraid to say anything, so nothing ever changes! What matters is the guests' experience and that's what I'm here to protect, but I get no fucking backup from you guys or the oblivious suits in the other room. And how are they supposed to know what's going on if you don't dare to communicate it to them! Fuck all of you fuckers. I've had it!"

Everyone in the kitchen stared at me – or this insane incar-nation of me – in complete silence. I stormed out but after a moment, I ducked into a side hallway to compose myself. I wanted to set a nice bonfire of the vanities with my uniform, but decided to rush back out into the dining room to minister first aid to the suffering and abused guests, considering whether I should call in the Red Cross. This was obviously inhumane and probably rose to the level of restaurant war crimes. Salmonella is chemical warfare, right? Back out on floor, Mr. P gave me a strange look that stuck with me for a long time.

At first, I felt badly for wounding a compatriot, but I also understood what that look meant. He felt betrayed but he also knew I was right. I had broken the code of silence that had kept him alive for so long, and it scared him. It was then that I finally realized he had never really been on my side. And I'm sorry to say that I suddenly saw myself in him. The way in which he sucked up to his bosses with no sense of pride, and for which I resented him deeply, reminded me of the way I was always sucking up to him and to our famous guests. And losing myself in the process. The parallel made me feel sick inside.

I'd dreamt of quitting many times before this, but now that I was on the verge of walking out, I just couldn't leave my guests wondering what was going to happen to their orders. It certainly wasn't their fault so why should they be disrespected? It's not my style. When I eventually left that night, I took a good look around. Everything looked different, but maybe I was seeing things clearly for the first time in years. With the house lights turned up, Mr. P's face looked paler and even more expressionless than ever. I noticed how his cheap suit had some unflattering permanent stains on it and how his red medallion print tie didn't seem to be of very good quality. There was a time when he took pride in his appearance but the corporate jocks had beaten the pride right out of him.

I also noticed the other employees' blank faces and flat affect like frozen cardboard figures. I looked at the shelves where we stored the polished glasses and noticed how they were stained and needed wiping. No one had time to do that anymore. The carpet had been changed a year ago in the dining room and was of course of a lesser quality than the previous carpet, so it was already fading and showing signs of wear. In past years, only the best would do, but now only the cheapest would. When walking through the kitchen, I realized it was dirty and the lighting was stark. Shortened staff, longer hours, and lack of pride had struck the kitchen as hard as it had the front.

Lola sat in her office staring at her computer; the greenish light from the screen illuminating her face in a hideous way. I walked through the lobby beneath the spot where the grand chandelier used to be and stepped across the echoing new floor. As I passed through, I thought about how the corporate death squad was planning to "upgrade" the garden area as well as the Cricket Room interior to make it more contemporary. No more Hollywood luxurious glam; they were now going for sterile, cold, angular, metal, glass, and plastic, and most of all, cheaper.

I took the elevator down to the changing rooms, and walking through the grocery-store lit hallway, I knew I'd never be coming back again. The romance was over. Pauli and the Cricket Room were breaking up; there was no more love. I had said what I needed to say and no one liked hearing it. Too fucking bad. I had unloaded ten years of accumulated insults, injuries, and opinions. Whether they were true or false perceptions didn't matter; they were mine and I had to stand by them.

With my credentials, I could work anywhere in this town. But I no longer wanted to work at the best place there is... or was. That says a lot. The fat paycheck, the fancy clientele... none of it mattered much anymore. I had loved my job. I'm good at it. Very good at it. I took pride in my work. But the incompetent, shortsighted management practices I was forced to follow ruined it for me.

Most waiters do burn out eventually – they tend to regard the job as an interim, as a temporary thing while they pursue other goals in their lives, and the stresses eventually outweigh the benefits. But I didn't go down in flames in the typical way. While it's true that I eventually did start pursuing my music again, I never looked at this job as second-rate. I had approached it wholeheartedly. Thanks to my early life in Europe, in which service is considered an art and requires prestigious training, and thanks to Jens showing me how to do it right and how to do it with flair, I took my work at the Cricket Room very seriously. If I had been given the tools I needed to do the job I envisioned, I might still be there. I never expected that my sense of self, my core beliefs about what is important in life, would be so sorely tested by a server job at the Cricket Room. And in that fight, the job had to lose. As a consolation prize – or maybe it's first prize – I learned a lot about myself and my values, my dedication, my ability to deliver quality work and maintain a high standard of professionalism. That's a hard-won lesson that I will always carry with me. Was it worth the cost? Yes. Not only did I win that first prize, I don't fear or wonder about the Rich and Shameless anymore. I no longer even respect them very much. I saw that they're just successful people (or heirs) who think they're more important than anyone else. Well, I beg to differ.

There was a time when I was very impressed with myself for getting and keeping this job, for working so closely to the glitz and glamour of Hollywood, and for being successful in such a competitive and thankless environment. I enjoyed rubbing shoulders with the Crowes, Stewarts and Depps of the world even if it was from behind a silver tray. I believed that they needed me, that I was somehow important and part of it all, and that perhaps I could be like them one day. When you spend forty hours a week immersed in the Cricket Room illusion, you begin to believe it. But my life couldn't be further from that reality. The illusion became a delusion. No matter how many $1,000 tips I made, I'd never catch up to them. I'd never be like them – and maybe that wasn't a bad thing. I'd never have their kind of money. But then again I'd never be their kind of shameless either.

After years of becoming accustomed to the thrill, I had finally evolved past that naïve impression of myself and my job, and came to realize that I don't care about having money, at least not the way the Rich and Shameless do. It's a means to an end, and necessary, but for them it's a religion. They place it on an altar above all else. Bottom line, what's impressive to me isn't money. It's when someone is dedicated to their art or studies because they truly want to share something that they're convinced others can benefit from. I needed to be that person. I needed to get back to who I truly am and stop kidding myself about this bullshit world centered inside the Cricket Room. I suddenly saw the work for what it was, I saw our clientele for who they were, and most importantly, I saw myself for who I am. And that's when I started growing again.

A huge sense of freedom overwhelmed me when I realized I was actually saying goodbye. Mr. P thought I was crazy, but we all know who's really wearing the straightjacket under his ill-fitting suit. All the money in the world isn't worth being miserable. I had to leave while I still had an ounce of myself left. Pride, self-esteem, and integrity can't be bought, not even by Johnny Depp.

Maybe I'll take some time off or maybe I'll open my own place; perhaps something totally unexpected will come along like floral design or Zoomba instructor. Or maybe I'll grow my hair back long, grow a beard, and become Swami Pauli. I'll give sappy life advice to bored LA housewives.

But all joking aside, whatever happens, I am walking away and not turning back. Bridge burned to the ground, check.

EPILOGUE

After I left the Cricket Room, I knew what I had to do to redeem myself in my own eyes, but I wasn't quite sure how to go about it. My immediate goals were to finish all of my writing projects, get back into a rock band, and reawaken my creative soul within. I had to take a chance on myself and believe that I can do it. But I was haunted by the question: why would things be different this time? I still had to make a living. This time, however, I felt a certain centeredness, a reassuring confidence I hadn't owned before. Believe me, I knew things would be a lot tougher than they had been for the last ten years and I knew there would be nights when I'd be sniffling in my bed wishing I could hide underneath that comforting security blanket that the Cricket Room provided for us working grunts. Yet this time, I couldn't go back. I wouldn't. I had to give it my best try, somehow.

It took some time to arrange my life so that I could pursue those ambitious goals. I had to make many unexpected adjustments due to my departure from the Cricket Room. My entire lifestyle needed to change. Juliana and I no longer had money to travel or eat out or drink fancy wines. I won't lie – it's been a tough lesson but one that has reminded me how most people of my trade really live, how people of my former (now current) income bracket are treated and how difficult and complicated our lives really are. No paid health insurance, no 401K. How could I have forgotten so quickly? I suppose because I'm older now, those things really make a difference. A most humbling experience indeed.

I dedicated a lot of time to my music, but to pay the bills I kept falling back into my old ways: service jobs. Through a placement agency in Beverly Hills I ended up working for an elderly man in San Marino for a while as his butler/chauffeur and when he became too ill and needed only medical staff, I had to move on. I then interviewed with Ellen and Portia to be the head butler at their Beverly Hills house. But luckily I didn't get that job and finally decided that day that I can't be that buttoned-up fucking boring cardboard figure of a waiter or butler that the Cricket Room had prepared me for so well. Instead I could see Dee Snyder's face coming at me full-screen, yelling *"I wanna*

241

rock!" I am no longer willing to sell out for comfort and security, and since Juliana is my biggest supporter and we don't plan on having any kids, why not live out my dreams, right?

Eventually, through a few different musical collaborations, I created and placed songs for three different films, and a TV show. I joined an Italian choir of 40 plus singers, and we trained for months for our performance of Mozart's Requiem. The concerts were backed by a 30-piece symphony orchestra and were held in Santa Monica and Pasadena. It was an amazing and gratifying experience and something I had always dreamed of doing.

In the meantime I stayed in touch with most of my old co-workers through e-mail and Facebook and met up with a few of them from time to time. I had lunch with Mr. P a few times and invariably came away with the feeling that he had become a thoroughly broken man.

Jens had come back from Denmark – apparently the Scandinavian lifestyle had been too slow for him and in less than a year he had run out of space to roam. The infamous thrill-seeking playboy could not be entertained enough to stay in Copenhagen, especially after a dark and dreary northern winter. His Angelino roots were screaming to return. Jens now works at a country club in Century City and has been keeping busy knocking around tennis balls with lonely wives, Andy Roddick and many others. I never knew it but Jens's passion for sports had always been piqued by tennis. He seems happy as a clam and is full of new stories that still make my jaw drop to the floor. I swear if I ever write another book it'll be about his life.

About a year after leaving the Cricket Room, I visited again to enjoy dinner with Juliana and a friend and to see all my old co-workers. It was amazing, the kinship and love I received. Mr. P rolled out the welcome mat and we were seated at the only four-top in the Cove. Oddly enough, right next to the Vanderpumps, with Courteney Cox in the booth next to them. When my friend asked if anyone famous was in the restaurant I had to laugh. It was just a typical night at the Cricket Room. The ambiance sparkled as always, and the same guitarist was there, on whom I had played that evil prank when Roger Waters was dining in the Cricket Room. He was singing in his best high-pitched falsetto voice, performing his softie versions of top ten hits from 1960 to the present. The waiters all hovered about, catching me up on the latest. There were hugs and kisses all around, and none of the faces were new although they had moved a few servers up from the lunch shift to fill my spot.

Both Juliana and I were astounded at the warmth and genuine kindness of the staff. It was evident that they all missed me. Mr. P even joked, *"Polli, go pour water on table 44!"* While the food hadn't changed, the dining room had undergone a solid makeover. There were new, luxurious crown moldings adorning the walls, some different pictures on the walls and some of the old ones had beautiful new frames. Overall the place looked even more rich and opulent, as if that were possible. The only mediocre change in the dining room was the ugly carpet. It was boring and institutional and couldn't hold a candle to the original huge motif design that I described early in my story.

The cozy seating in the garden area had been replaced with solid booths and chairs, sturdier tables and permanent overhead heating for night-time dining. The waiters told me that there were a lot of cosmetic changes but nothing that really made a big difference. There were now more service armoires placed strategically throughout the whole restaurant and two extra POS (point of service) computers, and the new GM offered benefits to all his employees – not just a select few as the last tyrant did. It gave me a sense of hope and at the same time a bit of sadness to think that perhaps if I had held out a year or so longer many of my suggestions might have been heeded. But let's face it, I wanted a change and a change I got. I have to admit it made things a little easier on me when Matt told me that despite the upgrades, they were still running the place like a five-star Denny's with a skeleton crew.

Should I have walked away and turned my back on an establishment that enabled a comfortable life for me? Would I have ever written this book if I had stayed? Or the screenplay I just completed? Would I have formed an original rock band, completed a 13-song album, appeared in a TV pilot and launched our video into heavy rotation on European music video TV stations? Our manager even got us onto the ballot for Grammy consideration in eight categories, which was a first for all of us in the band, and we are also planning a tour of Europe and Asia. In short, the future has never looked brighter.

I can't say whether any of this would have happened had I stayed in my relatively comfortable life at the Cricket Room. In life the unexpected happens and we can't do much more than try to hang on to ourselves as the road turns and twists. Funny thing is, I feel this band and this book are my best work yet, and deep inside I know that I could not have made it this far without my experiences at the Cricket Room to push me to my limits and teach me about myself and my abilities. I don't look back too often anymore, as my focus has shifted to enjoying life with Juliana and the future.

Thank you, Cricket Room, and I bid you a warm and bitter-sweet good-bye.

~ ~ * ~ ~

Follow me:

https://www.facebook.com/Pauli9641

https://twitter.com/Pauli9641

~ ~ * ~ ~

Made in the USA
Middletown, DE
11 February 2018